About the Author

Zhou Yongping, born in Shanghai in 1953 and rusticated in 1969, worked at the Information Office of Shanghai Municipality after 18 years of service with the Air Force Aviation Corps. He was the Director of Information and Culture Department of Overseas Chinese Affairs Office of Shanghai Municipal People's Government and Editor-in-Chief of Shanghai Overseas Chinese News.

Mr. Zhou joined Hong Kong-based Shui On Group in 1999, participated in and witnessed the development of Shanghai Xintiandi. Senior manager and assistant to Vincent Lo, chairman of Shui On, Mr. Zhou is also the founder and President of the Huaihai Road Economic Development Promotion Association since 2005.

Mr. Zhou has been a visiting faculty at Fudan University, Tongji University, Shanghai Jiaotong University and other colleges and universities as well as the China Executive Leadership Academy in Pudong for the Class of Leadership in Urban Development. He is also a guest professor at Tongji Zhejiang College.

EAST MEETS WEST

XINTIANDI
THE SHANGHAI NEIGHBOURHOOD
THAT CHANGED CHINA

ZHOU YONGPING

TRANSLATED BY XIE WEN

East Meets West

By Zhou Yongping
Translated by Xie Wen

ISBN-13: 978-988-8843-11-4

© 2023 Zhou Yongping

ARCHITECTURE

EB192

All rights reserved. No part of this book may be reproduced in material form, by any means, whether graphic, electronic, mechanical or other, including photocopying or information storage, in whole or in part. May not be used to prepare other publications without written permission from the publisher except in the case of brief quotations embodied in critical articles or reviews. For information contact info@earnshawbooks.com

Published in Hong Kong by Earnshaw Books Ltd.

New Foreword

China's urban development has shifted from its previous large-scale demolition and incremental construction to organic urban renewal. A swathe of buildings constructed in the past three decades in Shanghai are facing different destinies–those still standing are a testament to their superior engineering skills and architectural ingenuity, while others are falling foul of the bulldozers as a result of the builders' myopic focus on earning money. Dominated by skyscrapers, the city's skyline is a pre-eminent symbol of modernity. Yet most of them failed to impress. The century-old, low-rise *Shikumen* houses, however, have stood the test of time with its indigenous architectural feature and cultural identity.

When Xintiandi, a rejuvenated *Shikumen*-style district, opened to the public in 2001, it was an immediate and unexpected success, both at home and abroad. The old *Shikumen* alleys witnessed their decline in the second half of the last century and faced the threat of being demolished.

At the turn of the 21st century, Shui On has gone to great lengths to revitalize the historic buildings with a pioneering, preservation-oriented development concept. Xintiandi, certainly awe-inspiring in its staggering scale and intensity, has graced the city's skyline and proven a critical as well as commercial hit.

The young Chinese people come because they think it's trendy, the foreigners come because they think it's historically significant, and the old people come because they feel nostalgia. *Shikumen* architecture has now recovered all its former glory: it is the central gathering place for younger generations; it provides a scenic backdrop for wedding photographers and newlyweds;

and it caters to a trendy audience who is seen to patronize fashionable and vibrant environments.

Xintiandi has become a traditional townscape that evokes fascination from the young, and nostalgia from the old. As a window to the past and the future, to China and the world, Xintiandi has spearheaded preservation-based approaches to revitalization of historically significant buildings in Shanghai.

The Xintiandi initiative has sparked a series of commercial and leisure construction projects, including Sinan Mansions, an immense redevelopment of colonial mansions from the '20s and '30s, Tianzifang, a renovated labyrinth of traditional Shanghai alleyways, No.8 Bridge which was transformed from abandoned factory buildings, and a wharf converted from an old riverside warehouse, and started a wave of urban renewal efforts across the country.

Government officials from 31 provinces, municipalities and autonomous regions came to Xintiandi to study and bring back home its vision and model that had allowed it to retain the original charm and authentic flair of the historic buildings, in an attempt to achieve sustainable urban development where serial replication of a reliable if soul-deadening pro forma from one city to the next would no longer exist. In 2004, Xintiandi was designated as the 'Demonstration Base of National Cultural Industry' by the Ministry of Culture of the People's Republic of China.

Xintiandi's success is much more than just renovation of the old buildings, as what many people may have perceived, it has indeed contributed to China's sustainable urban development by introducing the new concept of "urban renewal" and "culture of urban public space". Instead of leveraging its proximity to the Huangpu River to deliver impressive panoramic riverfront views or relying on other scarce resources, Shui On painstakingly salvaged the area's *Shikumen* buildings that would otherwise have been razed for new development, in an attempt to evoke a sense of pride in the city's cultural heritage.

NEW FOREWORD

Xintiandi has also won accolades from international institutes and academies, such as the 'Award for Excellence' from US-based Urban Land Institute which described Xintiandi as "embracing the city's past while melding it with the commercial realities of modern urban living."

Enjoying an unrivalled location near three subway lines and two hospitals, the 52-hectare area encompasses the functions of living, working, shopping, learning and entertainment in one unique area. As an integral part of the 52-hectare redevelopment, instead of a standalone project, Xintiandi will be able to achieve sustainable development on a long-term basis.

Often imitated but never surpassed. I'm so proud that Xintiandi has withstood the test of time and been showing its vigorous vitality for two decades. It was rated among the "Top 20 Global Cultural Landmarks" by *Forbes* in 2016.

At the epicenter of Xintiandi's first phase is a national historic shrine, the Memorial Hall of the First National Congress of the Communist Party of China. According to the master plan of the *Taipingqiao Redevelopment Project* approved in 1997 by the Shanghai Municipal Urban Planning Bureau, only a few buildings were required to be completely preserved to feature a nostalgic atmosphere — those in the two blocks neighboring the site of the First National Congress of the CPC.

2001, the birth of Shanghai Xintiandi, also marked the 80th anniversary of the founding of the CPC. In 1998, local authorities decided to have the run-down *Shikumen* buildings within the protected site renovated by July 2001 in time for the 80th anniversary of the founding of the Communist Party of China.

As the developer of the redevelopment project, Shui On was faced with a tough challenge. Some experts from Shanghai Municipal Administration of Cultural Heritage suggested that the residents be relocated, the old *Shikumen* houses be demolished and new *Shikumen* buildings with a FAR (floor area ratio) of 1.8 be constructed as residential development, leaving Shui On little room to breathe since the relocation cost per square meter was much higher than that of a newly built apartment in Shanghai. Moreover, local residents in the 21st century started to favor 3-bedrooms apartments rather than the spatial structure of *Shikumen* houses. Replicated *Shikumen* residential development would have little market value.

Completing the restoration projects of the *Shikumen* buildings encompassing the Site by the end of June 2001 in time for the 80th anniversary was the most pressing requirement. I made it very clear to the management that the deadline could not be missed, or there would be serious consequences—we would all have to "jump into the Huangpu River".

We had to produce a feasible redevelopment alternative within a tight time frame, when inspiration suddenly struck me that the old towns in Europe were always dotted with charming cafes, lively breweries and beloved restaurants that were absent in Shanghai. Would there be a way to mix historic preservation and commercial real estate development, rather than continuing the residential function of the two city blocks?

People were initially wary of the pioneering initiative in *Shikumen* revitalization. At the height of the 1997 Asian financial crisis, banks were not lending, and my management team were not in favor of the plan. But I went forward even though a lot of people thought I was crazy. The wild idea turned out to be a trendy, award-winning landmark of the city that transcended the logic and stipulations of historic preservation.

The original name at the start of the project was "Regeneration of the Site of the First National Congress". After Shui On submitted a creative plan to restore the neighborhoods and keep it historically authentic while incorporating new commercial functions, both local authorities and the company considered the name inappropriate. After much deliberation and brainstorming, my team and I reached a consensus on the new name "Xintiandi"—the two Chinese characters abbreviated from the Chinese translation of "the first National Congress of CPC" could be combined into another character "Tian" which means

heaven, often spoken of in apposition to another character "Di" which means earth, and "Xin" which means new referred to the completion of this cross-century project in the new millennium — hence the powerful and lofty name.

After the project had come to its full realization in mid-2001, the then state leaders, accompanied by officials of CPC Shanghai Committee, visited the Memorial Site of the First National Congress of CPC, Xintiandi and Taipingqiao Park. At the viewing platform by the Lake, I was bestowed with the honor by Shanghai Municipal Government to brief the concept and practice of developing Xintiandi and the Park for the Leader of the Central Authorities who then spoke highly of our bold redevelopment ideas. On the same day, Xintiandi and the Lake Park became headline news on CCTV and other major national media outlets.

During the APEC Summit held on 20–21 October 2001 in Shanghai, foreign heads of state visited Xintiandi, including Russian President Vladimir Putin who had dinner of authentic Shanghai homestyle cooking at One Xintiandi. Global media coverage of Xintiandi has driven its reputation worldwide.

On July 1, 2021, the Communist Party of China will mark 100 years since it was founded in Shanghai. As the birthplace of China's Communist Party, the site of the First National Congress of the CPC will be the focal point as China celebrates the centenary.

The memorial of the First National Congress of the CPC, under renovation since this summer, will officially open to the public next year, with a newly built exhibition area, as part of multiple events set to commemorate the 100th anniversary. In addition, Xintiandi will also be celebrating its 20th anniversary. We are very much looking forward to the lively celebrations and exciting activities that will enliven the neighborhoods.

Disruptive thinking helps shape the future. After over forty years of interlinked reform and opening. China has been profoundly transformed and become the world's second largest economy. With economic reform at home and opening to engagement with the outside world, China is advancing toward national rejuvenation in constant pursuit of reform. I'm fully confident that Shanghai will ultimately become a global city of excellence and modern metropolis with international influence.

We should always remain true to our original aspiration and keep our mission firmly in mind. Though it's far harder to remain committed, staying steadfast in our aspiration and mission is what inspires us to continue to move ahead. As Shanghai goes through its rapid urbanization for the past three decades, improving the city's quality and standards guided Xintiandi to forge ahead.

In 1997, I suggested at the Shanghai Mayor's International Business Leaders Conference that Shanghai should create a creative, energetic, and entertaining environment equipped with full range of amenities as the focal point in the city center where locals and internationals can gather. Many of the participants probably did not expect that I would put my words into action and in four years' time, have created Xintiandi that has gained global recognition.

Shanghai was undergoing rapid urban expansion infused with standardization through wholesale demolition and large-scale construction 20 years ago when the Xintiandi project was first started. Most real estate developers didn't realize that preserving the city's historical and cultural heritage was the source of quality and differentiation. Cultural heritage sites were damaged accidentally or deliberately for more economic returns.

In fact, uniform architectural styles and stereotype patterns have resulted in standardization, ultimately harming distinctiveness and urban differentiation. Many cities are now having a deeper and more rational understanding of a vibrant urban community and recognizing the importance of preserving its cultural identity. Efforts have been made to regain the city's cultural glory by integrating architectural styles, urban skyline, waterway layout, streetscape features, multiple modes of

NEW FOREWORD

transportation. Many Chinese cities I have visited lately boast urban streetscape exuding strong historical fabric of the city that would not fall short of their Western counterparts.

With 20 years of experience and dedication, Xintiandi will continue to strive for excellence, innovation and upgrading, and contribute to making Shanghai a better city.

Who can read into the past can read into the future.

This book is a first-hand account of Xintiandi's growth trajectory and showcases the author's forward-looking perspective on Shanghai's historical and cultural heritage as well as its future development. Since its publication in 2015, this practical book has become an important teaching material in the Leadership Program in Urban Development and Cultural Creativity held by renowned colleges and universities such as Fudan University, Shanghai Jiaotong University, and Tongji University, and well received among government officials and business leaders.

This book has been collected by Shanghai Library as well as the internal library of the general office of Shanghai Municipal Committee. Available on Dangdang, Amazon and other online bookstores, this book, highly recommended by professionals and easy reading for the general public, has been reprinted twice. This edition marks the 20th anniversary of Shanghai Xintiandi and is dedicated to the 100th anniversary of the founding of the Communist Party of China.

Vincent H. S. Lo
Chairman of the Shui On Group
December 30, 2020

Preface

Twenty years is a long time. Two decades have passed since the opening of Shanghai's Xintiandi. Mr. Zhou's book is a factual account of the origins, design, and execution of this world famous, game changing, urban culture and entertainment destination. This new, English edition leaves no stone unturned, no fact unchecked, no contribution unrecognized.

When Mr. Zhou writes that he provided the bridge between Shui On Land and the Luwan District Government (now part of Huangpu District), he is being extremely modest. When he joined the Xintiandi team in January of 1999 there was only one man to whom he reported: Vincent Lo. An early, brilliant, and intrepid Great Urbanization of China pioneer, Vincent instinctively knew that he was in a class of one when he took on the Taipingqiao project. It was his mountain to climb. Vincent's guiding principle: "he who flies highest, sees the farthest", Vincent hand-picked Mr. Zhou to help his team "cross the Rubicon", to go where no developer in Shanghai had ever gone. Mr. Zhou could have chosen to use his communication skills to simply lavish praise on a Hong Kong prodigal son and promote his own aspirational agendas. Instead, he chose the intellectual high road and took on challenges that would help break new ground for both Shui On and the Luwan District. Mr. Zhou did not provide the bridge; he was the bridge. He never bragged about his unique qualifications, academic excellence. With carefully thought out, practical, sensible, reasoning strategies, he quietly went about helping put the right people in the right place to resolve complex approval and permitting issues. His book chronicles every aspect of this remarkable, epic journey into the past, present, and future

PREFACE

of the most modern, metropolitan, city in China.

This year, 2021, an exhibition of XTD archival drawings, photographs, and media documents brought Mr. Zhou and I back together. The exhibition, "XTD and Beyond", was hosted by the Shanghai Public Library No. 1. on Hua Hai Road. Much of the historical content came from the materials collected by Mr. Zhou in preparation for his original, Chinese, edition. Learning he would soon publish a new edition in English was great news. There are many XTD myths that will finally be dispelled for the English language community, both here in China, and abroad. Many people take credit for the success of XTD. Critics claim that XTD is a fake reproduction. Wannabees purloin the brand suffix, "Tiandi", hiring unscrupulous design and marketing firms to devise ways to emulate the commercial and cultural success of XTD.

XTD became Shanghai's model for all subsequent historic neighborhood re-development. Originally part of the French Concession, XTD's richly diverse urban fabric was created by a cross-cultural architectural exchange between the East and the West. The socio-economic value of the adaptive re-use of this human scale environment cannot be over-stated. The inherent human dignity of XTD's culture-based authenticity cannot be replicated, 3-D printed, or cultivated in the virtual world of DNA modified, artificial intelligence.

Mr. Zhou's book does not begin with his arrival at Shui On in early 1999. His research goes back to the very beginning of Shui On's presence in Shanghai. XTD was not Vincent's first investment in Shanghai real estate. But all others pale in comparison with XTD. Conceived in the late 90's, an Asia-wide economic recession made it difficult for real estate developers to borrow money. Vincent elected to risk his personal fortune. He was the sole owner of his company. He knew that all boats float in a rising tide of strategic capital investment. He would own the boats, not the bank. He was going to build a city within a city. He knew that creating a commercially and culturally successful

entertainment destination would add immeasurable value to the rest of Shu On's massive Taipingqiao development. He was going to change Shanghai and then change China. Vincent could see the forest.

Other independent, private developers, lacking any real vision, saw only trees. They were collecting, not creating, value. Only Vincent Lo saw far enough to recognize that the human spirit is not invincible. Policies that encourage the destruction of existing urban neighborhoods and rural communities can adversely affect a society's well being. His vision for a more humane approach changed my life, and the lives of those around him. What does it mean to live in Shanghai when all around you the city is changing? It is a question that continues to demand an answer. Mr. Zhou's book is a guided tour of a compelling and visionary response to this question. Shanghai Xintiandi should be on the shelf of every urban planner, architect, and real estate developer who wants to make the world a better place.

Benjamin T. Wood
December 5th, 2021

Foreword

Xintiandi (literally meaning *'new heaven and earth'*), the new landmark and name card of Shanghai, is a successful case that shows historical architecture invested with modern civilization.

From North America to Europe, from Asia to Oceania, Xintiandi is well-known to almost every continent in the world. Since its fame has spread far and wide across China, including mainland, Hongkong and Taiwan, many places are trying to copy the model of Xintiandi.

Why is Xintiandi so popular both at home and abroad?

Let's take a look worldwide to find the answer. The highrise buildings constructed during the urbanization process in the 19th and 20th centuries in the United States and Europe have shown signs of wear and tear. Recession and hollowing-out of the downtown areas in some cities have emerged. Some construction experts in the United States have proposed that the direction of urban development in the 21st century is urban regeneration, which requires activation of the cultural heritage of the 20th century. Some city planners in France advocate the development idea of "building cities on cities". How to invest historical architecture with modern civilization is a major issue for urban regeneration.

Xintiandi is essentially a successful case of regeneration of old buildings in the downtown area, which happens to be a global hot topic. Moreover, it occurs in China, where urbanization started not long ago. It has seized the curiosity of developed regions such as Europe, the United States and Japan. Construction experts and senior government officials from various countries who have been to Xintiandi all spoke highly of the project. In

China, government leaders and experts unanimously agree that Xintiandi has set a good example.

China embarked on urbanization at the beginning of the 21st century, catching up with developed countries at an amazing speed. The top of the city offers a spectacular panorama of a massive concrete jungle filled with immense skyscrapers, as if in New York, Tokyo or Hongkong. No more than one hundred high-rise buildings have survived through the centennial history of the Old Shanghai. However, in just 20 years thereafter, over ten thousand high-rises have sprung up in the city, 100 times that of the Old Shanghai.

Nevertheless, it is the historic buildings that could represent the image of Shanghai. The stones, bricks, iron doors and wooden windows left behind have preserved the spirit of entrepreneurship and innovation. Interestingly, while walking in the orderly arranged and well connected *Shikumen* alleys, many foreigners claim that this is the real Shanghai as it is one of a kind in the world.

As the urbanization processes unfold, China is facing a universal problem of homogenization—there is very little difference among the high rises in Shanghai, Tokyo, or New York. Perhaps it is the historic buildings with cultural heritage of the city that are the most culturally recognizable and vital. The reason why Xintiandi has such a charm is consequently self-evident.

A re-creation that integrated Chinese culture and Western culture, *Shikumen* (literally meaning 'Stone Warehouse Gate') has become cosmopolitan with its uniqueness and distinctiveness. *Shikumen* reached its heyday in the 1920s. By the late 1930s, *Shikumen* buildings were on their way out when Shanghai was invaded by the Japanese warlords and subsequently lost its position as Asia's financial center. Most *Shikumen* neighborhoods remained unchanged in their crowded state for more than 60 years until the economic reforms in the 1990s, when a *Shikumen* Museum was renovated to display the authentic restoration of

FOREWORD

the living space. In 2010, "construction techniques of *Shikumen* alley architecture" was recognized by the Chinese government on the national intangible cultural heritage register.

At the end of the 20th century, *Shikumen* residences were regarded as an obstacle to the modernization of the city by the people of Shanghai, who were desperate to replace them with new housing opportunities. Young people were looking forward to moving out of *Shikumen* residences and moving into modern apartments as soon as possible. Against this backdrop, large-scale demolition projects were carried out during the early phase of urban housing reform, leading to the demise of *Shikumen* residences. People of Shanghai were amazed at how Xintiandi has revived *Shikumen* — the old neighborhood of decay and overcrowding has been transformed into the city's new landmark and a hub of the city's trendiest fashion, dining and shopping. Having witnessed the constant price appreciation of the residential areas around Xintiandi which has become the benchmark for the downtown real estate prices, people of Shanghai have completely abandoned their prejudice against old *Shikumen*. Young people flocking to *Shikumen* alleys to take wedding photos has even become a fad.

Xintiandi has received several awards from the Chinese Government and been designated as the 'Demonstration Base of National Cultural Industry'. It has also won accolades from international institutes and academies, such as the 'Award for Excellence' from US-based Urban Land Institute and 'Architecture of Cultural Legacies' from the American Institute of Architects.

Xintiandi's success is not entirely based on luck. It has gone through risks and hardships. In late 20th century when people of Shanghai were demolishing the old *Shikumen* houses and building new apartments with overwhelming ambition, it was against the social trend and the longings of the majority to propose preservation of *Shikumen*. Under such circumstances, it took Shui On Land Limited, a Hong Kong-based company

headquartered in Shanghai, much courage and determination to develop Xintiandi. When many citizens and some people in power didn't understand and opposed to the reconstruction of *Shikumen*, the project was at stake.

I joined the Xintiandi development team in January 1999. My job responsibility was to bridge the communication between Shui On and Shanghai government, media and general public, so as to minimize friction and resistance in the course of development of this new project. I have witnessed and participated in the whole process that gave me the opportunity to closely observe and reflect on the key to its success.

The development and opening-up of the Pudong district have ushered in the era of Shanghai's urban construction, while Xintiandi marked a milestone for the city's entering a new phase. Mr. Chang Qing, dean of the Department of Architecture of Tongji University, has made a special comment, "Xintiandi is a benchmark of the contemporary urban renewal of Shanghai. Nevertheless, it is a limited edition that cannot be replicated." In fact, since its establishment ten years ago, Xintiandi has always been imitated but never surpassed. The key to its success remains a secret.

History without mystery is dull. This is where Xintiandi's charm lies.

At the beginning of the project, no one could tell what Xintiandi should look like since it seemed to be a far-reaching dream that only some believed in.

The ambiguous prospects for Xintiandi 13 years ago can now be clarified with certain patterns.

Benjamin Wood, the American chief designer of Xintiandi, has made some insightful comments. "It is a shallow understanding that the renovation of the old buildings led to the success of Xintiandi," said Wood, "As a matter of fact, Xintiandi is not only about the old buildings. It is a representative of the contemporary Chinese culture rather than the old culture which is perishing. Shanghai is creating its own new culture instead of introducing

FOREWORD

western spirit. I have noticed that many places are attempting to replicate Xintiandi, most of which I'm afraid will not succeed."

Mr. Wood's remarks, made in 2001, were abstract and eye opening. I didn't understand what new culture and old culture referred to. With the civilization and urban development of Shanghai in the past 13 years, we have grasped the differences that lie between the new culture and the old culture by learning from the experience and lessons.

- The attitude toward urban history (including old buildings and cultural traditions, etc.), whether to inherit and develop the cultural legacy or demolish everything and start over, draws a line between the new culture and the old.
- The philosophy of building and constructing, whether to open up and embrace the concept of transculturation or close off the connection with the outside world, sets the boundary between the new culture and the old.
- The mindset, whether to stay self-concerned or be considerate of others, forms the division between the new culture and the old. In the process of industrialization and urbanization, considering others involves taking into account history, future, environment and the descendants, while being self-concerned pursues only the immediate interest and profit maximization that will give rise to the consequence of environmental deterioration to be burdened by the future generation.
- The new culture behind leisure and fashion strikes a balance between maximum profit and minimum environmental degradation, between fast-paced urban life and slow-moving lifestyle, and between dedicating to work and prioritizing wellbeing.

This book is about the history of the establishment of Xintiandi, as well as my own perception of the new culture. Urban civilization is discovered through exploring and understanding the new culture (which is a different concept from civilization). Through the eyes of discovery, it is an impressive finding that people's mindset and behaviors are closely associated with urban architectural space, including pre-established habits and new manners built in recent ten years, and widths of the streets are subtly related to urban innovation capability. Moreover, the patterns of old city renovation have been discovered that the rolling process of integration and separation goes like a spiral curve.

I have tried to write about Xintiandi as much as I could, which has also been expected by some of my friends in the cultural and creative industry in recent years. I am neither an architect nor an economist. While I have witnessed the entire development of Xintiandi, this book is just a reflection of observation and thoughts from a personal perspective, subject to omissions or even errors. I believe time will be the fairest and toughest judge.

Zhou Yongping
Oct 1, 2014

Content

New Foreword   V
Preface   XII
Foreword   XV

PART 1   Xintiandi: a new cultural and social destination   1

Chapter 1	Entrance to Xintiandi	3
Chapter 2	The T-shaped intersection	13
Chapter 3	Central Fountain Square	21
Chapter 4	Songshan Packaging Station / Wulixiang Museum	39
Chapter 5	An extended back lane paved with history	59
Chapter 6	The South Block	81
Chapter 7	Taipingqiao Lake Park	93

PART 2   The Secret Formula for Xintiandi's Success   105

Chapter 1	The origin of Xintiandi	107
Chapter 2	The debate on restoration	133
Chapter 3	Turning Dust to Gold	161
Chapter 4	Shanghai's urban fabric in the next stage	185
Chapter 5	The success of a word-of-mouth marketing strategy	199
Chapter 6	Passion, the key to success	217
Chapter 7	Innovation is the admission ticket	241
Chapter 8	Protecting culture in urban regeneration	259
Chapter 9	Business operation determines the value	299

PART 3	A series of 'Tiandi' enlightment	**321**
Chapter 1	A new Initiative	323
Chapter 2	Reshaping Shanghai's social fabric	335

References 349
Postscript 351

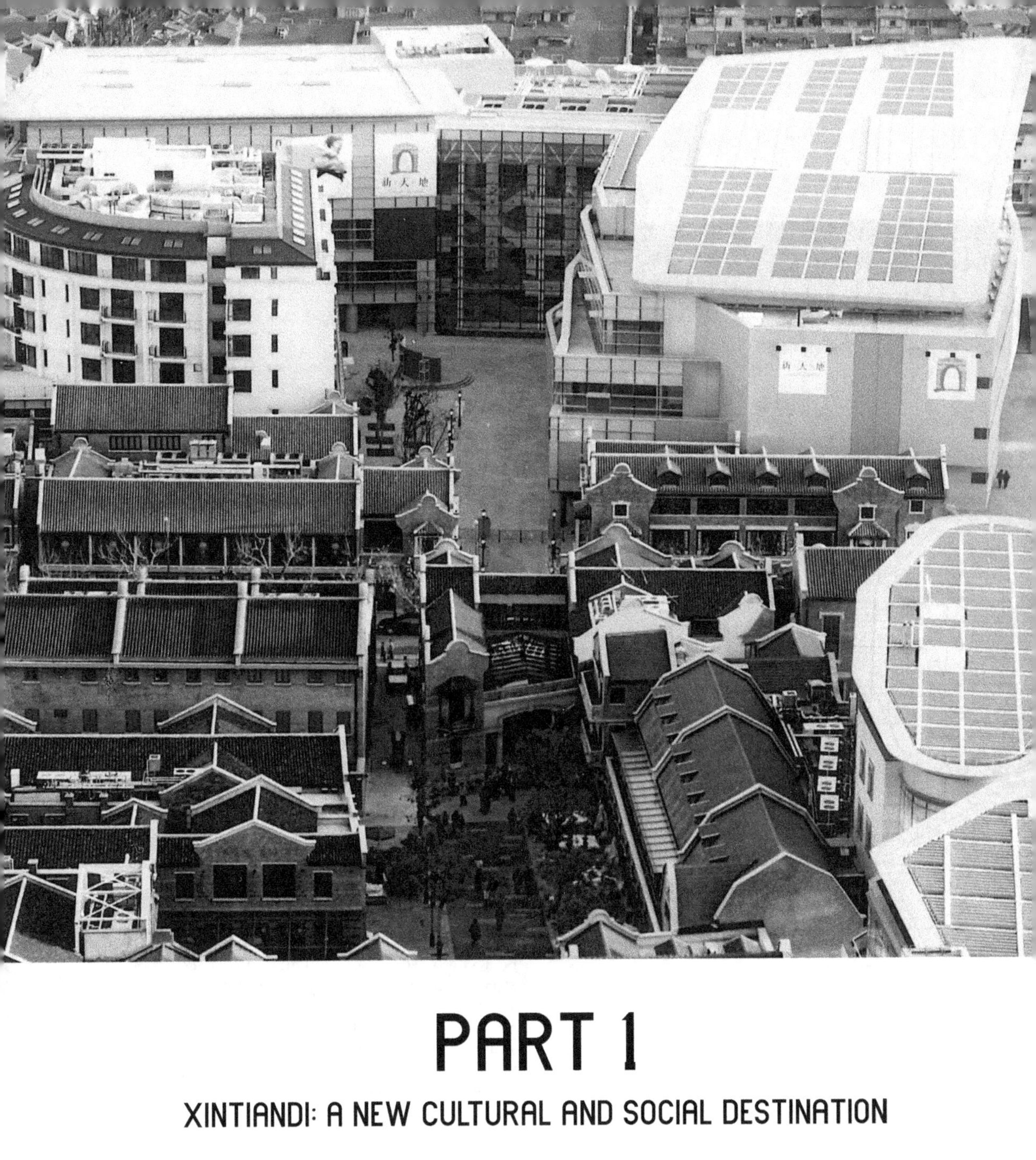

PART 1

XINTIANDI: A NEW CULTURAL AND SOCIAL DESTINATION

The real voyage of discovery consists in observing with inner peace and tending to the details where the cultural richness is hidden. Nothing is visible with an agitated and thoughtless mind.

1
XINTIANDI

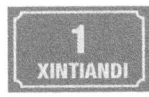

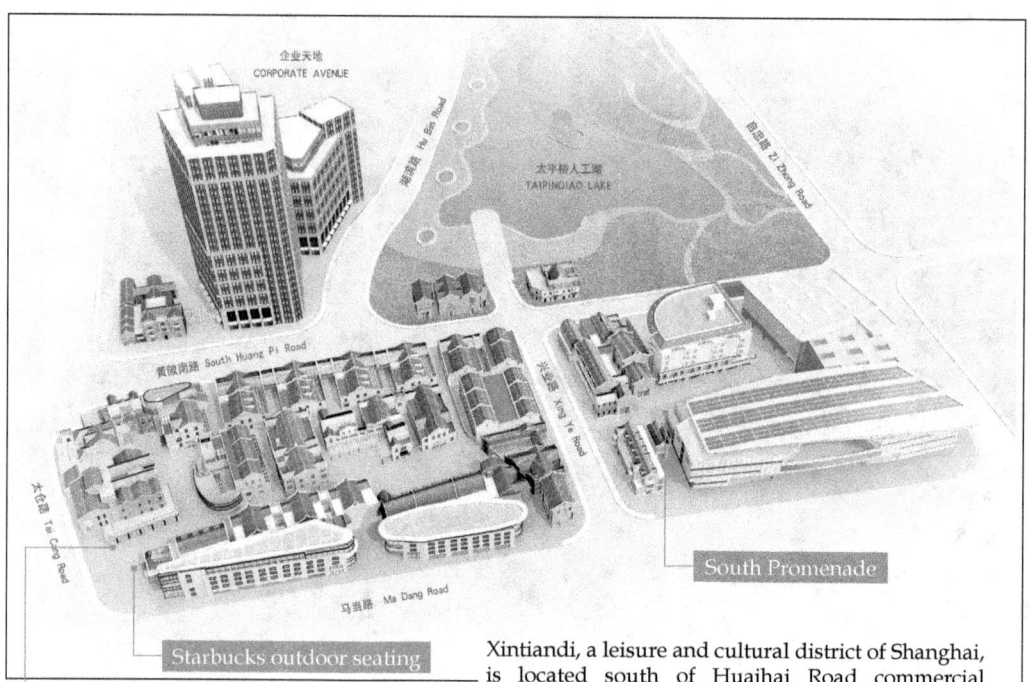

Xintiandi, a leisure and cultural district of Shanghai, is located south of Huaihai Road commercial street and split into a pedestrianized north and south blocks composed of reconstituted traditional *Shikumen* houses. It covers a site area of 30,000 square meters and a gross floor area of 60,000 square meters, receiving a total of 15 million visitors from home and abroad each year.

CHAPTER 1

Entrance to Xintiandi

Xintiandi doesn't take up a lot of space but has attracted much attention. Nevertheless, many tourists, both domestic and from abroad, often loiter at the entrance of the North Block and ask for directions to Xintiandi.

Most Chinese tourist attractions feature conspicuous signs such as tall architectural arch, plaques at scenic sites inscribed with celebrity calligraphy, tall walls or iron fences enclosing the area, ticket booths, etc., all of which are absent in Xintiandi. It wasn't an omission but a creative approach and new urban design utilizing the cultural atmosphere to achieve a natural transition.

Chinese culture and European culture are very different in terms of the deployment of functional areas. Walls and fences are widely used to divide the space into separate functional areas in Chinese culture, while European culture features a fusion of functional areas that blurs the boundaries and facilitate more convenient communications across the areas. Xintiandi is a representative of delivering the idea of cross-culture.

Xintiandi has its own cultural characteristics. The plaza at the entrance offers outdoor seating for about 30 guests with patio umbrellas of European flair. The seats are often fully occupied by people from all over the world, catching up with friends and family or watching the hustle and bustle over a drink at Starbucks.

With a modest but exquisite design, the entrance of *Shikumen* alley, where traditional Chinese breakfast such as soy milk,

With no archway or walls at the entrance, the gateway to Xintiandi is studded with a public piazza, where people can sit and relax for a cup of coffee and enjoy the streetscape.

sesame pancakes and Chinese crullers were once on sale, now interestingly blends with cafes that offer bread and cake. *Shikumen*, a place of cultural nostalgia for the local people is an eye opener for the Western tourists, while the outdoor cafes, a cultural identity of Western origin, provide a refreshing take for the locals. The entrance symbolizes a novelty for both Eastern and Western visitors and still retains a collection of reminiscences.

Xintiandi is a hybrid of historic elements and modern connections, a freely accessible block without doors or walls, and a welcoming embrace to the public.

The stone-paved pedestrian street that stretches across the cluster of *Shikumen* buildings neither resembles the traditional *Shikumen* alleys nor spans as widely as the high streets. These

ENTRANCE TO XINTIANDI

customer-friendly and refreshingly impressive alleys not only lead to the shopping malls but also revolutionize the lifestyle by offering upscale fashion brands, French cuisine, German snacks as well as trendy art studios.

Featuring plain brick walls, wooden doors painted glossy black and straight side alleys, the *Shikumen* houses that were once swarming with residents and hubbub now boast gentle music and elements of fashion. Pubs bring the thrill of rock music to the customers while the outdoor seating allows an invigorating touch of breeze. In an attempt to recall their cultural memory, local people are resigned to a farewell to the bygone love and determined to cherish the present.

People of Shanghai visit Xintiandi in the feeling of nostalgic roots, rediscovering beauty in the recollection of old times.

Fountains in European piazzas are an expression of Western culture. The fountain at the entrance of Xintiandi highlights the cultural ambience of the piazza, despite a narrow pedestal due to limited space. The steady flow of water fosters a slow-paced environment, encouraging the hurried city dwellers to slow down and take a break, savoring minutes rather than counting them before moving onto the next task.

Narrow alleys invite visitors to explore the labyrinth with excitement and anticipation, just like unwrapping the gifts.

Younger local descendants are lavish in their praise of the alleys: "My mom used to live here. How come I didn't realize its charm!"

Having caught sight of a reflection of their traditional culture in the uncanny resemblance between the old buildings and the terrace houses in London, Western visitors stand enthralled by the historic spaces that accommodate international cuisines and fashion design. The layout of the complex bears a close similarity to its counterparts in Europe, demonstrating a remarkably rapid urban development. Driven by curiosity, Western visitors take a seat in the outdoor café to savor the charm of the neighborhood.

After the First Opium War in 1840, the British, French and American colonial presences brought in Shanghai their architecture, blending Western elements with traditional Chinese buildings and bringing revolutionary changes to the unvarying style of Chinese residences. *Shikumen* houses originated near the Bund in the British concession around 1870. Western style terrace houses were adapted to Chinese conditions, with sub-alleys branching off of the main alley, symbolizing the meeting of East and West.

The plain brick walls, old roof tiles and interlocking alleys distinguish Xintiandi from the Nanjing Road shopping precinct, not only by the buildings, but also by the pavement which is an important detail likely to be overlooked. Smooth marble paving is widely used in most shopping precincts in China, while the pedestrian streets in Xintiandi area are paved with stone and recycled gray bricks of higher friction, embodying the architect's distinctive comprehension of leisure and cultural perception.

Pavements play a crucial role in the development of urban culture, as the paving materials mirror the rhythm of city life. The *Shikumen* alleys and urban streets in old Shanghai were square block stones (broadly rectangular quarried stones used in paving roads and walkways), also retained on Avenue des Champs-Elysées in Paris and in old town of Prague in Czech Republic. "Tange lu" (square block stones paved pathway) provides a moderate coefficient of friction, echoing a slow pace of city life, with permeability as its top advantage. The breathable gaps between Tange lu bear a resemblance to human skin texture, allowing the rainwater to infiltrate into the soil and be conserved in the groundwater recharge. The disadvantages of concrete pavements and asphalt roads, which are widely used in some cities in China, include poor permeability of rainwater that is collected by sewer system together with wastewater. The adoption of convenient concrete pavements and asphalt roads indicates an extremely eager pursuit of rapid urbanization in China. The smooth, mirror-like stone pavers used in the living room has been largely applied to the shopping precincts, glossy and expensive but slippery and dangerous especially for the old adults in rainy days.

Leisure culture empowers the urban residents to get off the treadmill and embrace a slower pace of life. The stone and recycled gray bricks paving has offered a moderate coefficient of friction, signaling a balanced mindset of gentle pace of life. Among all the metrics, a calm state of mind is the key index for a metropolis to stand out in the global competition.

With the development of ecocity underway, Tange lu is expected to stage a comeback in Shanghai and evolve with an integration of hi-tech rainwater harvesting and filters, turning the nature-blessed rainwater into the city's water recharge and reducing the urban heat island effects by deflecting radiation from the sun.

Development of urban culture entails philosophical contemplation on the urban space and tradition, rather than a blunt attempt to construct multiple cinemas, theaters or landmarks. Equally significant, architecture and pavement of a city bring art to urban life, spiritual fulfillment to people and accessibility to cultural development.

Exhausted by the hustle and bustle of urban life, people have ceased to appreciate the eternal cycles of nature and seasons. Much like a military strategist qualified by aptitude, experience,

Remodeled from the passageway where the demolished old Shikumen houses used to stand, the pedestrian street zigzags in the complex, harboring outdoor cafes along both sides.

The master plan of Xintiandi project features the space structure of main alley running through the site with branches of crisscrossing sub-alleys. The pedestrian street, functioning as the main alley, is paved with stone, visually contrasting with the recycled gray bricks paving of the sub-alleys in both material and color.

and education in the formulation and articulation of military strategy, an outstanding architect, in addition to building houses, incorporates nature inspired elements, from light to shade and wind to rain, into his design. The shifting outlines of the building at different times and weather conditions spice up a tedious life, impelling people to worship the power of nature through the media of architect.

The long stretch of the pedestrian street, interrupted only by the rich aroma of coffee and freshly baked bread as well as dance music in the air, is characterized by its smell, atmosphere, sound and color that distinguish Xintiandi from Huaihai Road commercial street and Nanjing Road shopping precinct.

Yet the most distinctive difference lies in the visitors of Xintiandi. Being the foremost characteristic of Xintiandi's cultural recognition, the customers that frequent the block are among the earliest adherents to simple living. Simple living promotes refraining from luxury and indulgence and advocates a change in mindset especially for the emerging affluents who kept buying to fill the void of acceptance and approval before eventually realizing that "less is more". They choose clothing and diet for bodily comfort rather than for showing off. Furthermore, they

A Shikumen *alley of Shanghai*

develop a detachment from electronic devices and devote time to spiritual inspiration. It is quality over quantity that manifests the essence of simple living.

The evolution of urban architecture demonstrates the return of modern intellectual culture and lifestyle.

The pattern of the stone pavement slabs in XTD, where the smooth and the rough surfaces alternate to create different plays of light and shadow in various weather conditions, demonstrates a fascinating cultural conception.

ENTRANCE TO XINTIANDI

Terrace houses in London

A main alley in the Shikumen *neighborhood*

Tange lu in Prague

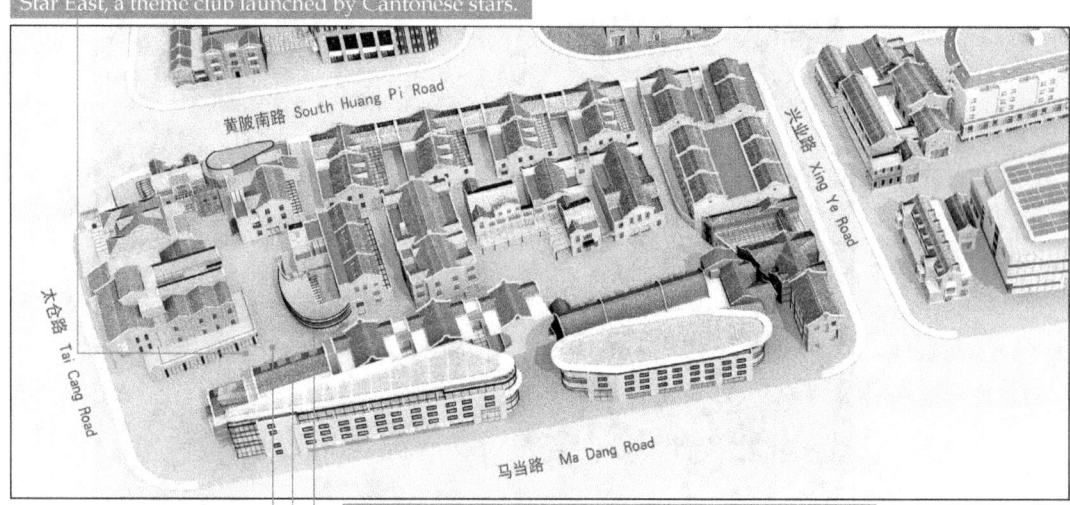

CHAPTER 2
THE T-SHAPED INTERSECTION

The first crossroad is a T-intersection that leads to the second trademark of Xintiandi where a curved glass structure comes into sight, housing Luna Restaurant and Bar, a Mediterranean restaurant. The integration of modern architecture in the cluster of the restored old houses has brought in a new flavor to the complex. The increment in the number of architectural elements of *Shikumen* residences from five or six in the past to eight or nine at present symbolizes a new development of *Shikumen* architecture, showcasing Shanghai's characteristic mix of modern and old.

The glass structure stands in conformity with the old houses, like a youngster encircled by the genial older adults. The harmonious fusion highlights the historical richness of the old buildings, exhibiting the city's progressive evolution.

Rather than completely refurbished, the exterior of *Shikumen* houses was renovated to be as historically authentic as possible to preserve every twist and turn of an evolving neighborhood. After erasing the trace of modern society on the exterior, including removal of air-con outdoor units, billboards, electric cables and laundry racks, the developer cleaned up the exterior with a high-pressure water gun to reveal its true color. The purification greatly enhanced the cultural quality of the old houses, like a piece of copper scrap found in grandpa's vintage chest turning into a priceless antique with rust wiped off and a complement of velvet pad and overhead light. In addition to restoring the structure of the old houses altered by its dwellers,

The connection between the glass structure and the Shikumen houses bears a resemblance to that of two generations. The developer opted for designs to reflect historical context and cultural climate of Shanghai over a high-rise with lucrative floor area ratio, curtailing the height of the structure at a lower level with additional removal of decorative spires, like a gesture of respect from the youngster to the old adults.

the renovation involves mending with surface curing reinforcing agents and damp-proofing agents.

These historical buildings now respectively house Starbucks Coffee from the U.S., Latina Grill from Brazil, Paulaner Brauhaus from Germany and Star East Nightclub from Hong Kong SAR. Each corner of the old houses deserves a close-up. A cup of freshly ground coffee in a quaint café characterized by exposed air-

conditioning ducts under the roof to signal industrial civilization, the echo of Shanghai vernacular music on a phonograph sitting under a modern painting, and feelings of coziness and nature evoked by the rustic log furniture with apparent annual rings, brings back familiar memories of the past.

When consulted if the thriving business of Starbucks owes to the rich flavor of its coffee, the supervisor shakes his head and smiles, "No, we don't sell coffee. We sell the sentiment of quality time and Shanghai nostalgia." Over a cup of cappuccino,

The internal lay-out has been strikingly altered. The compact living space, previously carved up into a living room, wing rooms, a kitchen and an enclosed courtyard, has been remodeled into an adjoining business area spacious enough to house a dozen of round tables, armchairs and even a stage with a grand piano.

locals and tourists fill their time with appreciating nice-looking passers-by and embracing the sunshine that can't be carried off with a cup of takeaway coffee.

The management of Luna repeatedly stresses that their selling point is the *Shikumen* house preserved in-store that inspires the recollections of the Old Shanghai days. The manager always takes the customers on a tour of the *Shikumen* historical building across the hall where three stone gate frames of 70 years of age and a stretch of gray brick wall stand, like the annual rings in the cross section of an old tree, reflecting the memories of Old Shanghai culture. The piece of wall, more like a stage setting, has witnessed the spontaneous moments improvised by streams of customers.

The look of the old alleys prior to renovation

The ambience conjures up scenes of the old times for the local diners: accompanied by the melodious bell of the Custom House on the Bund at dawn, the dwellers stepped out of the *Shikumen* residences, with a chamber pot at one hand and a coal stove at the other. The neighborhood sprang to life after a good night's sleep, amidst the shouting of the greengrocers selling freshly picked vegetables from a shoulder pole along the alley. Haggling over the price with the greengrocers, housewives and maids together with the kids sometimes received help from the neighbors to bag the best bargain.

Eating on the go, the hurried commuters rushed to the bus stop with a briefcase on one hand and a pack of sesame pancake and Chinese crullers on the other. The bustle of the peddlers, who were hawking traditional Chinese pastries along the alley, filled the neighborhood with liveliness.

The place quieted down at noon, when the older adults were

basking in the sun and women were knitting in the doorway. After school was over around three to four o'clock in the afternoon, the children reactivated the neighborhood, playing hide-and-seek, marbles and jump-rope. Along came a new batch of peddlers selling wontons, fermented glutinous rice balls and fried stinky tofu and craftsmen providing services such as sharpening scissors and repairing umbrellas and shoes. Young girls who spoke Wu Dialect from Suzhou (a neighboring city of Shanghai) were peddling blossoms of gardenia and white champaca in a sweet and soft voice, just like the fragrance of the flowers, while the craftsmen were shouting in loud and hoarse voices to drum up businesses. With distinctive tones of voice, peddlers succeeded in soliciting the attention of the kids who kept badgering their moms to buy them their favorite snacks or toys.

The play climaxed in the evening, the busiest time of the day, when women were burning coal in the stove to cook dinner in quick succession and talking about hot gossip in the communal kitchen. Food was served on the tables set in the alley for most

Luna Restaurant and Bar, a Mediterranean rustic restaurant, features an interior of Shanghai Shikumen alleys, epitomizing a lively dinner party in the 20th century when housewives served hot dishes on the tables set in the alley and the grandparents called the kids back for dinner. The scenes of pleasant-smelling dishes and hums of laughter, with the wave of demolition and reconstruction, are deeply rooted in the memory of the city, adding value to the cultural highlights of the restaurant.

An old lady cooking dinner in Shikumen alley

of the families, turning out to be a grand al fresco dinner party where residents shared bowls of pork and vegetable wontons, tried out neighbors' culinary skills and even joined dining tables. *Shikumen* residents extended the intimacy and sociability of lane life in their own way.

When night fell, the street lights cast a hazy yellow glow over the neighborhood. On a summer night, the alleys were packed with residents lying on cool bamboo lounge chairs, fanning themselves, shooting the breeze and playing cards. As the night wore on, the neighborhood piped down. Yet life moved on, and so did the play.

Shikumen buildings were where the scenes took place.

Since the practice of architecture is employed to fulfill the practical requirements, the prosperity of *Shikumen* buildings, incapable of keeping abreast of the times and changing urban lifestyle, has started to decline. Innovation made to *Shikumen* has proven a commercial hit. The historical characteristics of the original *Shikumen* settlements illustrate the cultural value of Xintiandi, justifying a high-priced cup of coffee sold here than on Huaihai Road.

Shanghai boasts numerous remarkable examples of modern architecture, such as the banks and trading houses on the Bund, European-style villas along Hengshan Road and the retail establishments on Nanjing Road and HuaiHai Road. Why are *Shikumen* buildings so overwhelmingly favored by local residents, domestic and foreign tourists as well as experts and scholars? While most of the excellent modern buildings are simple imitation and replication of Western architecture, *Shikumen* is a re-creation that symbolizes the meeting of East and West. Its uniqueness and originality are recognized by the world as emblematic of the city's identity. Despite the fact that *Shikumen* houses are barely holding on in modern living, the revolutionary spirit reverberates through history.

People's deep affection for *Shikumen* alleys is driven by their high esteem for revolution.

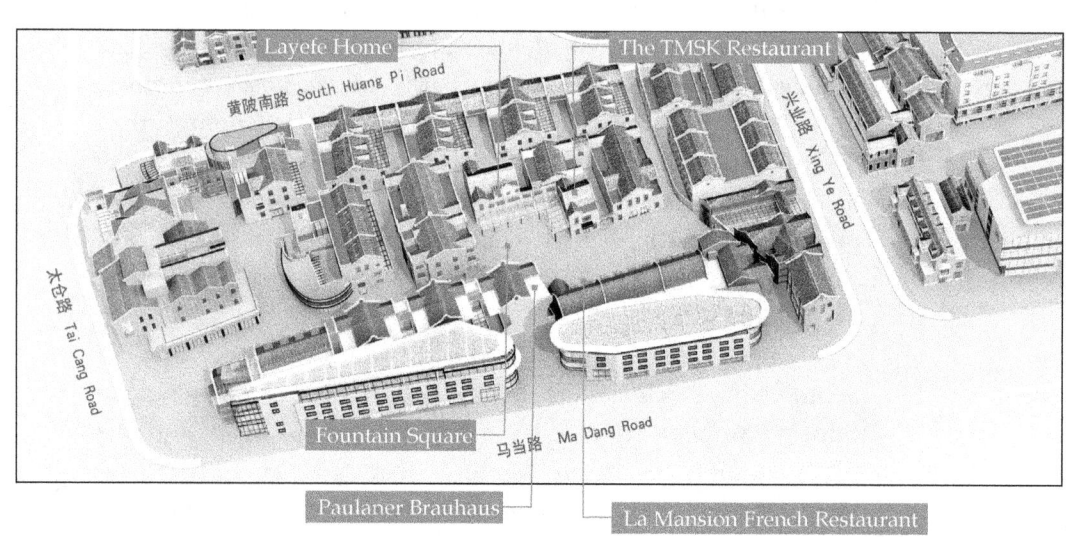

CHAPTER 3
Central Fountain Square

The stretch of the pedestrian street leads to a fountain square which is the third trademark of Xintiandi. Encompassing the square, the *Shikumen* buildings, despite their identical names, emanated from various developers and architectural designers according to historical archives. Albeit with distinctive presence, the buildings invite attentions to their namesakes instead of stealing each other's thunder, unlike other recently constructed buildings that strive to solicit the glare of publicity. The overemphasis on self-presence, just as each piece of musical instruments competes to stand out in an orchestra, will eventually break the finely wrought balance.

Urban architecture with mutual dependence mirrors the collaborative spirit essential in industrial production, while that with excessive self-emphasis reflects a decadent mentality of selfishness.

The fountain square offers the possibility to linger and enjoy the welcoming space, free from traffic and clouds of exhaust. The pedestrian street and three intricately designed lanes of distinct spans, with the widest broad enough for vehicular traffic and the narrowest hardly accommodable for two people, provide multiple entrances to the square, facilitating mass gathering and dispersion. The compound of a central square and lanes of different widths bears its convergence with a Parisian circular square from which a star of avenues radiates out.

Fountain of Blessings, sitting in the center of the square, shows three traditional Chinese mythological figures — the

EAST MEETS WEST

The fountain square is where the old houses used to stand. The inward focused design was conceived around a residential concept that invites visitors to the square, in contrast with some linear commercial streets in Shanghai.

CENTRAL FOUNTAIN SQUARE

Gods of Prosperity, Fortune and Longevity. The sculpture, an eye-catching photography spot favored by tourists, bears a refined interpretation of mingling Chinese and European folk culture.

Unnamed upon completion in the absence of the sculpture fountain, the square was nicknamed "Yifei Square" after Mr. Chen Yifei, one of China's most renowned contemporary artists, who leased the building on the east side of the square to house Layefe Home, a fashion brand of artwork that infuses quality with modern style.

The wide alley versus the narrow alley

The decade since Xintiandi's completion has proven that the nickname is more historically and culturally significant, not just because Mr. Chen was the forerunner of a new age in Chinese aesthetics, but because his representative of the emerging small

The sculpture group "Fountain of Blessings"

25
XINTIANDI

businesses of self-reliant production on the square notched a milestone in the history of Shanghai.

On entering the 21st century and new millennium, the world witnessed the start of the Third Industrial Revolution initiated by the Western pioneer. With manufacturing digitization as the core, the revolution has brought a paradigm shift, from centralized mass production that prevailed in previous industrial age to distributed, self-reliant production, exemplified by the revolutionary 3D printing technologies. Yifei Square is home to several small businesses in the cultural and creative industries, including Layefe Home, the TMSK restaurant, Shanghai Color, and Xavier.

Our first stop is Layefe Home. The two-story store showcases Chen's oil paintings, artifacts and homewares on the first floor and clothing and home décor on the second. Every piece of the exquisitely stylish vases, fruit bowls, tea sets and dishes epitomizes Chen's elements of art.

Puzzled by the mixed sale of artifacts and homewares, some consumers cast a speculative glance at Chen's dual identity as

Layefe Home offers a selection of clothing, oil paintings and household items on the second floor

both an artist and an entrepreneur.

An incorporation of hearing, sight and touch, electronic devices such as iPhone, iPod touch and iPad fall respectively in the scope of auditory sector, visual sector and tactile sector in the cultural and creative industry. Advocating the concept of visual culture which belongs to the visual sector, Chen is accomplished in areas of painting, industrial design, urban design, IT industry and clothing industry.

Layefe Home is both a retailer and a window to the concept of his "Great Visual Culture", while its factory, also possessed by Mr. Chen, is located in Tianzifang which is a touristic arts and crafts enclave in the vicinity of Xintiandi. The business structure bears a resemblance to that in the Agricultural Age when stores were in the front with factories sitting on the back. Dedicated to advocating small-scale self-reliant production, Chen Yifei is one of the pioneers in the East, whose name undoubtedly befits the square.

Mass production is characterized by production of large amounts of standardized products in a constant flow, in which production is detached from living and consumption, yet determines the mechanism of consumption. Small-scale self-reliant production, on the other hand, features customized manufacturing, a sensible mixture of production and living, and a dominant role that consumption plays over production. Consumers take the initiative to be the investors or manufacturers. The startup founders in the cultural and creative industry are primarily consumers who, evidently, have passion for life and live life to the fullest. Mostly from artists, fashion designers and intellectuals, these manufacturers promote their artistic flair and attitude toward life in the same way fashion insiders recommend the trendiest color, style or flavor to their appreciative followers.

Situated next to Layefe Home on the south side of the square, the TMSK restaurant is an exceptional representative of Shanghai cultural and creative industry. The restaurant presents a vivid illustration of a fairy tale land that blends together tea, fine

EAST MEETS WEST

The bar on the first floor of TMSK is a gorgeous length of art glass with thousands of liuli bricks pieced together. Lit from within, it takes up 1/3 of the space, exuding the feel of a highlighted oil painting.

The dark silhouettes of the customers stand out boldly against the illuminated bar.

CENTRAL FOUNTAIN SQUARE

The TMSK restaurant on the second floor features a colorful kaleidoscopic dome, inlaid with thousands of round liuli crystals. Light glints off the iridescent glass with the assistance of lighting control system.

Design of the ladies' restroom in TMSK is also imbued with artistry — water comes in thin streams from the stigma of a red lotus-shaped liuli sink.

The liuli sink in the men's restroom, with a pleasant earthy scent of the river bank, is shaped into dark green lotus leaves with a drooping seed pod. The restroom demonstrates a touch of Chinese culture, truly an experience worth coming for.

food, excellent wine and art of *liuli* (a form of archaic Chinese glasswork). The artistic Chinese glassware, instead of sitting for window display only, is now easily accessible in everyday life, sending a clear signal that the market need is where the cultural creativity extends.

With *liuli*-inlaid dome, orchid pool, table and chair sets, window lattice and restroom sinks, TMSK displays a dazzling interior as stunning as that of a crystal palace. In its staggering scale and splendor, it certainly is breathtaking to all the visitors that spontaneously walk and talk softly as if they were visiting a temple.

With bright red lantern-shaped bar stools and translucent *liuli* counter, the bar on the first floor creates a visual crush at first sight. The bold concept of cross culture is reinforced when the lantern stools meet the Western establishment and French wine clinks with Chinese Maotai.

The aisle on the second floor, like a time tunnel, stretches to a dimmer unknown where a new scene opens. With sizable eaves blocking the sun and sheer curtains keeping out the glare, the place is enveloped in soft light and shade with a close resemblance to a tranquil and noble imperial court of the Tang Dynasty at its height of power. What come into view are the intricately carved and painted beams as well as the upright totem pillars. The texture of Chinese culture, manifested in the standing lamps, winding corridors and glitzy glassware, proves that the enchanting Chinese design never fails to impress.

When asked about the source of the furniture and tableware, the management of TMSK would proudly reply, "We made everything on our own." Every single object in the restaurant, including paving, dome decoration, tableware and lighting fixture, comes from their own self-sustained factory in Minhang District of Shanghai. TMSK showcases art pieces from *liuli* Gongfang, Asia's leading crystal art brand, as well as an example of positive lifestyle. With TMSK having been invited into 2010 Shanghai World Expo and *liuli* Gongfang negotiating a tie-up

Live folk music in TMSK

with Shanghai Disneyland that is still under construction, this self-reliant enterprise is radiating its cultural impact with utmost endeavors.

Absorbing the traditions of several cuisines from Shanghai, Guangdong and of French and Italian cooking, TMSK takes pride in its new-wave Shanghainese cuisine endowed with cultural richness. Inspired by the European chefs who consider themselves as culinary artists and are often invited to meet and pose with the distinguished guests, the restaurant spares no effort to instill artistic sensibility into local chefs and prepare Chinese food that is as pleasing to the eye as it is to the palate.

Under the kaleidoscopic dome of the crystal world, diners are, in addition to the crystal tableware, gourmet food and nice wine, looking forward to some sound equally heavenly. Live folk music that combines Suzhou pingtan (a regional musical performance art form popular in part of south China) and Kunqu (one of the oldest extant forms of Chinese opera dating back to the beginning of Ming Dynasty) starts at nine sharp. Known as intangible cultural heritage, the traditional forms of folk music used to be favored only by older adults. With a magic touch by TMSK's artists and musicians, Pingtan and Kunqu have been infused with modern electronic musical elements, rising to fame as the "New Sound of China". Music has no boundaries. The iconic Chinese folk music is appealing to a wider audience from both home and abroad.

The hub of visual, auditory and palatal pleasure is founded by Loretta H. Yang, a two-time recipient of the Best Actress Award at the Golden Horse Awards, and Chang Yi, an esteemed Taiwanese film director. Albeit a latecomer to the realm of *liuli* culture that stretches back thousands of years, the couple was determined and resilient. Over a span of 11 years since its establishment, they used up all their savings, sold 3 houses and mortgaged 6 houses of all their family members in order to gain start-up capital. After much trial and error, they were able to master the lost-wax casting method. Healing Hand, one of their artworks, has greatly drawn international attention, symbolizing a revival of the lost art stifled at the end of Qing Dynasty and a reconnected bond between Chinese modern artistry and the art of *liuli* embedded in Han Dynasty two thousand years ago.

Chang and Yang's greatest contribution to Chinese *liuli* culture lies in extending the art to the general public as a part of the cultural industry. Motivated by the mission to present Chinese *liuli* to the world by penetrating people's daily life instead of putting on display in the museum, the couple endeavors to push the work of art to pass the boundaries of accessory and craft to incorporate it into modern living room and dining table. They hold on to their belief that improving the quality of life equates to overlapping aesthetics and life. Their artworks have been seen in sectors of construction, home decoration and household items. Committed to always transcending themselves and their international peers, they have, on behalf of the cultural and creative industry with self-reliant production in Asia, propelled "made in China" to "created in China" with their originality.

While TMSK and Layefe Home are the examples of joining aesthetics and creativity to dining and living, Shanghai Color and Xavier on the north side of the square have instilled them into clothing. Both retailers of clothing and accessories, they are recognized trendsetters specializing in fashion design, which is within the creative industry, rather than tailoring.

After the drop of New York City's apparel manufacturing industry, it has regained the throne as the world's fashion capital by transitioning to fashion design industry.

Richard Florida, founder of the Creative Class Group, asserts that countries with high concentrations of creative workers in science, technology, arts, design, music, entertainment, media, legal section, finance, business, healthcare and education exhibit a higher level of economic development. Florida refers to these groups collectively as the "creative class."

Creative workers in 1900 constituted only 5% of the U.S. labor force, whereas the percentage increased to around 10% in 1950 and 15% in 1980. It doubled to 30% in 2005, with a population of 200 million in the U.S., indicating a total of 70 million creative workers. The creative sector accounted for nearly half of all wage and salary income and 70% of discretionary spending, about US$2.1 trillion. Overshadowed by the creative economy, the service sector in the U.S. only collected 31% of all wages and 17% of discretionary spending. The Creative Class Group anticipates an increase of 10 million job opportunities generated by the creative economy in the U.S. by 2014. According to the Group's analysis, creative jobs represent 35%-45% of the total labor force in the developed Western countries.

Florida's research shows that the international economic landscape is spiky and most economic activities are concentrated in relatively few areas. The world is full of clusters where location matters. The talent-attracting regions, where creative talent migrates, generates higher regional income. Look no further than New York for its financial industry, Silicon Valley for its hi-tech industry and Los Angeles for its film industry as evidence of this phenomenon.

The square in the North Block has been home to the creative elites from Shanghai, Hong Kong and Taiwan since 2000, when Chinese design started to bloom in *Shikumen* areas. The clustering of these creative talents is the driving force behind Xintiandi's overnight boom.

The west side of the square accommodates all the restaurant tenants: Paulaner from Germany, La Maison from France and Ven-ice from Italy. Securing one of the outdoor seats is quite a feat especially in the evenings. These stores were meant to facilitate the development of the abovementioned self-reliant industries, yet they have generated much more income. Advocating the notion of producing and consuming simultaneously, both types, dependent on each other, showcase a trendy production mode and lifestyle.

Standing on the square offers a view of *Shikumen* buildings in the distance and high-rises up-close. One would recall the slogan printed on a billboard right at the entrance of the North Block—yesterday meets tomorrow at present—and ponder whether these revived old buildings stand for yesterday or tomorrow.

The high-rises undoubtedly represent the present. Shanghai's yesteryear, nevertheless, witnessed the straightening of meandering rivers to facilitate construction of roads and more than 9,000 *Shikumen*-style buildings in accordance with industry standards in the city's former colonial concessions. More than 10,000 high-rises have been erected according to industry standards in the course of the city's reurbanization in the new century.

Having rolled off the assembly line, today's food and beverage products are mass-produced in line with the industry standards, allowing for no individuality. Serial replication of the cities and commercial streets in China which infamously gave the country a "thousand cities with the same face" comes at a price—it may result in profit maximization, but ultimately harming distinctiveness and urban differentiation.

Serial replication, smog pollution, food safety and online shopping have posed new challenges to the development of China's urbanization and industrialization, urging a transition of mode of production and living. Crisis has, however, put forward an opportunity to wake people up from self-fulfilling euphoria.

Hence, the code of Xintiandi's vitality has been cracked. Who exactly activated this score of *Shikumen* houses?

Was it the Western architects? Not exactly. The growths of the industries and the city are tightly interlocked. With the injection of self-reliant production businesses, old *Shikumen* houses have regained vitality.

The team of architects evidently plays a crucial role. Not all architects are able to study the self-reliant production and architectural form in such depth, which proves Mr. Wood is one of the best.

It can be induced and even concluded that the iconic Xintiandi symbolizes the transition of production mode in Shanghai. The restored *Shikumen* houses are a testament to the vision that historical architecture will hold up both the new industries and modern life.

Despite the fact that emerging industries have sprouted over Xintiandi, Tianzifang, the Bridge 8, M50 and hundreds of other cultural and creative industry parks, mass production is still the mainstay of the city's production mode. Industry parks are therefore established to facilitate the growth of the self-reliant production businesses.

Unaware that they are engaged in a great cause, some of the parks presume it to be another themed real estate project. Driven by a business mentality, the parks impose an impulsive rent increase on the up-and-coming brands, only to suffocate the startups as well as the prospects of the parks. With the demise of the creative industry and consequently the cultural texture, it would only be a matter of time for the parks to wither.

EAST MEETS WEST

Window graphics and interior of Shanghai Color

Founded by a Taiwanese couple Kuo Cheng Feng and Wang Hsiao Hu, the store is nestled in a Shikumen house on the north side of the square. It sells women's scarves, satchels, apparel and accessories designed by the couple, accentuating the elements of Old Shanghai in the 1920s such as calendar posters, qipao (a type of body-hugging dress of Manchu origin) and social dance. The masterpieces "dancing qipao" and the "multi-colored parrots" exemplify a high standard of craftsmanship.

Australian fashion designer Anthony Xavier Edwards created his own namesake brand in one of the old houses. The spare, hip space displays Edwards's flamboyant designs that guarantee no two outfits are identical. It has attracted an international following, including the consular wives. With a special slogan – Proudly made in China, the outlet is the source of inspiration for a vast array of designer brands popping up in the vicinity in the next 10 years.

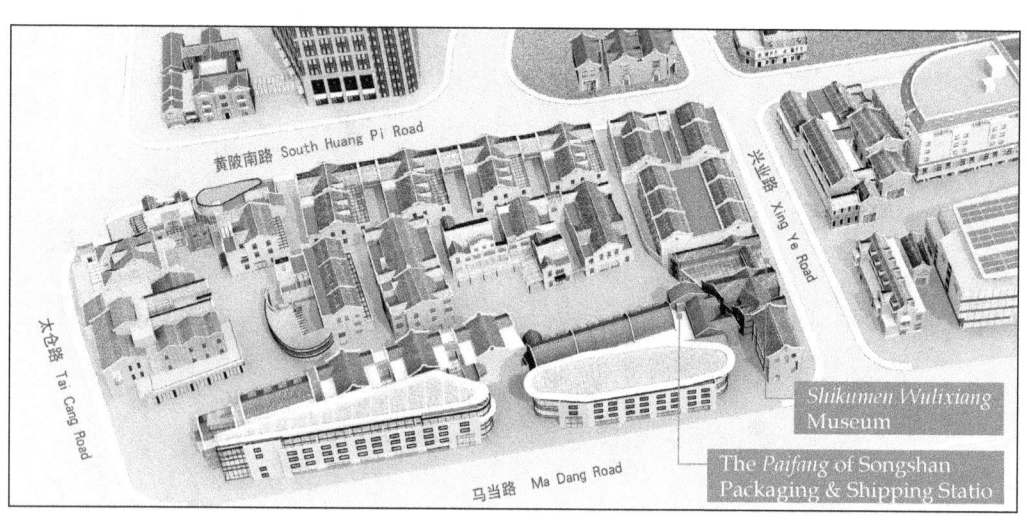

CHAPTER 4

Songshan Packaging Station / Wulixiang Museum

Running south of the square, the broadest pedestrian street in the complex, albeit uncompetitive in terms of width compared to that of Huaihai Road and Nanjing Road, is characterized by outdoor seating and an comfortably spacious car-free area that encourages interaction among the pedestrians.

With a tight space, fundamental facilities, antiquated furniture and air that is filled with smoky coffee aroma, the cafés provide affordable exquisiteness, bourgeois ambience and a taste of indigenous culture.

Walking on the gray brick pathways creates an illusion of a street full of Latin bars in Europe, bewildering the pedestrians as to where exactly they are strolling.

Local people are inspired to reminisce about the old days here—the establishments are where their living room, bedroom and kitchen used to stand. It feels like only yesterday that mom was calling the kids back for dinner, evoking nostalgia through a display of domesticity.

Mr. Ruan Yisan, an expert on historic preservation of China and professor of Tongji University, has been calling for an end to the demolition of *Shikumen* houses. The professor insists that the alleys should be retained, and so should the path to the city's history.

The path, composed of different historical episodes, links yesterday to present and stretches all the way to the future.

EAST MEETS WEST

40 XINTIANDI

SONGSHAN PACKAGING STATION / WULIXIANG MUSEUM

(Left/right) The Dunheli **Paifang** *was exempted from demolition in the process of urban regeneration, thanks to the remnants of the black-painted characters on the stone pillar: Songshan Packaging & Shipping Station. The characters exemplify a precious piece of history of the city engraved on the old buildings.*

China's urbanization drive has ushered in a new era when the spirit of preservation reverberates through the city's development that saves scores of historic buildings from the wrecking ball, by endowing them with vigor and vitality.

The preservation of the Dunheli *paifang* (a traditional style of Chinese architectural arch) is exactly an exemplification of protecting cultural heritage. After bulldozers knocked down the outer walls on the alleys of Dunheli, in accordance with the construction plan, keeping the *paifang* would only erect a barricade for the crowd.

The remnants of the black-painted characters on the stone pillar of the *paifang*, however, captured the attention of the foreign architects who eventually decided to keep it on hearing the story that took place in the late '60s and early '70s in Shanghai.

Today the *paifang* is a popular photography backdrop favored by some foreign visitors, but they are unaware of the cultural background, nor is the young generation of China.

EAST MEETS WEST

The courtyard of Shikumen, *a transitional space between the front gate and the inner house where both relaxation and chores take place, offers a sense of safety to the residents. Some even turn it into a garden, adding vibrant color to life.*

Inscribed with historical imprints, these characters witnessed an extreme expression of education movement in China's history. The Great Cultural Revolution, launched in 1966, denied the school admissions that had primarily been based on academic performances. Schools and universities were closed with the college entrance exams cancelled. Urban intellectual youths were mobilized to go to the countryside to be re-educated by the peasantry and to better understand the role of manual agrarian labor in Chinese society. Songshan Packaging and Shipping Station, a luggage transfer center of the railway station, provided luggage check-in service for the urban youths.

With termination of the Revolution and initiation of the historic Reforms and Opening-Up program, the college entrance exams were restored in the 1980s. However, in only 20 years, Chinese education system goes to the opposite extreme—the exam-oriented education system, a filtering process with fewer students at the higher end of the educational ladder, comes at the cost of students losing their imaginations and creativities.

The paint of the characters fades over time, nevertheless, it offers a constant reminder of the past and the present, signaling the arrival of a turning point for the standardized education and copycat architecture.

When we are deprived of key information to guide us, history is the only true teacher we should turn to. History moves in a spiral. We travel through time in a circular trajectory, our distance increasing from an epicenter only to return again. It is, therefore, vital for a nation, a country or a city to treasure and preserve its historic origins as past cycle and present pattern bring insight into the future.

Shikumen Wulixiang (literally meaning "home" in the Shanghai dialect) Museum in the Xintiandi area is one of the city's origins.

According to the Taipingqiao redevelopment project plan, the area measures 52 hectares and covers 23 *Shikumen* blocks, 22 of which are to be demolished, leaving only one intact to house a miniature history museum as a preservation of the historic origin.

The sitting room is a public area for family reunion and social activities. Against the wall sits an old fashioned square table seat eight people (representing a group of legendary immortals in Chinese mythology), accompanied by two old-fashioned wooden armchairs on both sides. The portrait of Buddha or ancestors are placed on the wall facing the main door where the residents could express veneration to the ancestors and carry out divine worship to pray for a better life.

Sitting on the south side of the North Block of Xintiandi on Xingye Road, the museum presents Shanghai life as it was around the 1920s in a *Shikumen* house.

Wulixiang means "home" in Shanghai dialect. For every local resident, the word "*Wulixiang*" warms the heart, as a vast majority of Shanghai residents were born and raised in *Shikumen* houses.

This *Shikumen* house occupies a gross floor area of 513 square meters, with 9 rooms on the first and second floors and an attic with exquisite decorations on the third. The museum, composed of the sitting room, east wing room and west wing room on the first floor, the front rooms, east wing room and west wing room on the second floor, as well as *Tingzijian* (a small room located at the turn of the staircase), kitchen and attic, integrates items of everyday life of a three-generation family into the architectural setting, showing a typical Shanghai household in a *Shikumen* neighborhood in the 1920s.

The internal structure of the *Shikumen* houses, unlike that of a modern condo which features three bedrooms, a living room, a dining room and a bathroom, exudes the ideal lifestyle, aspirations and value orientation of the people of Shanghai, who began to set foot in the city in mid-19th century. Taking influence from their previous rural life and reality of a high housing cost in the city, the dream house should possess a courtyard and a sitting room where the residents could express veneration to the ancestors and carry out divine worship to pray for a better life.

Shikumen houses entail an assemblage of heritage conservation and bold innovation, in concordance with the city's pursuit of efficiency while spatially retaining the cultural traditions of Chinese farm life—the composition and layout of alleys, courtyard walls, courtyards, sitting rooms and wing rooms manifest the traditional household hierarchy and ties of kinship.

Shikumen buildings in Shanghai dates from the 1860s when the British developers began to build dwellings that resembled Western terrace houses as a response to the influx of Chinese into foreign settlements. The construction workers, who came from the adjacent Zhejiang Province, told the foreign architects that the British terrace houses couldn't accommodate the lifestyle and cultural traditions of the Chinese people—absence of a courtyard would lead to insecurity and lack of a sitting room would deprive the family of a public area for reunion and social activities. With the collaboration of both parties, the incorporation of the Chinese traditional Sanheyuan (a compound with houses on three sides) into the Western terrace house exterior symbolized the meeting of East and West.

The defining characteristic of a *Shikumen* building is its prominent main gate. Typically, the gate features intricate baroque style lintels and stone frame, with twin doors made of heavy wood, painted glossy black and installed with beast head shaped knockers. The gate, favored by Shanghai residents in the concessions, bespeaks safety and social identity.

A solid gate guards our home and keeps the intruders away.

After the First Opium War when the doors of the country and cities were forced open by the Western colonies, the gate of our house required extra reinforcement. The developers consequently framed the gates with stone, similar to the way iron hoops were used to enclose barrels. This brought about the original documented name for such buildings to be "*Shigumen*", which in Shanghai dialect meant "gate framed with stone", but over time corrupted into the similar-sounding "*Shikumen*".

The period spans 151 years, from 1860 when *Shikumen* first appeared to 2011 when "construction techniques of *Shikumen lilong* architecture" was recognized by the Chinese government on the national non-physical cultural heritage register.

The choice of its heyday in 1920 to 1930 for the temporality of the display is to commemorate the glorious moments during that period when Shanghai became Asia's financial center and the world's sixth most cosmopolitan city, the Communist Party was established and the character of Shanghai was defined. *Shikumen* architecture has accommodated industrial civilization, commercial civilization, urban lifestyle, Shanghai's indigenous cosmopolitan culture, the spirit of the Communist Party and the *Tingzijian* literature during that time.

The museum, however, signifies only the return to an idealized past when *Shikumen* were the undivided, private properties of wealthy, local, middle-class families. The period thereafter bore witness to the vibrant street life behind the glamour, when abundant *Shikumen* culture became the cornerstone of urban public culture that consummated the character of the city.

The Japanese invasion of Shanghai in August 1937 completely disrupted the property market in Shanghai, resulting in a grand relocation of investments and talented people to southwest China. The Japanese army cut off the sea and port access to Shanghai. With the blocking of international trade, Shanghai soon lost its position as a primary commercial and financial hub of Asia which drastically altered the population structure of *Shikumen* residents. The finance and trading employees had

SONGSHAN PACKAGING STATION / WULIXIANG MUSEUM

Tingzijian, *a closet sandwiched between staircases and floors, often with the patio above and the kitchen below, is usually the darkest, hottest, coldest and most disagreeable room in a traditional Shikumen house. In better times, families used them for storage or servants' beds. The progressive young writers, who lived in these tiny rear rooms in the 1920s studied arduously and wrote prodigiously, giving rise to* Tingzijian *literature which played an integral part of Chinese literature.*

The attic on the third floor is a triangular-shaped space under the sloping ceiling. Light streams into the attic through a window on the roof, which is called "tiger window" as the word "roof" sounds like the Chinese translation of tiger in Shanghai dialect.

The gate lintel features intricately carved Baroque-style swirl-like pediments

escaped, while people who stayed in the occupied city suffered on a daily basis and were obliged to lease out some of the rooms in order to survive.

The phenomenon blossomed after the start of the aerial bombardment in the Chinese zones by the Japanese army in an attempt to deter Western colonies and Chinese troops — refugees rushed into the unoccupied concessions and French Concessions from the Chinese zones, leading to dramatically increased demand for housing in the concessions. The real estate agents took the opportunity to match the refugees in search of a dwelling and the *Shikumen* residents looking for a tenant. The agents encouraged the landlords to subdivide the rooms, fragmenting the whole *Shikumen* space into residences inhabited by dozens of families.

Apart from the lifestyle, the influx of the refugees brought a vast array of new businesses such as workshops, factories, inns, grocers, restaurants, tiger stoves that sold boiled water, schools, theatrical troupes, newspapers, and bath houses. Alley life of the humble working class epitomized struggles at the bottom of the society. The original *Shikumen* alleys with its sole residential function were transformed to a hub of dwelling, business,

SONGSHAN PACKAGING STATION / WULIXIANG MUSEUM

The Shikumen *sub-alleys are part of a semi-private space.*

industry and entertainment, posing an excessive burden on *Shikumen* residences that led to its downfall.

While *Shikumen* residences were on their way out, alley culture was cultivated in the long process.

When *Shikumen* residences were still undivided, the alleys were tranquil. The residents were entitled to a fairly spacious house and seldom made use of the public space. After the single-family residences were turned into structures that housed several families, the living space for each family was downsized to 10 square meters, depriving the residents of the right to keep their daily life, such as eating, personal hygiene, reading, hanging the laundry, washing chamber pots, lying on lounge chairs and showering, to themselves. The residents' private life unfolds in the sub-alleys in broad day light and yet considered typical. The phenomenon, if observed in a developed country, would be protested by the neighbors or even engender prosecution. The *Shikumen* residents, obviously, had subconsciously taken it for granted that the sub-alleys were part of a semi-private space.

Residents used their own faucets and meters.

The upsurge of group leasing turned the private space into communal. Kitchen, courtyard, patio and corridor were shared and unwritten rules for social interactions were followed.

For instance, the kitchen, measuring 8 square meters, was shared by 7 or 8 households with the same amount of coal stoves sitting cheek by jowl with each other. The residents had to precisely calculate the area allocated to them and their neighbors to safeguard their own interests.

Same rule was applied to lighting. The compact kitchen was interestingly equipped with 7 or 8 light bulbs while one would suffice to light the place up. During the rush hour in the evening, each household switched on their own bulb, in compliance with the unwritten rule, to steer clear of being gossiped or jeered at.

The rules shaped the city's mindset, directly impacting on Shanghai's attitude towards external relations and trading. Shrewd Shanghai businessmen, highly keen on profit calculation, would rather terminate the business partnership if the counterpart would make more profit.

In light of this, negotiations between Shanghai and foreign enterprises often came to naught since the onset of China's Reform and Opening-up in the 1980s, driving the foreign businesses to establish factories in Guangdong province where businessmen were more decisive and less envious.

Shanghai people's shrewdness cost them a large number of business opportunities. On the other hand, their adherence to the spirit of contract, deeply embedded in the character of the concessions, provided a springboard to a considerably high contract performance rate.

Despite the fact that living in these dense quarters could easily create disputes between neighbors, they resolved conflicts in a way that allowed them to return to the status quo in the shortest possible time. Grudge was dissipated when one helped the other to take back the laundry hanging in the courtyard in a rainy day or offered a meal to the neighbor's child prior to his late arrival. A piping hot bowl of homemade wontons in return on the second day showed a gesture of goodwill, further strengthening the relationship. The alley life has nurtured the urban culture of "seeking common ground while reserving differences".

The residents also flexed their inquisitive nature. Upon spotting a stranger, women sitting in the alleys would come forth to greet him, give direction and probe into his intention, undoubtedly scaring off ill-purposed intruders. Owing to the alley culture that protected the neighborhood from burglary, the back door was left ajar at night, convenient for the residents to enter or exit the house. The inquisitive nature prompted for the sake of the public interest, which was in essence civic consciousness categorized in industrial civilization, embodied the city's culture in public spaces.

Shikumen residences, dating from early 20th century, bore witness to the development of the alley culture that manifested local people's lifestyle, mindset and behaviors at that time. A century has passed, and it is still fascinating and worth preserving.

Since the re-urbanization process of Shanghai started at the end of 20th century, a huge swath of *Shikumen* buildings have been razed, leaving the invaluable alley culture unrooted. Inquisitiveness has been replaced by indifference and public relations are handled in an extreme manner. It is high time that the culture was revived.

Shanghai started to demolish *Shikumen* houses and favor tall apartment buildings to better accommodate the residents. A desirable apartment is comprised of two bedrooms, a study, a dining room, a kitchen and a bathroom.

Growth in affluence has escalated people's pursuit of living space expansion from 120 to 200 even 300 square meters with home theatre, library, and gym.

More is less and less is more. When it comes to the unity of opposites, in other words, it's all about the balance. While excessive desire leads to bigger houses, it directly results in a significant decrease in the frequency of possible visits to public

The chamber pots, hidden inside wooden chairs, are exhibited in the museum.

The former Singaporean statesman, Lee Kuan Yew, was standing in front of the chamber pots during his visit.

places. Children of the nouveau riche prefer to stay at home and indulge in internet and computer games. Leeching off their wealthy parents, they cut off their social networks and shun their social and family responsibilities. The expansion of space is inhibiting their creativity and suppressing their independence, giving rise to a series of misfortunes for the family.

The misfortunes resulted from violating the ethics of Taoism. The ancient philosopher Lao Tzu believed that he who is attached to things will suffer much, as he revealed the essence of Taoism in Tao Te Ching, the most influential Taoist text: having little gives one access; having much leads one astray.

Relentless pursuit of larger space exemplifies the redirection of people's passion to things that can never fulfill, distracting them from the very life they wish they were living.

Shikumen Wulixiang Museum leaves us thinking about the relationship between size of living space and subjective well-being.

The urban planning in Singapore has demonstrated efficient utilization of spaces based on a people-centric principle. The living space for each household is limited to 45 to 60 square meters, compact but ample. In an attempt to encourage people to pause and enjoy the public spaces, the government has endeavored to build a smart and happy city by sprucing up the gardens, leisure streets, parks, libraries, museums, theaters and cinemas as happiness lies in the joy of social interaction, sports, labor and adventures.

Pursuing an appropriate size of living space in Shanghai will be the dominant concept in the near future.

Among the items exhibited in the museum, several wooden chamber pots, often undervalued and scoffed at, are vanishing in Shanghai without much notice.

They have, however, grabbed the attention of a Singaporean statesman and thinker, Lee Kuan Yew, who has engineered Singapore's economic miracle. In the fall of 2001, a photographer from Shanghai captured the moments of Lee Kuan Yew standing in front of the chamber pots and posing questions about the culture and history of *Shikumen* with relish.

The chamber pots have, as a matter of fact, reflected the evolution of Shanghai people's lifestyle with the development of the society and manifested the changes in the mode of production. The waste collected by the chamber pots was essentially part of an ecological chain connecting the urban and rural areas. The waste, carried to the countryside by boat, was then transformed into organic fertilizer, nourishing the soils that produced crops. The harvested produce was subsequently delivered back to the city. This cycle repeated itself ad infinitum, maintaining the delicate balance of the Earth's ecosystem instead of polluting the waters.

The introduction of the flush toilets exempted people from cleaning chamber pots, resulting in a campaign for eliminating chamber pots during the urban regeneration in the 1990s. People rarely think about where the waste has gone after the flush. Instead of nourishing the soils, the bodily waste is transported to sewage treatment plants after harmless treatment. Eventually the sewage effluent is discharged into the ocean along with the industrial wastewater.

Although the ocean has for all time been the ultimate sink to dilute the waste, it has its limits. As predicted by the environmental protection experts, the city, with a population of 10 million, has the capacity to handle the discharges to coastal waters for 50 years. With its population rocketing to 20 million, how long can the city hold on? Where will the discharges go in 20 years?

The Shanghai municipal government is currently working on the urban strategic planning for the next 20 to 30 years. The sewage water could be, from a different perspective, collected and reused in separate channels from the industrial effluents. Environmental protection essentially entails reverse logic starting from the waste.

"With every drop of water you drink, every breath you take, you're connected to the sea." said Sylvia Earle, an American marine biologist. It is a microbial process that most of the oxygen production on Earth comes from the ocean which absorbs and stores substantial amounts of organic carbon. When the water vapor combines to form heavier cloud drops which can no longer "float" in the surrounding air, it can start to rain, snow, and hail.

No water, no life. No blue, no green.

The discharges we are posing on the waters will trigger mass extinction of marine organisms, leaving the future generations polluted water bodies that will take a considerable amount of financial and material resources to restore.

The increasing popularity of sanitary toilets in urban areas has cut off the source of organic fertilizer for the rural areas. Meanwhile, the agricultural production mode is under transformation: the frequency of use of inorganic fertilizer from the Western countries became more intensive. Inorganic fertilizer is better-received than organic fertilizer since the application of the former leads to soaring yields of crops with no odor. People were not aware of the health risks of the chemical residues on the plants brought to humans and of the fertilizer brought to the soil itself.

People have been punished by breaking the laws of nature as the damage done by modern methods has taken its toll on traditional ecological supply chain in circular economy, resulting in cancer incidence and hardened farmland. The crisis has made it indispensable for transforming the production mode and lifestyle.

The "organic vegetable" from Tony's Farm emerged as a new term in Expo Shanghai 2010. Organic agriculture became a label of healthy diet recognized and purchased by top earners with modern mindset. The owner of the farm, an MBA graduate at Fudan University, left for the countryside of Qingpu District to rent a chunk of land measuring 66.7 hectares and set up an organic vegetable farm. After spending 6 years on removing chemical residues from the field, the modern farmer started to apply organic fertilizer to the soil. The organic produce didn't come cheap: organic leek cost as much as 80 yuan per kilogram. Despite varied comments, diet started to be broken down into three grades: healthy, semi-healthy and unhealthy, partially depending on different types of fertilizer used to the soil.

While the chamber pots are displayed only in the museums,

flush toilets are believed to play an eternal part of our life. Presence of toxic elements in rice and vegetables with human health hazards has spurred market demand for organic crops. Will the concept chamber pots regain its lost glory?

The development of healthy eating will probably stimulate the organic fertilizer market in the near future. Odorless and stylish plants will be established in the urban area of Shanghai, purchasing human and animal feces from the residents to produce organic fertilizer. With residents' enthusiasm for waste classification on the rise, the chamber pots are likely to stage a comeback as the organic fertilizer collector.

Separating drinking water from non-drinking water is one of the greatest achievements in the 21st century. Technology will certainly be developed to distinguish between organic and non-organic fertilizer in the manure treatment.

The replacement of chamber pots with toilets showed an innovative development in human lifestyle, yet posed serious threats to the ecosystem. Therefore, the toilets are on the cusp of change as the sustainable development of mankind requires preserving the ecological integrity of ecosystems in which they reside.

Thus, it can be seen that the chamber pots in the museum are one of the marks of historic origin that we should preserve to bring insight into the future.

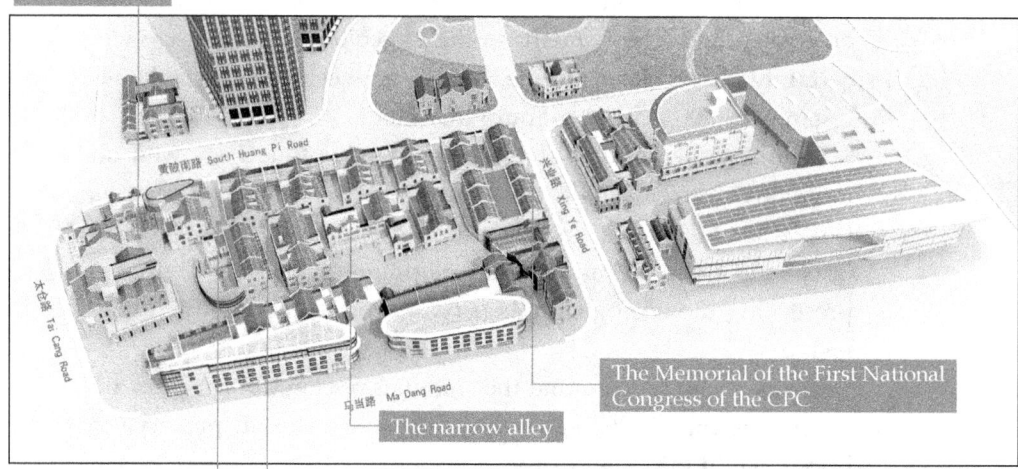

CHAPTER 5

An extended back lane paved with history

Across the narrow sub-alley that stretches from the end of the pedestrian street lies a back alley, the fourth trademark of Xintiandi.

The back alley is characterized by *Shikumen* buildings of three or four stories, with a brick path winding through, quiet and secluded.

Constructed in 1911, completed in 1933 and renovated in 2001, the back alley was reinvigorated in Expo Shanghai 2010. Having witnessed a century's rise and fall, the dilapidated alley resumed its historic feel of the 1920s and '30s when Shanghai was the leading financial center in Asia and known as the "Paris of the East". Presently, the city is striving to regain its glory as the global financial hub in the 2030s.

Once a symbol of poverty and backwardness, the back alley today features simplicity, charm and modernity. It has become a popular photography spot for the tourists and a favored setting for Chinese newlyweds' wedding photos. Families come to reminisce about the past, while the youngsters, with high-fashion clothing matched with an equally epic hairstyle, stride towards Ark Live House, a rock and roll restaurant from Tokyo. *Shikumen* houses are nothing more than a photo backdrop or a historical site to the young generation.

At the southernmost end of the back alley sits the site of the First National Congress of the Communist Party of China (CPC), while the northernmost is One Xintiandi, a private members' club. The back alley, like a time tunnel that spans a century from

Xintiandi features a long back alley interlocked with six sub-alleys. The back alley, leading off the pedestrian street, serves as a fire escape route as well as directing foot traffic to the commercial establishments, encouraging the visitors to wander through and explore the alleys for some refreshment in a café or tea house.

1921 to 2010, has witnessed the start of the great anti-imperialist and anti-feudal revolutionary movement, the unprecedented Cultural Revolution, the onset of China's Reform and Opening-up, as well as Expo Shanghai 2010.

This place attracts thousands of domestic and international tourists every year to visit the tangible historical buildings and, more importantly, to listen to the invisible echo of its history: what fascinating stories have happened in the century and what caused its rise and fall?

The *Shikumen* buildings are not just bricks and mortar, but an expression of value and emotion in every detail. A historical retrospect surprisingly shows that the constructors and residents of the *Shikumen* houses along the back alley in 1911, 1921 and 1931 were the revolutionary entrepreneurs and elites, a generation passionate about driving change and committed to leaving the place better than they found it.

The house at the south end of the back alley, 76-78 Xingye Road, was at that time the sojourn residence of the Wuhan-based official Li Shucheng and his brother Li Hanjun. The latter set up a communist party organization with Chen Duxiu and hosted the First Congress of the Chinese Communist Party, a secret meeting held among thirteen delegates, including Mao Zedong, Zhang Guotao, and Dong Biwu. Chen Duxiu used to live at 21 Jiyili on the back alley, while Chiang Kai-shek, a Chinese Nationalist

AN EXTENDED BACK LANE PAVED WITH HISTORY

Ark Live House offers dream-fulfilling live performances every night, from pop to rock, jazz to folk. Young rock n roll lovers come to Xintiandi for the exciting and thrilling experience in Ark.

Shikumen alleys are only a favored hang-out for the younger generations

The memorial on 76 Xingye Road is where the first National Congress of the CPC was held in July 1921. Behind the iron fence is the back alley of Xintiandi.

politician, stayed at 369 South Huangpi Road.

Shanghai was thriving in 1921. It was the most open city in China, requiring no papers or visas of any sort for entry. Being the perfect breeding ground for new ideas and technologies, the city became a hub of Marxism and European construction techniques of trains, cars and skyscrapers. Shanghai was home to a hybrid mixture of Chinese and Western culture, making it the perfect place, instead of other coastal cities, for the establishment of the Communist Party of China.

As one of the most attractive international cities, Shanghai was the paradise for foreign adventurers and aspiring young people from all over the country. The story of Mr. He Chujing, one of the migrant workers in Shanghai, who managed to build a *Shikumen* house at the north end of the back alley by his own efforts, was a typical example of how hard work paid off. When Mr. He fell in love with Miss Ha Xiumei, a young lady from a wealthy family, in 1903, her father set his face against the marriage. Influenced by modern civilization, Ha Xiumei broke through the shackles of feudal ethics and eloped with Mr. He.

With 20 years' assiduous efforts, the couple saved enough money to build a three-story *Shikumen* house on 328 South Huangpi Road (now the site of Xinjishi restaurant on the North Block). Many people have been moved by their story, including Wu Changshuo, a renowned painter, who offered a painting of his as a token of congratulations.

The extended back alley boasts an abundance of stories, some of which are still going on while others have played a vital role in the history of Shanghai's urban development as well as in China's modern history. The back alley is an outdoor exhibition hall of urban historical development with a display of invaluable collections.

We've noted that the pivotal reason behind the degradation of the old houses, after conducting a careful look into the history, is the group leasing.

How did it come into being?

There were two major outbreaks of group leasing in the centennial history of *Shikumen*. The first one was in 1937, when the Japanese invaders bombed Zhabei District. The middle class in *Shikumen* fled to the southwest of inland China, while a large number of refugees rushed into the concessions from the Chinese zones, leading to dramatically increased demand for housing in *Shikumen*. It was common for a single *Shikumen* residence to be inhabited by three or four families. The change in structure of the *Shikumen* neighborhoods, from the dominant upper-middle class to a crowd of refugees, was the beginning of its downfall.

The Shikumen *house on 328 Huangpi Road now houses Xinjishi, a Shanghainese Restaurant*

The courtyard and chambers of Xinjishi

The second one was in 1966,

when the Great Cultural Revolution revealed itself in an extreme form. Red Guards (a mass student-led paramilitary social movement mobilized and guided by Chairman Mao Zedong) marched into *Shikumen* houses in a campaign to eradicate the "Four Olds" (i.e., old customs, old culture, old habits, and old ideas) and cultivate the "Four News" (i.e., new customs, new culture, new habits, new ideas). They destroyed historical relics and decorative motifs on the exterior of *Shikumen* buildings, smashing all the baroque style lintels and traditional auspicious patterns from so-called "feudal" "capitalist" or "revisionist" culture.

Red Guards invaded and occupied He Chujing's house on 328 South Huangpi Road and drove the family out, turning it into "Red Guard headquarter" and "Red Guard national reception station". The family returned to their home when the first wave of private property seizure was over.

Unexpectedly, the second wave started before long. The rebel Red Guards wearing red armbands were strolling along the back alley, looking for "big-character posters" on the walls indicating that this family had gone politically astray. They then broke in and seized the property. He Chujing passed away before the liberation, but his son He Shuhong became the target again. The Red Guards took position of their rooms and shoehorned the family into the attic on the top floor. The rebel factions, who were under poor living conditions, moved into the upscale houses in central locations, such as Nanjing Road, Huaihai Road and Hengshan Road, by means of so-called revolution.

There were altogether three waves of house seizures during the decade-long Cultural Revolution in Shanghai, striking a disastrous blow on *Shikumen*. A single residence, already inhabited by three to four families, had to house more families of looters. The phenomenon of group leasing was exacerbated, resulting in crowded and disorderly dwellings packed with dozens of households. He Shuhong's house, for example, was inconceivably occupied by 11 households of rebel factions. These

(Left) Located in the back alley, the gateway of Changxingli-1932 was built in 1932. The red inscriptions on the stone pillar which reads "Great Chairman Mao steers the country through revolution" bears an imprint of the Cultural Revolution in 1966. At the beginning of the Reform and Opening-up, people tried in vain to cover the red inscriptions with white paint, leaving behind the traces of thoughts and behaviors in 1978. The gateway, imprinted with historical narratives, bears witness to the development of the country.
(Right) Weeds pushed through the gaps on the gateway of Changxingli-1932

new tenants, with poor living habits and ignorance of house maintenance, expedited the degradation of *Shikumen* residences through overuse or neglect.

The residents' yearning to escape the dwellings and predicament of group leasing marked its ultimate downfall. The growing trend of hollowing out *Shikumen* neighborhoods reflected the fact that the rise and fall of the city is determined by people's faith and trust rather than the building's condition. In the 1980s, years after the end of the Cultural Revolution, people's thoughts were still confined to the ideology of eradicating the old and cultivating the new. Urban modernization was mistaken for demolition of old buildings and establishment of new ones, leading to the abandonment of *Shikumen*.

The wholesale destruction of dilapidated buildings and reconstructions signified desertion of Shanghai's historical architecture.

In the mid-90s, Luwan District Government broke through the rigid forms of ideology and brought in advanced urban development concept during the regeneration of the *Shikumen* blocks along both sides of Huaihai Road.

EAST MEETS WEST

A row of old Shikumen houses in Yongqingfang have been converted to model houses of Xintiandi.

AN EXTENDED BACK LANE PAVED WITH HISTORY

Restored baroque style lintels of Yongqingfang alley which were originally smashed during the Cultural Revolution

The Hong Kong developer Shui On Group, granted the development rights for the project, revolutionized the redevelopment planning to reserve the old buildings, restore the exteriors while keeping it historically authentic and gut renovate the interiors with installation of modern amenities. With residences repurposed into commercial complexes and private spaces converted into public areas, the result showcased traditional dwellings that best represented a locality.

The government and local *Shikumen* experts were blown away by the refreshing idea that preservation of historical buildings could harmonize with modern urbanization. This revolutionary spirit reverberated through the two-square block development as well as the city's ideology.

Shikumen buildings have been revived.

The Xintiandi initiative sparked a series of revitalizations of historical buildings in the center of the city, including *Shikumen* houses in Tianzifang and Jianyeli, garden houses such as Sinan Mansions, and abandoned factories such as Bridge 8.

The effect of Xintiandi project on urban regeneration is monumental and revolutionary, acknowledged by all concerned.

In 2001, much international media attention was given to this revived *Shikumen* neighborhood. During the press conference held in the memorial of the first National Congress of the CPC on 30th June, Western journalists were most concerned about the relationship between Xintiandi and the site of the first National Congress of the CPC. A Western reporter aggressively challenged Ni Xingxiang, the curator of the memorial, that the site seemed to be encompassed by capitalism. The allegation, attributing poverty to socialism and regenerated Xintiandi to capitalism, epitomized the cold war thinking and cultural hegemony that persisted in the mindset of some Westerners.

Ni responded, "I disagree. Xintiandi symbolizes China's Reform and Opening-up as well as urban modernization."

Reform represented invention and Opening-up implied fusion, while Xintiandi embodied concentration of both. Ni made it very convincing that preservation of *Shikumen* buildings was, in addition to skyscrapers, a concrete illustration of urban modernization. Xintiandi demonstrated significant headway made in the mindset of Shanghai's urban development.

Reporters from CNN, a U.S. TV channel, and the *China Times*, a daily Chinese-language newspaper published in Taiwan, interviewed the management of Shui On for deeper insights.

The management shared their unique perspective. In the early 20th century, China was stricken by poverty and backwardness as a result of disintegration of feudalism, tangled warfare among the warlords, and invasion by Western powers. In 1921, 13 Chinese scholars, filled with patriotic enthusiasm to salvage the country through assimilation of European communism, declared the birth of the CPC in a *Shikumen* house on 76 Xingye Road, depicting a grand blueprint for national rejuvenation. The CPC was committed to overthrowing the rule of semi-feudalism and semi-colonialism through revolutionary measures and building a new socialist country of equality, freedom, prosperity and strength. Countless revolutionaries have sacrificed their lives for the independence, democracy and prosperity of the country today. Decades have passed and Xintiandi has become a global village where Chinese people and visitors from the developed countries gather together to dine and relax on an equal footing. The grand vision outlined by the 13 delegates has been realized in Xintiandi, revealing the true relationship between Xintiandi and the memorial.

The CNN reporter didn't pursue the reason for building Xintiandi. He probably forgot to mention it, or maybe it didn't even cross his mind.

It is no exaggeration to say that this historic district's rebirth is all because of the restoration of the CPC memorial. Without the initiative to preserve the memorial, the swath of *Shikumen* buildings would have been razed and replaced by modern high-rises.

In 1998, in order to celebrate the 80th anniversary of the

founding of the CPC, CPC Shanghai Municipal Committee decided to revamp the memorial of the first National Congress. The municipal government was unnerved by the report from Shanghai Municipal Administration of Cultural Heritage that the neighborhoods in the vicinity of the memorial had been included in the urban regeneration scope, therefore the memorial would be dwarfed by the encompassing high-rises to be constructed. Shanghai Municipal Administration of Cultural Heritage suggested that the memorial, together with its neighboring historic buildings, should be preserved. Since the site of the first National Congress of CPC is a major historical and cultural site protected at the national level, the *Shikumen* house should remain intact while retaining the authenticity in terms of the environment and atmosphere on the founding of the party. On this account, CPC Shanghai Municipal Committee came to a decision that the site of the first National Congress and its adjacent two *Shikumen* blocks should be preserved.

The decision was both a challenge and an opportunity for Shui On, who eventually consummated the innovative Xintiandi project.

The original name at the start of the project was "Regeneration of the site of the first National Congress", which was deemed too political for a commercial real estate project. After much deliberation, brainstorming and inspiration, the team reached a consensus on the new name "Xintiandi": the two Chinese characters abbreviated from the Chinese translation of "the first National Congress of CPC" could be combined into another character *"Tian"* which means heaven, often spoken of in apposition to another character "Di" which means earth, and "Xin" which means new referred to the completion of this cross-century project in the new millennium.

The history of the memorial is intertwined with the culture of the *Shikumen* houses in Xintiandi, with a finely wrought balance of patriotism and fashion embedded in the details: the residential quarters in Xintiandi area were remodeled into commercial complexes with a range of restaurants and retail establishments while the residence on the CPC site was converted into a memorial and opened to public to remember the great development history of the Party; entry to Xintiandi is free of charge as the site cancelled the admission fee since the beginning of the new century. The free admission symbolizes the city's cognitive focus on public space culture. When some cities are busy developing cultural heritage attractions to generate more income, the CPC memorial offers free entry, indicating the headway made of Shanghai's urban civilization.

One Xintiandi, a private members' club, is situated at the north end of the back alley. The number One is only a symbol of locality rather than a sign of special meanings. This gorgeous house, built in the 1920s when Shanghai was in its heyday, was on the decline and ultimately inhabited by 36 households after the Sino-Japanese War and the Chinese Communist Revolution.

A massive restoration has helped it return to its original glory in the new century. The house is now an upscale club for domestic and international prestigious guests including government officials, politicians, entrepreneurs and celebrities that make frequent appearances on TV. One Xintiandi illustrates the city's rise from hardship to glory in microcosm.

During the Expo Shanghai 2010, One Xintiandi has received a significant number of guests every day. After the six-month run, the Expo had attracted well over 70 million visitors, while the number of visitors to Xintiandi topped 10 million, equivalent to over 14 percent of the expo's volume.

Though little known to the general public, One Xintiandi also pitched in with the running for host of the expo. In 2002, the delegation from the Bureau of International Expositions (BIE) went to Shanghai to make on-the-spot investigations and Xintiandi was on its list of inspection visit.

Vincent Lo, chairman of Shui On, hosted a feast for the delegation on behalf of Shanghai Organizing Committee, accompanied by influential Western entrepreneurs and investors in Shanghai. The delegation was impressed by the exquisite elegance of the house and the delicate food and wine, but it was the aspiration of the foreign enterprises for Shanghai's success in the selection that played a decisive role in the final vote.

Expo Shanghai 2010 highlighted and promoted Shanghai as one of the world's greatest metropolises. One Xintiandi not only bore witness to the event, but also played an active role.

There were thousands of villas in Shanghai, some of which were more magnificent and famed than One Xintiandi. What contributed to its glory in the Expo? What was the most valuable treasure in the old house that captivated the foreign heads of state, entrepreneurs, and celebrities?

The house features a front yard and a back yard. Overlooking the courtyard are square shaped corridors on both second and third floors, bringing in light into the courtyard that brightens the hallway on the first floor. All the rooms are characterized by spatial distribution in the living room dining room combo, with Chinese elements embedded in the quaint tables in simple design, armchairs and cabinets from Ming Dynasty, and antique style blue and white porcelain. Yet the rooms also exude a strong sense of European culture with the presence of the fireplaces, crystal chandeliers, velvet carpets, and classical oil paintings. A careful mix of Chinese and Western cultures is displayed in the house with an elegant touch that is representative of Shanghai's irresistible indigenous cosmopolitan style.

On the first floor there is a spacious hall, achieved by knocking together the living room and two wing rooms to accommodate about 100 people. The hall is left spacious on purpose to highlight the scale model of the Taipingqiao Redevelopment Project in the center, with walls adorned with paintings and armchairs and table tucked into the corner.

It would be too quick to draw the conclusion that the heads of state were merely captivated by the style of the old house. Instead, what to see, where to dine, whom to meet with reflected their attitudes.

AN EXTENDED BACK LANE PAVED WITH HISTORY

One Xintiandi, a three-story villa with a European-style balcony, stands firm with an innate grandeur despite the vicissitudes of the past.

Former Italian President Giorgio Napolitano walking out of One Xintiandi.

The real charm of One Xintiandi lies in the innovative ideas of the urban regeneration plan, embodied in the work of calligraphy on the wall of the courtyard: yesterday meets tomorrow at present. The ideas conveyed in the cursive script, created by the well-known Shanghai-based calligraphy artist Han Tianheng, has been showcased in the scale model.

China's massive urbanization began at the beginning of the 21st century, when leaders from inland provinces visited coastal cities to brainstorm and get inspired with new ideas. The urbanization of Shanghai initially focused on solving the major issues of people's livelihood by providing more affordable housing units. It is about to enter a new phase, after several stages of urban development, that prioritizes walking, transit, and integration of industrialization and urbanization.

The concept of the Taipingqiao Redevelopment Project echoes the focus of this phase, showing potential contribution of modern service industry to GDP as well as respect for historical heritage, natural environment, and the rights of our future generations. The mindset behind the revival of historical and cultural heritage

The wife of the Governor-General of Australia looking at the scale model in One Xintiandi.

with modern civilization is what enthralled the foreign heads of state and Chinese government officials for inspection.

Most of the Chinese government officials have been to Xintiandi, while each of them had their own perspective of the scale model.

For the mayor of Wuhan, urban regeneration required comprehensive planning with phased implementations. According to the Mayor, the land of city used to be subdivided into smaller pieces and allotted to different developers without proper planning, resulting in urban sprawl and homogeneous competitions. The phenomenon was also manifested in urban development that is discontinuous, scattered and decentralized. Wuhan was in desperate need of a developer with innovative mindset like Shui On to produce a comprehensive plan and ensure step-by-step implementation.

Meanwhile, the officials of the Tibet Autonomous Region were enlightened by the idea that the aging property could be renovated and revived while the indigenous cultures remained intact. Six months later, CCTV channel broadcast a report that

The corridors above the courtyard of One Xintiandi have been restored to preserve the historical authenticity, with newly made wooden handrails and well preserved 1925 ornamental iron fences.

AN EXTENDED BACK LANE PAVED WITH HISTORY

The soul of Xintiandi lies in the innovative ideas of the urban regeneration plan, embodied in the work of calligraphy on the wall of the courtyard: yesterday meets tomorrow at present.

The remodeled hall on the first floor of One Xintiandi.

a swarth of old Tibetan residences at the foot of Potala Palace in Lhasa had been saved from the wrecking ball and renovated with new technologies to preserve its historic flavor. Water supply, drainage and heating systems had been installed. The residences had become a popular spot for the Tibetans.

The officials from Hangzhou, capital city of Zhejiang Province, interpreted the project as a space of openness, similar to an undergoing project in their hometown that removed the iron fences of the six major parks encompassing the West Lake to offer free admission to all the visitors. Ticket sales would hence play a minor role in the tourism economy which, on the other hand, would incur more spending from a larger influx of tourists.

The Director of the Development and Construction Administrative Committee of Hangzhou had been to Shanghai seven times by 2001 to explore the new ideas of commercial recreation and tourism business in an attempt to spur tourism spending in Hangzhou. In addition, the Secretary of the Municipal Party Committee personally visited Xintiandi with officials from the Committee, the municipal government, the National People's Congress, and the Chinese People's Political Consultative Conference to invite Shui On to build a Xihu Tiandi in Hangzhou that would bring the concept of leisure business and construction of urban public space.

The Governor of Liaoning Province and the delegation were most fascinated by the story behind demolition of old houses and creation of artificial lakes. Were the large-scale regeneration projects commanded by the government or initiated by the developer? How were the interests balanced among the government, the residents and the developer?

The governor was impressed by the collaboration between the government and the enterprise on improving ecological sustainability, cultural environment and the value of downtown land prior to development of real estate, likened to the agricultural cycle where preparation of soil with manure and fertilizer preceded harvesting.

AN EXTENDED BACK LANE PAVED WITH HISTORY

The notion of prioritizing environmental protection over property development has set a new benchmark for many developers in China who have realized that preservation of historical buildings is not a burden but an opportunity for better investment returns by increasing the value of the land.

One Xintiandi has to some extent taken up the responsibility to be the window of Shanghai for international publicity. In the first few years after Xintiandi's completion, One Xintiandi had received 800 groups of government delegates amounting to 20,000 people annually. The numbers have dropped by half in the following years, yet still dismayingly high. The story of Xintiandi has been spread nationwide, bringing Shui On both corporate reputation in the real estate industry and commercial opportunities of urban renewal in cities such as Hangzhou, Wuhan, Chongqing, Foshan and Dalian.

A stone sculpture at the entrance of Xihu Tiandi, a redevelopment project in Hangzhou by Shui On, features Westlake, lotus and a millstone which dated back to Southern Song Dynasty.

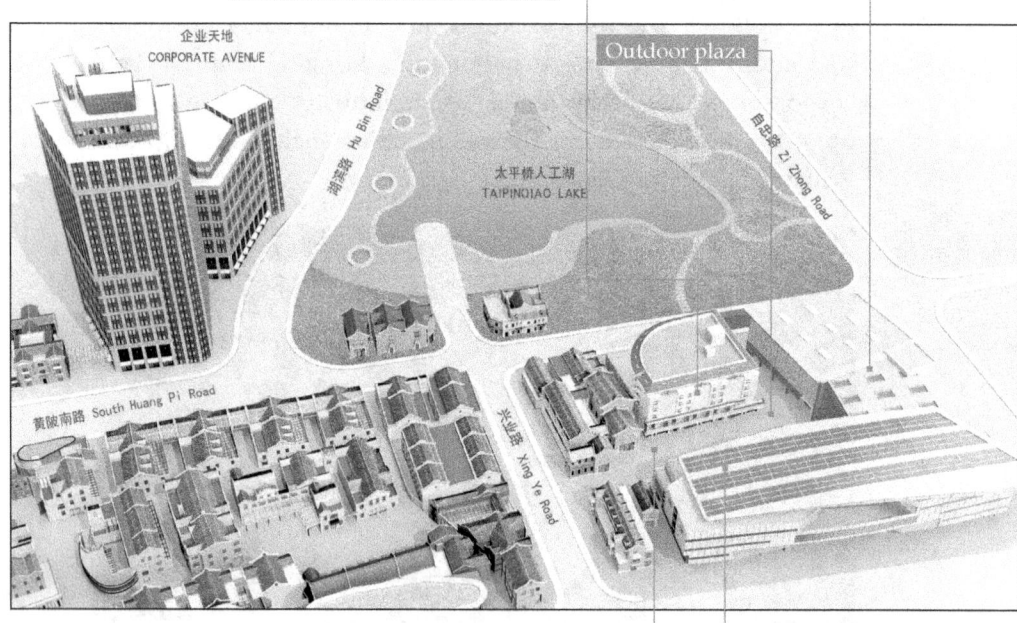

CHAPTER 6

THE SOUTH BLOCK

Western visitors, standing at the intersection of Xingye Road after strolling through the North Block, often wonder if the opposite block that boasts modern architecture is the genuine fifth trademark of Xintiandi.

Chinese tourists visiting Arc de Triomphe of Paris share the same feeling. Their bucket list only includes the area between Place de la Concorde and the Arc de Triomphe that showcases the world-renowned masterpieces distinguished for their sizes, antiquity, and architectural interest: Notre Dame de Paris, Champs-Elysées, Eiffel Tower, and the bridges and sculptures on the Seine River. While La Défense, a business district located behind the Arc de Triomphe that contains high-rises and the most emblematic buildings in France, is not worth a visit to the Chinese tourists as Shanghai is already home to more iconic skyscrapers. There is no doubt that if you want to witness the marvels of modern architecture, Manhattan skyline is the place to be.

The historical area of the Avenue des Champs-Elysées built in the 19th century is the ideal representation of Paris for the Chinese tourists, while the *Shikumen* houses are likewise a symbol of Shanghai for the foreign visitors.

While the old *Shikumen* houses, known for being crowded and disorderly, epitomizes Old Shanghai, what role does it play in the future of the city?

Still take Paris as an example. The historical area of the Avenue des Champs-Elysées is regarded as representation of Paris by

The mobile souvenir carts in the plaza of the South Block

Chinese visitors, while Parisians argue that this place has been taken by tourism. It is the Saint-Germain-des-Pres Quarter that is frequented by the locals and considered the quintessential Paris neighborhood.

The quarter dates back to the 17th century. Boulevard Saint-Germain, traversing the 5th, 6th, and 7th arrondissements, is most famous for crossing the quarter from which it derives its name. The 6th arrondissement is located in the heart of Paris' Left Bank. It is home to the atmospheric Saint-Germain-des-Prés Quarter and the Latin Quarter. Jean-Paul Sartre, Honoré de Balzac Sartre, Auguste Rodin, and Pablo Picasso are some of the famous names associated with the area.

This Parisian neighborhood with centuries-old literary and artistic roots harbors more than 50 cinemas, 200 galleries and 520 cafés. Philosophers, artists, writers, politicians and college students have made this quarter their regular haunt.

In addition to being a hub of universities, Saint-Germain is a place of intellectual vibrancy and artistic vibe. This historical quarter has witnessed the past of Paris and will undoubtedly be the heart and soul of its future.

While Xintiandi is where yesterday meets tomorrow at present, where exactly in Xintiandi are emblematic of the past, present and future of the city?

The modern glass façade buildings in the South Block exhibit the present narrative of Shanghai's urbanization and industrialization, and the *Shikumen* neighborhood in the North Block is an evident illustration of both the past and future of the city. The city's future is a logical extension of its past and present. The *Shikumen* buildings in the North Block have seen the city traveling through time in a circular trajectory and returning to its starting point, a historical space that accommodates both self-reliant production businesses and new civilizations.

Upon its debut, Xintiandi received divided popularity: the North Block was swarming with people while the South Block was devoid of visitors. Neither the tourists nor the local residents deemed South Block a part of Xintiandi. Their reluctance to step in the block registered their disapproval.

As a result, the marketing department contrived to enliven the South Block by putting delicately festooned mobile souvenir carts between the entrance and the modern shopping mall.

Many visitors asked the developers why they had to tear down the *Shikumen* alleys in the South Block. Their retention or demolition had been the subject of a heated debate in the course of the regeneration which will be covered in later chapters.

To Mr. Wood, the principal architect of Xintiandi, the place promotes broader thinking and is a genuine cradle of culture and new ideas. The historical buildings of a city, acting as a catalyst for its evolution, should neither stand alone nor be completely demolished to make way for new ones. The city's revolutionary spirit derives from its past, reverberates through its present and flourishes in its future.

The spatial structure and asymmetrical balance are unfortunately absent in Shanghai's architectural landscape which harbors significantly more modern buildings than historical ones.

EAST MEETS WEST

The asymmetrical balance of the architectural style of the North Block, punctuated with some modern buildings, and the South Block, dotted with several old Shikumen houses, exemplifies a fusion of modern and old and a blend of conservation and evolution.

THE SOUTH BLOCK

The strategic urban planning of Paris has identified the danger of irreversible transformations and the irrevocable damage it would inflict on the continuity of the cultural heritage and, more importantly, the city itself.

This lesson was lost on most people of Shanghai, not to mention the sweeping slum clearance still to come. Serious citywide consideration is eagerly awaited.

Just like a person's self-awakening can't be forced as there's no prescription for enlightenment, urban development can't be propelled through imitation of the Western culture.

Young and unstoried, the mall in the South Block spans four floors. The first to the third floors, originally occupied by restaurants of Hong Kong, Taiwanese and Southeast Asian styles, now offer clothing brands.

The Xintiandi UME International Cineplex, built by the very renowned Mr. Ng See Yuen, a Chinese director, producer and writer of independent film companies in Hong Kong, is situated on the top floor together with LifeZtore, a total solution provider for home lifestyle products, whose Art Director is Alan Zie Yongder, a multifaceted artist of Chinese descent.

The interior of LifeZtore

Born in Shanghai, director and producer Ng See Yuen moved to Hong Kong at a young age. Ng is widely recognized as one of Hong Kong's most influential and visionary independent filmmakers. He is credited with spotting and grooming talented actors and actresses.

The Cineplex shows in six theatres which create a mixture of lively and cheerful tone and nostalgic atmosphere for movie patrons. The cinema is popular among locals for showcasing the classic Shanghai movies featuring iconic movie stars in Old Shanghai, such as Zhou Xuan, Zhao Dan, and Jin Yan. A great place to catch up on the latest Hollywood blockbusters prior to other cinemas, the Cineplex, benefiting from Ng's resources in film distribution channel, has magnetized a great many loyal patrons.

The only art store of self-reliant production in the South Block, LifeZtore, backed by the Asian Development Bank, sells an array of handmade art works with premium quality, including furniture, vases, and porcelain housewares. In the 18th century, the imported Chinese ceramics and silk gained popularity among the nobles in Britain and France, while the wealthy Chinese consumers are now fascinated by the luxury brands of clothes, handbags and watches from France, Italy and Switzerland as a result of the demand for social recognition. Expecting the Chinese luxury brands to stage a comeback among the European countries sometime in the near future, the Asian Development Bank had the foresight to invest in the vanishing Chinese traditional handicrafts at the turn of the 21st century.

It might take years for the original Chinese brands to emerge. Despite little patronage of LifeZtore, Mr. Zie held the belief that they were pioneering a trendy lifestyle that would prevail in ten years. He concluded that with the continued growth in China's economy and comprehensive national power, the Europeans would be captivated by our brands as we were by theirs at the moment.

Preparation started in no time. Mr. Zie frequented the nearby

THE SOUTH BLOCK

Shanghai Museum to stock creations from the well-established Chinese civilization. As he put it, "Shanghai Museum boasts a large collection of precious Chinese cultural relics—Yangshao painted pottery, bronze ware of the Han Dynasty, and Buddha statues in grottoes of the Tang Dynasty, just to name a few. They are, however, only on display behind the glass, remotely pertinent to everyday life. Chinese civilization needs to be revived to interact with our life, infusing the cultural and creative industries with originality."

Loretta Yang and Chang Yi, founders of TMSK, who resurrected the wax casting technique that had been lost for more than two thousand years and reintroduced it into the international arena, have forged a world-renowned luxury brand known for its outstanding artistic endeavors and high standard of craftsmanship. An environment which encourages and promotes originality and free thinking in individuals needs to be fostered. Few people have the courage to stray from the norm and to challenge the status quo. Loretta Yang and Chang Yi attributed their originality to "enduring tribulations, embracing setbacks, honing creative artistry and crafting works of art".

Although Mr. Zie could endure the long wait for the breakthrough, LifeZtore was eventually priced out of the market by the soaring rents.

Nestled in the South Block, the small but exquisite 88 Xintiandi Boutique Hotel houses 53 rooms and suites. Popular among the celebrities, Hong Kong and Taiwan stars in particular, 88 Xintiandi has been patronized by Ricky Martin, known as the "King of Latin Pop", Yao Ming, an international basketball star, and Hong Kong movie stars including Jackie Chan, Chow Yun Fat and Andy Lau.

In 2003, Tung Chee Hwa, the then Chief Executive of Hong Kong, was supposed to stay in the presidential suite of Jinjiang Hotel on his vacation in Shanghai with his family, as arranged by the local government. They, however, opted for 88 Xintiandi, as Mrs. Tung preferred its superb service and extraordinary taste.

EAST MEETS WEST

The city harbors an array of four- and five-star hotels, mostly of European and U.S. origin, such as Portman, Hilton, Shangri-La, and Langham. 88 Xintiandi is among the few that are representative of Shanghai's indigenous cosmopolitan culture. The upscale rooms, rather than its spectacular lobby, capture the essence of a boutique stay.

A comfortable bed and a well-appointed guest room deliver a good night's sleep essential for every traveler. Each of the hotel bed features typical Chinese characteristics, encompassed by floor-length curtains and intricate woodwork derived from the ancient Chinese bed dating back to the Ming and Qing dynasties.

Each room offers six pillows with different firmness that keep the guests cozy and well-rested during their stay. The comforter that absorbs, stores, and releases heat to regulate body temperature manifests the hotel's effort to go to great length to pamper their guests. The comforter, crafted to absorb extra heat after the guest takes a shower and release the heat when it's cold in the morning, helps to maintain a more neutral temperature.

The closet in the guest room is characterized by its traditional look derived from the Ming and Qing Dynasties with an adjustable closet rod catering to guests of different heights as Western guests are generally taller than their Asian counterparts. The rods are adjusted in line with the guests' height estimated by the hotel staff upon their check-in at the front desk.

Regulars will find the two bathrobes in the closet embroidered with their names for a personalized touch. Bathrobes of a different color are available specially for ladies, accentuating a heartwarming female concept.

Guests are welcomed by a softly-lit room with fluffy carpet, dreamy melody and aromatized air where they indulge themselves in the peace and serenity of nature's absolute equilibrium. The hotel offers a retreat for the guests who will be spoiled with first-class service after a long-haul flight with a touch of indigenous culture.

Guests are overwhelmed by the hotel's attention to details

The guest room of the 88 Xintiandi Boutique Hotel

after check-in: the room is equipped with an air purifier and humidifier to enhance the air quality and maintain ideal temperature and humidity levels. Imported air purifying device has been placed under the bed to capture microorganisms, ensuring that the guests enjoy a carefree stay away from allergens and bacteria. The windows in the room, unlike the sealed ones in a five-star hotel, can be opened and offer an expansive view of an open park with an artificial lake and lush green trees.

It is noteworthy that the background music of the hotel flows through the room in the absence of the guests in an attempt to prolong the lifespan of the wooden furniture, including the bed, table, chairs, closet and cabinet. The wooden furniture is artistically made, and yet the form and flow of the wood and the tree is not lost, but remains alive. When the owners have reverence for the wood as a living material, it will treat the guests well. Soothing music such as Sound of Angels and Sound of Wellness are played to help pacify the guests as soon as they enter the room.

There was a time when the toilets that had been sanitized had, instead of a seal placed on top of the cover, some rose petals floating in the water. Ladies were deeply touched by the nice gesture invented by the hotel itself.

The hotel features a smooth checkout process that requires no waiting time for room inspection after the bills are settled. The guests are welcome to take away the music CDs, books or towels in the room to their hearts' content, free of charge, as a token of hospitality from the hotel. Rooms are inspected for any belongings the guests have left behind so as to be returned promptly. All the supplies are also replenished before a new guest arrives.

88 Xintiandi didn't participate in the national hotel rating system, yet has developed its own impeccable service standard. This gives rise to reflective thinking about the hotel rating system in China: who launched the system? Will China develop its own system acknowledged worldwide since the hotels in China are currently following in the steps of their European counterparts.

Hospitality and upscale service must be put into practice. 88 Xintiandi has its own instrument to measure the dimensions of service quality: when tea is served, the cup handle must face towards the guest for his or her convenience. A glass of wine must be slightly tilted and gently placed on the table as a token of respect. Friendly eye contact must be maintained for three seconds as a gesture of sincerity when the staff greets the guests.

A waiter once noticed some creases in a guest's suit and politely reminded him when serving breakfast. The guest replied that he was too busy to have it taken care of. The waiter responded with an offer of assistance despite the fact that ironing was not among his job responsibilities. Ten minutes later, a well pressed suit was delivered to the guest. Spontaneous and self-directed services certainly embody the hotel's culture of excellence.

Despite its smaller size, 88 Xintiandi has been the pioneer to showcase a sprout of original creativity and design rather than pursuit of culture of service in European hospitality industry.

THE SOUTH BLOCK

Attentive service with eye contact 88 Xintiandi

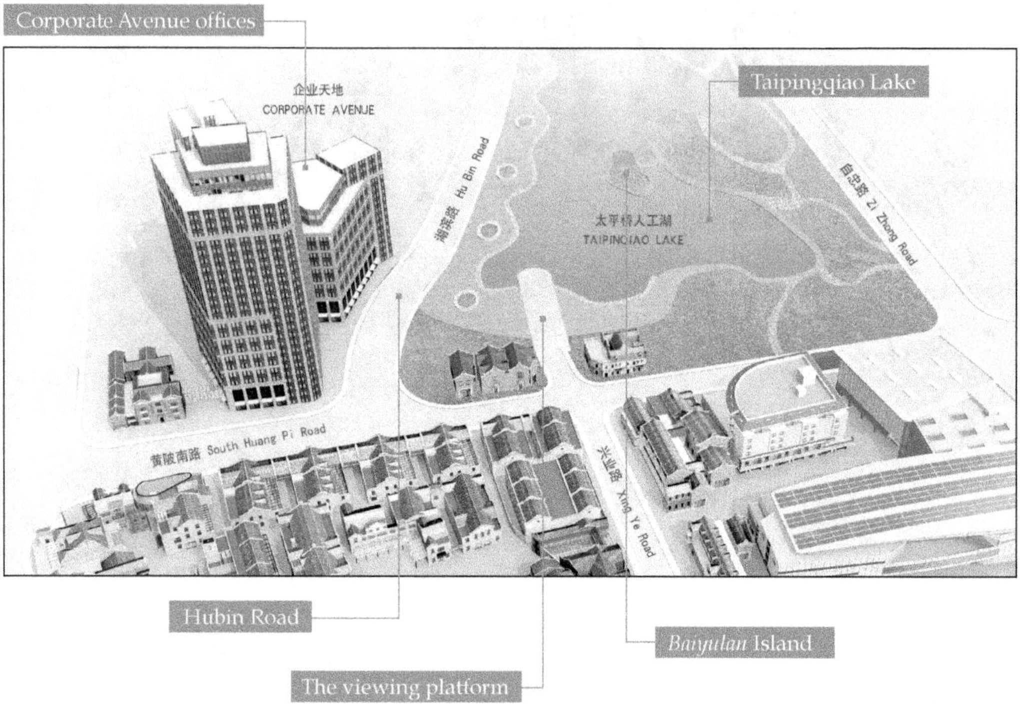

Corporate Avenue offices

企业天地
CORPORATE AVENUE

Taipingqiao Lake

湖滨路 Ho Bin Road

太平桥人工湖
TAIPINGQIAO LAKE

自忠路 Zi Zhong Road

黄陂南路 South Huang Pi Road

兴业路 Xing Ye Road

Hubin Road

The viewing platform

Baiyulan Island

CHAPTER 7

TAIPINGQIAO LAKE PARK

A short stroll from the architecturally and culturally salient *Shikumen* neighborhoods eastward along Xingye Road, Taipingqiao Lake Park is in bloom with lush green trees and jeweled with an artificial lake. A breeze provides a slight ripple to the mirror-like surface of the lake. One of the most romantic getaways in downtown area, the park features well-arranged buildings on the left bank of the lake and densely covered woods on the right with a winding path cutting through.

The Park was completed in June 2001. Astonished and puzzled by the construction of an artificial lake on the site of former residential neighborhoods, tourists and visitors were eager to find out why a lake, instead of profitable properties, was created in the city center of skyrocketing land values.

An artificial lake was blueprinted in the Taipingqiao Redevelopment plan completed in 1996, with a planned area of 4 hectares. As advised by the then Shanghai Mayor Mr. Xu Kuangdi, the lake was reduced to 1.2 hectares with the remaining 2.8 hectares converted into green parkland. A man-made lake, lacking the capacity of self-purification and subsequently likely to suffer from stagnation and foul odors, would be therefore invigorated by the green plants beneficial to the health of the lake ecosystem.

3800 neighborhoods and 50 enterprises and institutions were relocated and clusters of old houses were knocked down to make way for Taipingqiao Lake by leveraging human effort. The broad lake zigzags east–west, flowing beyond sight. Most lakes, uniformly round or square, resemble swimming pools, while the designers of the Lake have stricken a balance of asymmetry with a perfectly irregular presentation.

Questions then arose about the intention to build an artificial lake in the heart of the 52-hectare land.

Unlike building designers, regional planning architects have to employ a comprehensive approach to the regional planning with a broader notion of culture. As one of the leading architectural, urban planning and engineering firm that has made influential contributions to urban design approaches in many metropolises such as San Francisco, SOM patiently conducted a study of the regional culture rather than directly replicating the formular of an American city. The team of architects noticed that Taipingqiao area was crisscrossed by a network of creeks a century ago, the major ones being Zhaojia Bang (Chinese equivalent of creek), Datie Bang, Nanchang Bang, Beichang Bang. One of the multiple bridges over these creeks, Taipingqiao, spanning over Datie Bang, was one of the principal arterial roads to Laoximen, a history-steeped corner of Shanghai.

Having scrutinized the historical context and cultural climate of Taipingqiao area, SOM sensitively integrated the new development into the city's existing fabric.

During the first urbanization of Taipingqiao area in early 20th century, the French Concession authorities impressed the people of Shanghai with land reclamation to create new roads and real estate properties. At the end of the century when the regeneration took place, the area, embellished with a beautiful body of water, was a revelation to the public.

Taipingqiao area had been a compact and walkable district for nearly a century, characterized by a market that offered food, household goods, meals, haircuts, and even showers at its heart. Shunchang Road snack street connected the market with the outer ring of establishments of intellectual abundance including the Great Wall Cinema, Songshan Cinema, Yalu Shuchang (a storytelling teahouse), Yueguang Theater, middle schools, primary schools, art schools, law schools and Fazangjiang Temple, one of the most prominent Buddhist temples in Shanghai. All of the abovementioned establishments were within walking distance that took less than half an hour, with streets of appropriate width for cyclists and pedestrians.

The redevelopment plan didn't expand the area to accommodate vehicles and traffic lights that would otherwise hinder walking and bicycling.

With preservation of the original street width and creation of an artificial lake, the planning took a giant step forward to facilitate the cyclists and the pedestrians with easy access to the metro station.

When visiting Taipingqiao Lake, the Deputy Secretary-General of the UN couldn't help but exclaim: "Amazing! Amazing! It's something we can't do in New York right now." At that time, the average residential property sale price in Shanghai stood at 3000 yuan per square meter, one tenth of that of New York. The epic redevelopment of the Taipingqiao area would by no means be accomplished in 2010, when the sale price increased 680% as compared to a decade ago. The sky-high compensation for residential relocation would make it impossible to relocate the 3800 households within 40 days.

In early 20th century, the veteran city planners of the French Concession placed a market in the center of this area, demonstrating strategic spatial planning for urban areas with accurate positioning. Having enough food remained top priority for the average citizens. The market encouraged public interaction on a daily basis, providing a more livable environment for the locals.

In early 21st century when the Shanghai citizens were better-off, houses and cars eclipsed food to take top spots in people's demands. What about 10 years later when both demands have been met? It will definitely be a blue sky and clear water that this area has to offer a decade earlier, an epitome of great foresight of the future urban environment.

EAST MEETS WEST

Photographed in early February 2000. The residences at the central Taipingqiao old block were being torn down to build a lake.

Photographed in early June 2000, the third day of water injection after the completion of the artificial lake. Taken four months later than the left one, this photo is a symbolic manifestation of urban foresight and city visions.

The first urbanization of Taipingqiao Lake featured land reclamation to create new roads and real estate properties while the second urbanization carried out a century later is characterized by construction of an artificial lake on the site of former residential neighborhoods.

Nature inspired artificial lake

The intention behind, which most people didn't envision, was to shift the urban center from Huaihai Road to Taipingqiao Lake Park which used to be a residential area attached to the former. Now the 14 office buildings in the east section of Huaihai Road and the premium offices in Corporate Avenue constitute a central business district to the north of the Lake Park.

What a smart move!

The change of urban spatial structure has more importantly shaped public behavioral norms, modes of thought and urban cultures.

The process of the redevelopment in this area has been a struggle to bridge the old and the new. The residents of the *Shikumen* neighborhood are worse off than but greatly outnumber the white-collar workers in Corporate Avenue offices and the wealthy residents of the upscale community. Social opportunities have been reinforced when the new residents overlap with the indigenous dwellers, the rich meet the poor, and modern civilization intertwine with traditional culture. The

Lake Park, therefore, has promoted public interaction through shared experiences such as morning workouts and evening promenades.

Serving as a vital green lung amid a body of concrete, the Lake Park also fosters emotional interaction and bonding through monthly or weekly activities including concerts, musicals, fashion shows, and auto shows on Hubin Road and Baiyulan island of the Lake.

Annual Chinese New Year Countdown Gala is prepared at the Lake Park to celebrate the most exciting moment while the city is stepping into the new year.

All of the residents in the vicinity of Taipingqiao area, new or old, share cultural identity and take pride in where they live. This gives rise to a thorny problem for the developers, where the compensation for residential relocation has skyrocketed by 10 times in 2010 as compared to a decade before.

The indigenous residents, whose quotidian life used to orbit the Lake, traded voluntary relocation for incredibly high compensation. Despite the limited living space, the residents lamented the demise of the distinctive sociability and ambience of life in this area, unparalleled by any modern comfort in the suburban mansions.

This has posed a question that never occurred to us: is the Lake publicly or privately owned? Do the artificial lakes that have sprung up during the urban renewal process belong to the developers and investors?

Mr. Wood once addressed an urban planning forum in Shanghai on the architectural planning along the city's major rivers to be complemented by public buildings, such as cultural centers, museums, shopping malls and restaurants, that offered panoramic view to the public.

The forward-looking government made a bold decision to retain the ownership of Taipingqiao Lake by investing 600 million yuan in the residential relocation package for the indigenous dwellers. Shui On, having sponsored another 400 million yuan for the construction of the Lake, the parkland and the underground garage as well as long-term park maintenance cost, was granted the development right of the land encompassing the Lake in return.

A balance among the government, the private sector and the needs of the people was reached, epitomizing Chinese wisdom of moderation and political height.

Not everyone has foresight as strategic as Vincent Lo, whose plan was initially voted down by almost the entire board. His move was widely derided in Hong Kong's real estate industry as artistic emotion instead of business acumen. The Lake Park and Hubin Road cover an area of 5 hectares, grand enough to accommodate residential structures and office buildings of about 180,000 square meters that meant a potentially quick turnaround in profit. Yet, Lo went forward with his plans.

The debate on the construction of the Lake recalled the heated discussion in respect of the Bund in 1869 that whether the western bank of the Huangpu River stretching from Yangjingbang (now

Thousands of people gathering at Xintiandi New Year's Eve Countdown party

Performer-audience interaction.

East Yan'an Road) to Huangpu Garden (now Huangpu Park on East Beijing Road) should function as a pedestrian path or commodious wharves and large warehouses. All relevant parties were widely consulted by the municipal councils.

Given the increasing demand for warehousing as a result of the rapid development of trade at that time, most businessmen were in favor of building wharves and warehouses.

Edward Cunningham, a former board member of the Shanghai Municipal Council of the International Settlement (SMCIC), wrote a letter in Yokohama to strongly oppose the plan to use the river frontage of the Bund for wharves shortly after he retired from the position of SMCIC chairman.

"The sole beauty of Shanghai is the Bund ... It is the only place where the residents can get fresh air from the river in an evening promenade, the only place of the settlement where there is a free outlook," Cunningham wrote in the letter. "Shipping is not the main element in commerce. It is one of the courses adjunct like pack-horses and drays. The Exchange, the Banks, the Counting houses hold the basics of commerce and where they are located there always is the best quarter, the greatest throng of commercial life," wrote this far-sighted man.

In his opinion, the presence of shipping would bring only noise and dusts, which would scare off those financial institutions. Although retired, Cunningham was still influential and this four-page letter had affected opinion of the SMCIC board that eventually made the Bund Shanghai's most celebrated vista.

Among all the other unknown wharves and warehouses along both sides of the Huangpu River, the Bund, crowned as a world architecture museum, offers a sweeping perspective of the city.

If history has lessons to impart, they are to be found par excellence in such recurring patterns.

Accompanied by the municipal government officials on June 12, 2001, Jiang Zemin, the then President of the People's Republic of China, paid a visit to the memorial of the First

National Congress of the CPC, Xintiandi and Taipingqiao Lake and Park.

Former Mayor and subsequently the Party Committee Secretary of Shanghai, Jiang knew the *Shikumen* alleys like the back of his hand and felt responsible for providing the residents with modern amenities without destroying the historical culture of the decades-old terraced houses.

Restoration made to the existing *Shikumen* houses encompassing the Memorial to keep its former glory miraculously proved a commercial hit that even brought tax contributions to the country.

Vincent Lo was bestowed with the honor by Shanghai Municipal Government and Luwan District Government to brief the concept and practice of developing Xintiandi and the artificial lake for President Jiang at the viewing platform by the Lake.

The presence of the Lake Park was then broadcast to the entire country on CCTV and other major national media outlets on the same day.

To the east of the Lake stand scores of old blocks to be regenerated, awaiting the government and the developers to spearhead another renewal with new insight and resourcefulness. A landmark of urban ecological harmony and diversity, Taipingqiao Lake has illustrated the charm and invigoration of local civilization.

Moreover, the local daily evening news culminates in a display of Shanghai's iconic landscape, including the gorgeous views of the Bund and Taipingqiao Lake view with reflections of the city.

Having preserved dozens of gray-brick *Shikumen* dwellings, Xintiandi maintains the atmosphere of the original neighborhood and obscures the view of the modern structures springing up around it. Shanghai, the pounding commercial heart of the world's largest communist country, is a tangle of such contrasts.

China and the West implemented different development

EAST MEETS WEST

Gorgeous night view of the reflection of the cityscape in the water of Taipingqiao Lake

strategies in the 21st century. The United States and Europe have entered a post-industrial era after the third Industrial Revolution. Detroit, the Motor City in the U.S., underwent the largest municipal bankruptcy in the U.S. history in 2014. The government decided to invest in hi-tech industry, such as 3D printers, to revitalize the city's social and economic dynamics through a self-sufficient, local and modernized economy.

Driven by cultural differences and innovative thinking in the course of re-urbanization, the West has been working on the revival of historical and cultural heritage with modern civilization.

China's industrialization is characterized by a transformation toward a fast-growing economy based on mass manufacturing. Serial architectural replication may result in urban modernization,

TAIPINGQIAO LAKE PARK

ultimately harming distinctiveness and urban differentiation. Replicas of skyscrapers, boulevards and central plazas from the urban landscape in Europe in the 19th century and the U.S. in the first half of the 20th Century all provide notable examples of China's approach to simulating Western historic architecture, posing a confusing problem for the generations to come: where is our urban distinctiveness and national culture?

The new wave of urbanization, as indicated by the implementation and practice of the Xintiandi project, rests on the city's historic origin that we should preserve to bring insight into the future.

PART 2
THE SECRET FORMULA FOR XINTIANDI'S SUCCESS

Make people understand that their voice is valued.
Rich and varied perspectives lead to the core issue.
Truth springs forth from the clash of opinions.
The sparks of creativity ignite innovation.

Huaihai Road, a commercial street with a Parisian sensibility, is the preferred destination of local residents.

CHAPTER 1

The origin of Xintiandi

The revitalization project of Xintiandi has won a big success and garnered a great deal of international attentions and admiration. The true story behind Xintiandi's success uncovers the history of its evolution.

Now let's rewind back to the spring of 1990.

On April 18, 1990, Li Peng, the then Premier of China, announced in Shanghai the development and opening-up of Pudong, a district of Shanghai located east of the Huangpu River. Having reduced the gap of prosperity between the areas separated only by the Huangpu River, the development strategies by the Communist Party of China and the State Council have ushered in vivid dynamics of rapid urbanization.

Puxi, on the other side of the Huangpu River, was also a beneficiary. Having completed its urbanization in the first half of the 20th century, Puxi witnessed a downfall of the once glorious commercial streets, high rises and stretches of the *Shikumen* neighborhoods after a turbulent half-century.

A new wave of re-urbanization occurred in Puxi area to bring back its glory.

The construction of the first line of Shanghai Metro in 1992, indicating the arrival of the city's subway era, reshaped the urban spatial structure and the way people lived and worked.

As transportation got faster, cities got bigger. The development of the suburb is governed by its accessibility — which is to say, by the reasonable speed of transport to reach. With the arrival of the new mobility mode, some of the urban dwellers moved to

EAST MEETS WEST

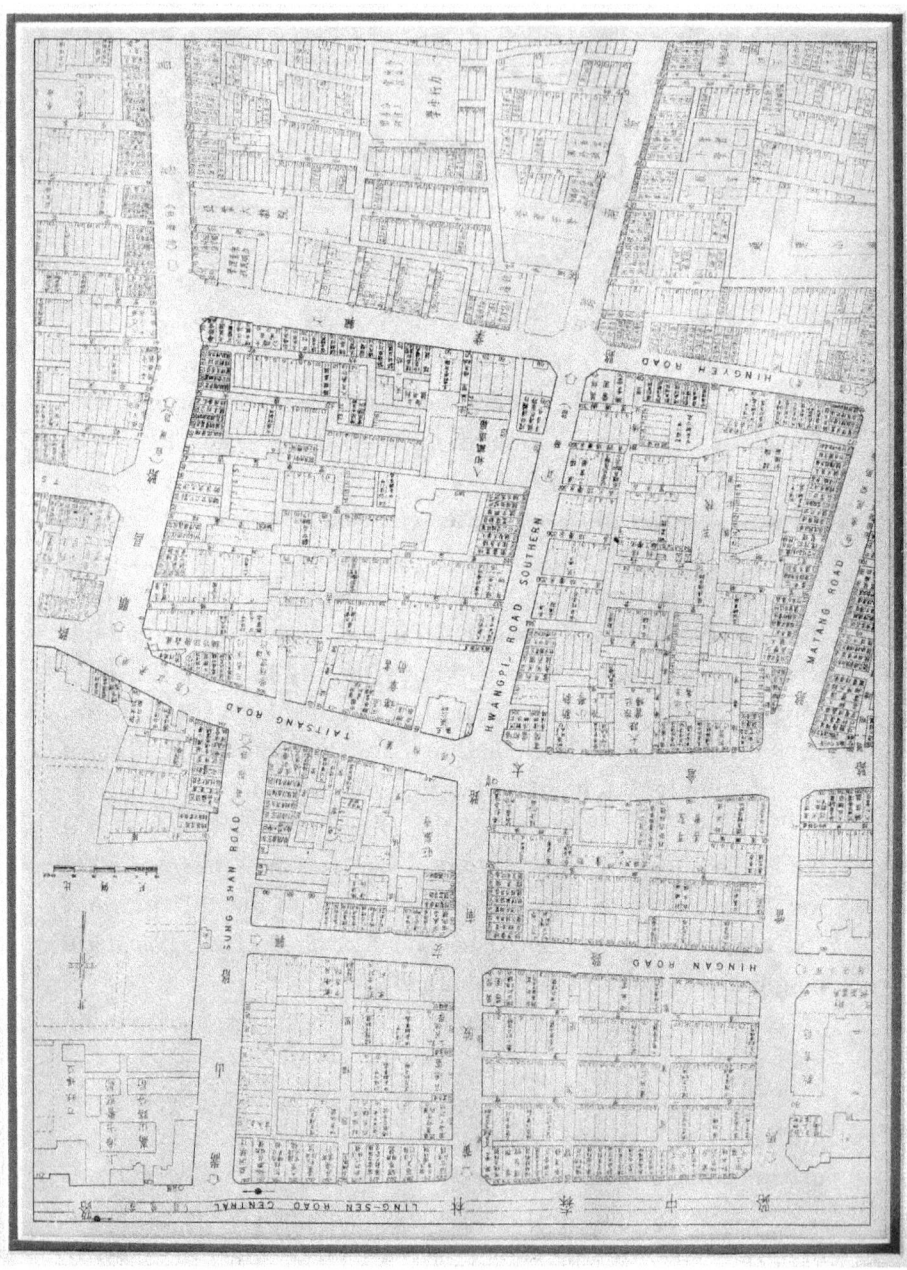

Floor plan of the Taipingqiao area in the '40s.

THE ORIGIN OF XINTIANDI

The farmer's market of Taipingqiao old quarters in the '90s.

the outskirts, bringing prosperity to the newly accessed territory and indicating potential decline of the once-thriving city center.

A sail boat must forge ahead or it will be swept downstream.

A section of the proposed Metro Line 1 would run underneath Middle Huaihai Road which was located in the former Luwan District (later merged into Huangpu District) in central Shanghai.

In order to move challenges towards opportunities, Huaihai Road had to undergo a thorough spatial reconstruction to occupy its dominant position in the city. The district launched a renovation program to replace the traditional business model of Huaihai Road with modern format.

The district government put the two-kilometer-long Middle Huaihai Road Commercial Street into hibernation: all shops were closed and traffic was prohibited to facilitate the underground excavations and concrete pipe installation. Roadside establishments along the one-kilometer-long east section of Middle Huaihai Road were demolished to make way for a new central business district with 14 office buildings.

The combination of the brand-new subway and business model required more room for growth, taking a whirl of change around the *Shikumen* residential area on both sides of Huaihai Road.

The Mayor of Luwan District asked the district planning director to devise a redevelopment plan of the old *Shikumen* blocks located one kilometer south to the east section of Middle *Huaihai* road. The result was the Taipingqiao Redevelopment Project that included the land parcel where Xintiandi was later conceived.

The functional orientation of the blocks was high on the list of priorities. At the beginning of the 20th century, this area, as planned by the French Concession authorities, was mainly composed of residential neighborhoods complemented by a little community commercial function during the first urbanization process.

Would the redevelopment plan follow the original functional orientation to handle the housing supply shortages by substituting the *Shikumen* houses with new residences?

Solving housing problem would definitely enhance the livelihood and well-being of the people and promote the political accomplishments of the government.

Nevertheless, instead of following the social trend, the district government coordinated with the municipal government to implement the urban development strategy: Shanghai was to transition from an industrial economy to a service economy focused on international business, trade and finance, building a new image of the city as an international financial hub and modern metropolis. The government's sustainable reconstruction plan helped to make connections between the long-term vision and short-term actions so that the city would always stay ahead of changes in the 21st century.

In 1992, Shanghai's regeneration process was in an exploratory phase where neither the planning department nor the local architects had sufficient capacity and appropriate urban planning experience to tap the opportunity for development which urbanization represented. A forward-looking framework to outline the district's collective vision of the future of Taipingqiao old quarters and to identify long-term strategic priorities for making that vision a reality was crucial to the transition.

The broad-minded district government made a bold decision to invite the best urban designers to weave the urban planning concept adopted in developed countries into the Taipingqiao Redevelopment Project.

Lacking international contacts and the capacity to select the right architects, the district government thought of a trustworthy friend—Vincent Lo, chairman of Hong Kong-based Shui On Group.

When opportunity knocked, Shui On answered the door.

Just awarded one of Hong Kong's Ten Outstanding Young Persons, Vincent Lo partnered with the Shanghainese Communist Youth League to build the City Hotel on Shaanxi Road in the city center. This pleasant experience laid foundation for future partnership, as the then District Mayor was the Youth League secretary and representative of the hotel project at that time.

City designers can be subdivided into architects and urban planners which are two distinct categories. Architects and urban planners both play a part in determining how a community will look, but the specific focus of their work is different. While architects design buildings, urban planners determine where buildings will go and how land will be used to meet community needs.

When planning an expansive urban area of tens of square kilometers, some cities invited world renowned architects, who, all too often, presented planning schemes disconnected from the

Gentle and well groomed, Vincent Lo, one of the most consistently successful foreign investors in China, is known as 'King of Guangxi (connections)' among foreign property developers.

day-to-day realities and needs of the community despite a perfect look of every single building.

Urban planning can have a profound impact on a city for decades if they are properly conceived and systematically executed. Therefore, integrating knowledge from the "right person" is essential for getting the project "right".

Entrusted by the district director, Vincent Lo engaged Skidmore, Owings & Merrill (SOM), a global architectural, urban planning and engineering firm, to appoint its best urban planner as the chief designer to work on the master plan.

SOM has a long history of innovation in sustainable architecture and design. Its foresight plays a pivotal role in the excellent interpretation of the government's vision and implementation of the plans adapted to local context.

The district government's goal to "stay ahead of changes in the 21st century" didn't specify the time frame within which all this has to occur.

People might wonder about the importance of setting down the scheduled time.

A specific time frame determines when the urban plan should be conceived and executed. Should the time frame fall on the beginning of the 21st century, modernism oriented urban planning would best fit the redevelopment plan in which the city is a fundamental spatial unit that must be zoned according to different functions.

With a very backward automobile industry in the 1990s, Shanghai featured zero functional zoning where production, living and shopping were mingled together: the machines downstairs were making banging noises; the residents upstairs were cooking and doing laundry; next door could be a primary school or a nursery school or even shops and tiger stoves.

The modernity local residents have been yearning for feature areas with designated zones based on different functions such as an industrial zone, a residential zone, a shopping zone and a recreational zone. Multiple generations can live separately in their own dream house which includes a living room, bedrooms, a study, a dining room and a kitchen, complemented with a private car.

The relatively compact urban form of the city, driven by people's dreams and desires, will be gradually replaced by a more decentralized and dispersed urban structure.

Modern urbanism was once the mainstream urban model in the United States, forcing pedestrians and vehicles to compete for the same territory—with vehicles overwhelmingly winning the battle.

In the mid-90s, most of the cars on the roads in Shanghai were government owned cars used by its officials. The cars would, based on SOM's estimation of the development of Shanghai's automotive industry, clog the limited street space and discharge exhaust fumes in a couple of decades. The citizens would be pushing to reorient urban areas away from cars in favor of pedestrians by then.

Incorporating walkability into urban planning has become a clarion call of contemporary urbanism. Should the district government plan to fulfill its vision by 2020, contemporary urban centers must provide various options for good-quality public open spaces to facilitate their use by pedestrians, public transport and contain fine-grained urban functions to adapt to work-life integration.

City visions represent shared, and often desirable, expectations about our urban futures in a couple of decades. As societies advance and history progresses, improvements are indispensable and almost inevitable. When others are constantly dealing with new crisis, people with foresight, on the other hand, have developed the habit of spotting issues ahead of time.

After careful consideration and discussion, SOM decided to apply the New Urbanism that arose in the United States in the early 1980s to the Taipingqiao Redevelopment Project, as the city center would be focusing on service-dominated economy instead of primary industry. The area after redevelopment should, therefore, feature greater integration of spatial structure rather than dispersion.

The forward-looking redevelopment project was endorsed by both the government and Shui On.

It took four years, from 1992 when the planning concept was put forth to 1996 when the controlling detailed plan was approved. It took another six years to officially start construction in January 1999. Once the plan was finalized, it remained unchanged for 18 years, during which its vitality, foresight and scientificalness were demonstrated as time went by.

A successful urban renewal project sometimes takes two or three terms of office to accomplish, where the incumbent government paves the way for the next. In some Chinese cities, however, the speed and scale of urban planning bring challenges, including meeting accelerated demand for political achievements, with a lack of patience and foresight. Conflicts are on the rise, resulting in hasty formulation of the aims and operational goals of the projects.

Shui On was also invited to participate in the regeneration project of tens of hectares of land in another administrative region of Shanghai. Eager to endow the weathered quarters with new elegance, the local government put forward the requirements of "developing the master plan, relocating the residents, embarking on construction and unveiling the new look within the year".

To meet all the goals and purposes of the government, the architect Shui On had invited made a quick design that referenced the functional zoning approach in the United States that transformed the condemned buildings into modern residential district designated for a single function that segregated work from life. Having prioritized shanty town reform over visionary urban planning, the local government neglected the potential integration of industrial territories into the urban environment, allowing no room for creating organic architectural and cultural development.

When work life integration became the new norm in Shanghai

in 2004, the development mode of Taipingqiao community that blends work, life and leisure has garnered much recognition and set a new benchmark throughout China for the rest of the industry to follow. The increase in the value of land in the immediate area has also provided vindication of Xintiandi's success.

Priority was given to the development of the modern service industry in Shanghai in 2005. When the municipal government was selecting the most representative modern service industry cluster, Taipingqiao topped the list.

Low-carbon mobility, which became a trendy transport mode in Shanghai in 2010, nicely dovetailed with the core concept of Taipingqiao community that advocated walking and public transportation.

The conventional practice of urban renewal entails the following patterns: first separate urban areas into various specialized mono-functional zones, then encourage mixed-use zoning that blends residential, commercial, cultural, institutional, or entertainment uses. The evolution may take years or even decades to materialize.

SOM produced a master plan that envisioned a dynamic mix of commercial office space, retail, preserved historic buildings, public parks and cultural facilities near the well-recognized Xintiandi and Taipingqiao Lake, rejuvenating the old downtown housing quarters into a compact and walkable district.

A poster child of the New Urbanism, Xintiandi was also closely associated with the development of subway which altered the city's appearance and accelerated the pace of urban life.

Leisure, on the other hand, helped to forge a more balanced slow-paced lifestyle in the fast-forward culture. There were times to go fast and be busy—but there were other times to put the brakes on and slow down.

A showcase of the city's fast-paced development, Xintiandi is a style hub that connects leisure pace to speedy subways.

In the 52-hectare Taipingqiao Redevelopment Project, how was the shape, boundary and area determined?

Well, there was a story behind the decision.

Since the first bid project for land leasing conducted in Hongqiao District in Shanghai in 1990, the government has been leasing the subdivided land parcels in the run-down inner-city areas to different developers, earmarked for commercial, residential or industrial properties. This, however, resulted in isolated and inconsistent real estate projects that undermined the potential for integrated neighborhoods, prompting the authorities to rethink its urban development model.

Urban community, a global concept that caught the government's attention, was the framework that helped Taipingqiao Redevelopment Project to encompass the functions of living, working, shopping, learning and entertainment in one unique spot.

A multi-functional urban community requires large-scale land lots. So how much area should the new Taipingqiao community cover?

Taipingqiao old area was bordered by Huaihai Road Commercial Street to the north, Xizang Road, a boundary road between Huangpu and Luwan District, to the east, and Chengdu Elevated Highway to the west, leaving no room for expansion in these directions. Extending south seemed to be the only option.

Nevertheless, if the southern border extended to Xujiahui Road and Middle Jianguo Road, the project would cover an area of one square kilometer, accounting for nearly one-seventh of the entire Luwan Administrative District. Handing such a project over to a Hong Kong developer on an unprecedented scale posed potential political and economic risks to local authorities, which was beyond their capacity to control and manage.

If the border stretched to Middle Fuxing Road, the project would only occupy an area of 40 hectares, 4 of which had been appropriated for the construction of the artificial lake. The remaining tight space for residential development south to the lake would lead to inequitable marginal benefit for Shui On Land to enjoy.

The final decision was based upon two factors: The district government planned to renovate all poor quality and small size public rental housing with no toilets, or those in the worst conditions that lacked private toilets and kitchens, most of which were located in the north of Hefei Road; on the other hand, the redevelopment budget was estimated at between 30 billion to 40 billion yuan, way above Shui On's ten-digit assets. A consensus was finally reached on Hefei Road bordering Taipingqiao redevelopment area to the south, fixing the total area of the project at 52 hectares.

The project was approved by the Shanghai Municipal City Planning Administration in 1997.

In the same year erupted the Asian financial crisis when panicked Hong Kong real estate developers and banks withdrew from the market in droves and the property market in Shanghai plunged into a major recession.

Taipingqiao Redevelopment Project was launched despite the blow of the financial storm. Hong Kong developers traditionally financed the working capital needed for construction of leisure and commercial zone and artificial lake with the cash inflows from the residential and office units sold.

In 1998, the original plan had to be adjusted with the intent of showcasing the site of the first National Congress of the CPC and its adjacent blocks by 2001 in time for the 80th anniversary of Communism in China as well as the October convention in Shanghai of the Asia-Pacific Economic Cooperation (APEC).

The local authorities envisioned a wave of media attention in China and overseas reporting the historic conservation of the first National Congress of the CPC as an iconic urban landmark after China's 20 years of reform and opening up.

Given the context of the economic downturn, local government and Shui On decided to avoid the risk of undertaking residential or commercial office development immediately. Instead, the strategy was to firstly develop the historic conservation zone and the major landscaped park which would hopefully increase the popularity of the project.

Shanghai Municipal Administration of Culture Heritage, having demonstrated a willingness to embrace concepts widely adopted by the international professional community, was involved to supervise the redevelopment project since the site of the first National Congress of the CPC was a "Major Historical and Cultural Site Protected at the National Level". The Administration augmented the political and cultural significance of the CPC site through protecting the historic *Shikumen* buildings and preserving the historical and cultural atmosphere of the neighborhood at its proximity, requiring the new design be sensitive to historic buildings and compatible with them in terms of height and character of the property and environment.

Challenged by the rules that only *Shikumen* buildings, for which local residents might have little relish to dwell in in the 21st century, were allowed to be constructed after the old ones had been demolished, Shui On had little room to breathe on a seemingly thorny project that required a FAR of 1.8 and a massive capital investment of 1.4 billion yuan, half of which would be expended to facilitate the relocation of the 2,300 households in two blocks and half on renovation, resulting in a higher cost per square meter than that of a newly built apartment in Shanghai.

Crisis inevitably spurs innovation. Mr. Lo, as a frequent traveler around the world who is most fascinated by the old streets in every city he goes to where old buildings have seen the cultural history and economic development and given people a sense of place and connection to the past, recalled the old towns in many European and American cities where cozy pubs, age-old restaurants and charming cafés line cobblestone streets. He believed that the CPC site and the neighborhood at its proximity would serve as the perfect snapshot of contemporary urban development in Shanghai. Xintiandi would be to Shanghai what the St Germain street is to Paris, Fisherman's Wharf is to San Francisco or Ginza is to Tokyo.

THE ORIGIN OF XINTIANDI

While the Bund and Nanjing Road shopping precinct are among Shanghai's most Western cityscapes and celebrated vistas, *Shikumen* buildings exude a nostalgic narrative of Shanghai's modernization and set a new benchmark for style.

Great things never came from comfort zones. Instead of settling for the ordinary, Vincent Lo, mastermind developer behind the project, was willing to risk the unusual. Other than the input of creativity, inspiration and impulse, a great partner would play a pivotal role in setting the innovation in motion.

The famous Café de Flore located at the corner of Boulevard Saint-Germain and Rue Saint-Benoît in Paris

Founder of Thompson & Wood and then Wood & Zapata, architectural firms that spearheaded many redevelopment projects in the '80s and '90s, Benjamin Wood, who revitalized Boston's 150-year-old Faneuil Hall into a world-renowned marketplace that attracted millions of visitors annually including students of Harvard and MIT, captured Mr. Lo's attention.

Known as the expert of protection, rehabilitation and redevelopment in the planning and design realm, Mr. Wood explained that the success of Faneuil Hall Marketplace, which was being fast replicated around the world, stemmed from having retained the intangible value of the historic fabric.

Culture was recognized as an integral part of urban development linked with acknowledging diversity in cultural heritages and values. To create a new culturally sensitive urban development model, the role of cultural practices and values in sustainable development must be explicitly recognized, supported, and integrated into planning in a systematic and comprehensive way.

EAST MEETS WEST

Mr. Wood disdained the punctilious historic preservation which maintained all of the things in their original places, and neither did he consent to razing all the old rabbit warren of unique Shanghai-style houses. Ever mindful of the precinct's authentic history, he proposed restoring and repurposing them for an upscale and trendy entertainment hub, while maintaining the original character of Old Shanghai in this site.

Seeing eye-to-eye with Wood's vision, Vincent Lo believed he had found the right partner after much contact and communication with Mr. Wood in the States.

The two had a very interesting conversation.

According to Mr. Wood, buildings weren't static. Dynamic building prototypes required constant renewal and rejuvenation in order for the building to maintain its value over a lifespan of hundreds of years.

He said, "I don't believe you should proclaim things dead and turn them into museums. I believe you should breathe life into places. That's my goal. I want to make living areas, where people can eat, drink and enjoy themselves."

This struck a chord with Vincent Lo!

As Mr. Wood put it, "preservation shouldn't be an end to itself… traditional structures should be evaluated for their modern value and not simply preserved blindly." Only those architectural features that gave the area its unique character would be preserved. The restoration would utilize original bricks and tiles, black doorframes, window shades, and knockers to keep the buildings true to their original appearance.

It had become a commonplace idea in contemporary architecture that social and technological shifts occurred at fast pace. Everything would need to change at coordinated moments in time to ensure the viability of the whole.

It was open to us, through our own efforts, to give history, in our case, some new and unprecedented turn.

Teaming up with this visionary architect, Vincent Lo anticipated a refined cluster of traditional brick town houses that would exude social richness and historical narratives by sensitively integrating the new development into the city's existing fabric.

Their vision for Shanghai went beyond the immediate historical context and concerns of the city because they came from outside of it. In particular, Wood's outsider perspective and his unique design approach were instrumental.

Mr. Lo said that Xintiandi would be built into a centerpiece of the city, incorporating modern architecture to turn it into an iconic ritzy and glitzy leisure, shopping, fashion, dining, entertainment, and residential area and make it one of Shanghai's favorite complexes with a concentration of culture and lifestyle, and a range of hotels, restaurants, cafes, book stores, shops, and boutiques. It would cater to a variety of audiences — white-collar workers, business people, expatriates and tourists.

Hence began the clash of wits between an Asian businessman and a Western architect, and a re-creation was born out of the sprawls of *Shikumen* housing.

Faneuil Hall Marketplace, the dark red building in the picture and a once-rundown warehouse on the wharf, has been transformed into a vibrant complex of restaurants and shops by Benjamin Wood and inspired festival marketplaces around the country.

The author in Faneuil Hall Marketplace

Mr. Benjamin Wood, the principal architect of Xintiandi

Summary of the *Shikumen* Neighborhoods in Taipingqiao Area

Plot 107

Number	Name	Address	Time/Year	Number of Households	Floor Space /m²
1	Hongyili	Lane 138, Taicang Rd. Lane 15, Xing An Rd.	1912–1936	23	
2	Fuxingli	Lane 110, Taicang Rd.	1931	10	580

Plot 108

Number	Name	Address	Time/Year	Number of Households	Floor Space /m²
1	Wuxingli	Land 300 & 310, South Huangpi Rd. Lane 91 & 101, Madang Rd.	1914	82	5580
2	Zunshan Welfare Association	Taicang Rd.			

Plot 109

Number	Name	Address	Time/Year	Number of Households	Floor Space /m²
1	Yongqiangfang	South Huangpi Rd.			
2	North Shudeli	Land 374, South Huangpi Rd. Lane 80, Xingye Rd.	1911	21	1446.7
3	Dunrenli	Land 117, Madang Rd.			
4	Fuzhili				
5	Yudeli	Land 344, South Huangpi Rd.	1933	28	920
6	Changxingli				
7	Jurenli				
8	Dahuali				
9	Fushouli	Lane 191, Taicang Rd.	1917	4	406.7
10	Mingdeli	Land 139 &147, Madang Rd.	1923	34	2733.3

SUMMARY OF THE SHIKUMEN

11	Jipingli				
12	Dunrenfang	Land 117, Madang Rd.	1923	10	853.3
13	Qinyufang	Land 111, Madang Rd.	1917	10	406.7
14	Ciyunfang	Lane 96, Xingye Rd.	1919	11	726.6
15	Shudeli	Land 374, South Huangpi Rd.			

Plot 110

Number	Name	Address	Time/Year	Number of Households	Floor Space /m²
1	Fayili	Lane 54, Xingye Rd.	1925	7	1233.3
2	Yuqingfang	Lane 68, Shunchang Rd.	1930	26	1633.33
3	East Jiyili	Lane 119, Taicang Rd.	1914	45	5580
4	Fushengli	Lane 30, Shunchang Rd.	1930	4	446.7
5	Changdeli	Lane 24, Shunchang Rd.	1926	12	680
6	Deshengli	Lane 10, Shunchang Rd.	1925	18	706.7
7	Yanqingli	Lane 121, Taicang Rd.	1911	5	720
8	Jiyili	Lane 119, Taicang Rd.	1914	45	5580
9	Tianyifang	Lane 40, Xingye Rd.	1922	7	573.3
10	Tongyili	Land 337 & 349, South Huangpi Rd.	1929	15	1566.7

Plot 111

Number	Name	Address	Time/Year	Number of Households	Floor Space /m²
1	Chengqingli	Lane 108,, Shunchang Rd.	1928	71	5140
2	Jiwufang	Lane 210, Zizhong Rd.	1925	61	7360
3	Zixiangli	Lane 244, Zizhong Rd.	1925	20	700
4	Junyili	Land 429, South Huangpi Rd.	1923	25	2386.7
5	Xindeli	Land 419, South Huangpi Rd.	1912–1936	8	446.7
6	Yunshengli	Land 381, South Huangpi Rd.	1912–1936	4	1020
7	Shunchangli	Lane 31, 41, 51 & 61 Xingye Rd.	1914	24	2093.3
8	Fengdeli				

EAST MEETS WEST

Plot 112

Number	Name	Address	Time/Year	Number of Households	Floor Space /m²
1	Yonganli				
2	Wangdeli	Land 430, South Huangpi Rd.	1919	18	2053.3
3	Renshouli	Lane 139, Xingye Rd.	1929	23	1780
4	Jingxili	Lane 151, Xingye Rd.	1929	6	193.3
5	Renjili	Lane 322, Zizhong Rd.	1929	63	4766.7
6	Huifeng Villa	Land 458, South Huangpi Rd.	1938	15	1546.7
7	North Shudeli	Land 374, South Huangpi Rd.	1911–1916	21	1446.7
		Lane 80, Xingye Rd.			

Plot 113

Number	Name	Address	Time/Year	Number of Households	Floor Space /m²
1	Xihuli	Lane 317, Zizhong Rd.	1928	98	7373.4
2	Cianfang	Lane 394, Hefei Rd.	1924	48	4146.7
3	Pingyuli	Lane 328, Middle Fuxing Rd.	1925	9	660
4	Yongyuli	Lane 320, Middle Fuxing Rd.	1925	17	2126.7
		Lane 307, Zizhong Rd.			
5	Chengsuili	Land 482, South Huangpi Rd.	1924	9	720
6	Dunrenli	Lane 257, Madang Rd.	1925	7	513.3

Plot 114

Number	Name	Address	Time/Year	Number of Households	Floor Space /m²
1	Tianheli	Lane 239, Zizhong Rd.	1922	104	13333.4
2	Fukangli	Lane 250, Middle Fuxing Rd.	1921–1936	30	2306.7
3	Sanyuli	Lane 234, Middle Fuxing Rd.	1921–1936	12	
4	Sanqingli	Lane 180 & 206, Shunchang Rd.	1911	80	4993.3
5	Ruikangli	Lane 219, Zizhong Rd.	1931–1936	13	793.3
6	Guangmingli	Lane 288, Middle Fuxing Rd.	1921–1936	17	1160

SUMMARY OF THE SHIKUMEN

7	Sanrangli	Lane 170, Shunchang Rd.	1921–1936	34	560
8	Guifuli	Lane 135, Shunchang Rd.	1929	22	2220
9	Ruiqingli	Lane 255, Zizhong Rd.	1921-1936	3	380

Plot 115

Number	Name	Address	Time/Year	Number of Households	Floor Space /m^2
1	Ruihuafang	Lane 285, Middle Fuxing Rd.	1920	79	6520
2	Anjili	Lane 168, Hefei Rd.	1921–1936	10	973.3
3	Guangmingcun	Lane 278, Nanchang Rd.	1921–1936	12	1953.3
4	Caishifang	Lane 30, Shunchang Rd.	1927	15	1240
5	Chengyuli	Lane 221, Middle Fuxing Rd.	1923	41	5906.7
6	Guahuali	Lane 239, Middle Fuxing Rd.	1920	38	3226.7
7	Weihouli	Lane 263, Middle Fuxing Rd.	1919	26	3026.7

Plot 116

Number	Name	Address	Time/Year	Number of Households	Floor Space /m^2
1	Guiyunli	Lane 242, Jinan Rd.	1923	14	886.7
2	Songqingfang	Lane 232, Jinan Rd.	1919	23	1433.3
3	Xingpingli	No. 26-36, Lane 279, Shunchang Rd.	1926	12	1046.7
4	Renshouli	Lane 139, Xingye Rd.	1929	23	1780
5	Xianchengli	Lane 14, Hefei Rd.	1911	36	1113.3
6	Shudeli	Lane 260 & 270, Jinan Rd.	1903	31	1953.3
7	Shuxiangli	No. 15-25, Lane 279, Shunchang Rd.	1931	11	1000
8	Ruikangli	No. 72-79, Lane 279, Shunchang Rd.	1935	8	466.7
9	Dingxingli				
10	Dongshenli	Lane 64, Hefei Rd.	1923	2	466.7
11	Yanshouli	Lane 325, Shunchang Rd.	1923	1	440

Number	Name	Address	Time/Year	Number of Households	Floor Space /m²
12	Dexiangli	Lane 82, Hefei Rd.	1928	1	453.3
13	Xiangshengli	No 34-36, Lane 14, Hefei Rd.		5	526.7
14	Xianchengli	No 2-32 & No. 48-52, Lane 14, Hefei Rd.	1921	22	2586.7

Plot 117

Number	Name	Address	Time/Year	Number of Households	Floor Space /m²
1	Taihefang	Lane 163, Zizhong Rd.	1919	24	3480
2	Tingyunli	Lane 160, Middle Fuxing Rd.	1919	62	5493.4
3	Wenxianli	Lane 170, Middle Fuxing Rd.	1922	14	806.7
4	Wubenfang	Lane 182, Middle Fuxing Rd.	1932	4	460
5	Hezhongfang	Lane 188, Middle Fuxing Rd.	1921	22	746.7
6	Shoufuli	Lane 205, Shunchang Rd.	1920	51	5146.7

Plot 118

Number	Name	Address	Time/Year	Number of Households	Floor Space /m²
1	Yonganli				
2	Wangxianli	Lane 164, Ji'an Rd.	1921–1936	11	760
3	Guangyuli	Lane 144, Ji'an Rd.	1921–1936	42	3660
4	Changxingli	Lane 126, Ji'an Rd.	1921–1936	6	1340
5	Rongshengli	Lane 156, Dongtai Rd.	1921–1936	28	2040
6	Xiangchengli	Lane 93, Zizhong Rd.	1921–1936	7	813.3
7	Xinpingli	Lane 121, Zizhong Rd.	1921–1936	10	1053.3
8	Baoanfang	Lane 113-159, Zizhong Rd.	1921–1936	13	
9	Shananli	Lane 165, Ji'nan Rd.	1921–1936	2	
10	Baoshanli	Lane 173-175, Ji'nan Rd.	1921–1936	1	
11	Xi'anli	Lane 185, Ji'nan Rd.	1921–1936	2	

SUMMARY OF THE SHIKUMEN

12	Jing'anli	Lane 185, Ji'nan Rd.	1921–1936	28	3433.3
13	Shaoanli	Lane 207 & 217, Ji'nan Rd.	1921–1936	5	1026.7
14	Jiuanli	Lane 225, Ji'nan Rd.	1921–1936	6	680
15	Derenli	Lane 126, Middle Fuxing Rd.	1924	16	1486.7
16	Shandeli				
17	Fulinli	Lane 106, Middle Fuxing Rd.	1921–1936	49	2813.3
18	Yinxingli				
19	Demingli	Lane 99, Zizhong Rd.	1928	14	1080

Plot 119

Number	Name	Address	Time/Year	Number of Households	Floor Space /m²
1	Yongkangli	Lane 243, Ji'nan Rd.	1905	16	1206.7
2	Pingjili	Lane 275, Ji'nan Rd.	1921	21	1606.7
3	Gaoshengli	Lane 166, Ji'nan Rd.	1915	19	520
4	Dechengli	Lane 146, Zhaozhou Rd.	1908	18	986.7
5	Zhichengli	Lane 126, Zhaozhou Rd.	1926	34	2573.3
6	Changpingli	Lane 328, Ji'nan Rd.	1931	12	566.7
7	Danfengli				
8	Xixiangli	Lane 87, Middle Fuxing Rd.	1921	52	1273.3
9	Yuanchengli	Lane 113, Middle Fuxing Rd.	1915	58	5246.7

Plot 120

Number	Name	Address	Time/Year	Number of Households	Floor Space /m²
1	Liyangli	Lane 508, South Xizang Rd.	1912–1936	4	342.7
2	Chundeli	Lane 528, South Xizang Rd.	1912	52	3346.7
3	Deyili	Lane 343, 339, 349, Dongtai Rd.	1922	19	1673.3
4	Ruianfang	Lane 40, Zhaozhou Rd.	1912	12	
5	Renbenli	No. 56 Sublane, Lane 528, South Xizang Rd.	1921–1936	3	620

6	Tianyoufang	Lane 26, Zhaozhou Rd.	1921—1936	15	733.3
7	Huichaoli				
8	Yonganli	Lane 23, Middle Fuxing Rd.	1904	1	260
9	Yangweili				
10	Sanruili	Lane 73, Middle Fuxing Rd.	1915	9	513.3
11	Dexiangli	Lane 78, Zhaozhou Rd.	1921	29	2626.7
12	Wubenli	Lane 284, Dongtai Rd.	1927	8	1000
13	Tianlaifang				
14	Houdefang	Lane 200, Zhaozhou Rd. 148—175	191—1936	26	2606.7
15	Youyuli	Lane 7, Middle Fuxing Rd.	1930	5	146.7
16	Yuqingli	No. 49-53, Lane 528, South Xizang Rd.	1912	5	153.3
17	Shaoyili	Lane 303, Ji'nan Rd.	1912—1936	1	233.3

Plot 122

Number	Name	Address	Time/Year	Number of Households	Floor Space /m^2
1	Xing'anli	Lane 15, Zizhong Rd.	1927	17	2726.7
2	Quanyuli	Lane 412, South Xizang Rd.	1928	27	1860
3	Dunrenli	Lane 426, South Xizang Rd.	1928	5	680
4	Chongshanli	Lane 438, South Xizang Rd.	1921—1936	10	693.3
5	Ruyili	Lane 454, South Xizang Rd.	1929	8	700
6	Renshouli	Lane 167, Dongtai Rd.	1928	4	713.3
7	Annafang	Lane 177, Dongtai Rd.	1928	7	706.7
8	Yonganli	Lane 32, Middle Fuxing Rd.	1923	5	1260
9	Ziyangli	No. 1-9, Lane 64, Middle Fuxing Rd.	1935	11	7793.4
10	Meiquanli				
11	Rongshengli	Lane 156, Dongtai Rd.	1921—1936	28	2040
12	Wendeli	Lane 163, Jitai Rd.	1921—1936	10	700

SUMMARY OF THE SHIKUMEN

Number	Name	Address	Time/Year	Number of Households	Floor Space /m²
13	Jixiangli	Lane 125, Ji'nan Rd.	1921–1936	8	
14	Dahuali	Lane 37, Zizhong Rd.	1929	26	3726.7
15	Rendeli	Lane 121 &123, Ji'nan Rd.	1921–1936	14	2173.3

Plot 123

Number	Name	Address	Time/Year	Number of Households	Floor Space /m²
1	Dingchangli				
2	Baoanli	Lane 9, Dongtai Rd.	1936	16	1166.7
3	Yuanjifang	Lane 29, Dongtai Rd.	1921–1936	8	633.3
4	Ruyifnag				
5	Wenyuanfang				
6	Yuanshengli				
7	Chengdeli	Lane 15, Liuhekou Rd	1915	6	526.7
8	Fuyuli				
9	Zhenhuali	Lane 301, Madang Rd.	1928	45	6193.3
10	Minshenfang	Lane 346, South Xizang Rd.	1915	1	860
11	Hongfuli	Lane 356, South Xizang Rd.	1932	27	1686.7

Plot 124

Number	Name	Address	Time/Year	Number of Households	Floor Space /m²
1	Dingxiangli	Lane 57, Liuhekou Rd	1912–1915	35	2180
2	Chang'anli	Lane 257, Middle Jinling Rd	1910	21	1953.3
3	Fuyuanli	Lane 60, Zizhong Rd.	1913–1921	54	3440
4	Leyili	Lane 88, Dongtai Rd	1913	35	1813.3
5	Hengdeli	Lane 16, Dongtai Rd.	1910	24	1460
6	Huaishengli				
7	Yishouli	Lane 45, Chongde Rd.	1911 Front	3	180
8	Kangningcun	Lane 36, Dongtai Rd.	1936 Front	3	120

Plot 126

Number	Name	Address	Time/Year	Number of Households	Floor Space /m²
1	Qingpingfang	Lane 119, Chongde Rd.	1923	41	2226.7
2	Peifuli	Lane 91, Chongde Rd.	1927	36	3860
3	Lanxinli				
4	Tongjifang	Lane 105, 113 &125, Ji'nan Rd.	1908	35	1533.3
5	Dunrangli	Lane 98, Zizhong Rd.	1912	8	540
6	Xinfuli	Lane 78 & 80, Ji'nan Rd.	1912	9	1346.7
7	Yiyeli	Lane 20, 28, 36 & 40, Ji'nan Rd.	1920	24	2320
8	Yirunli	Lane 79, Chongde Rd.	1925	11	646.7
9	Shunyuanli	Lane 60, Ji'nan Rd.	1920–1926	17	806.7

Plot 127

Number	Name	Address	Time/Year	Number of Households	Floor Space /m²
1	Renjieli	Lane 69, Shunchang Rd.	1928	5	680
2	Renlingli	Lane 153, Chongde Rd.	1928	16	1260
3	Xinhuacun	Lane 143, Chongde Rd.	1937	16	1286.7
4	Liangshanli	Lane 24, Ji'nan Rd.	1931	8	713.3
5	Qing'anfang	Lane 64, Ji'nan Rd.	1924	6	793.3
6	Yonganli	Lane 89 & 99, Shunchang Rd.	1927	39	2906.7
7	Yongchenli	Lane 78, Ji'nan Rd.	1929–1936	15	713.3
8	Huaibenli	Lane 111, Shunchang Rd.	1928	12	1426.7
9	Gengyunli	Lane 96, Ji'nan Rd.	1929	5	873.3
10	Kangjili	Lane 106, Ji'nan Rd.	1917–1931	18	1713.3
11	Guifuli	Lane 135, Shunchang Rd.	1929	22	2220
12	Songbailu	Lane 124, Ji'nan Rd.	1931	1	580
13	Hanzeli	Lane 162, Zizhong Rd.	1926	8	646.7
14	Jishanli	Lane 141, Shunchang Rd.	1924	6	1160

SUMMARY OF THE SHIKUMEN

		Plot 128			
Number	Name	Address	Time/Year	Number of Households	Floor Space /m²
1	Renyili				
2	Fengboli	Lane 33, Taicang Rd.	1924	3	686.7
3	Tongfuli				

		Plot 129			
Number	Name	Address	Time/Year	Number of Households	Floor Space /m²
1	Yuanqingli				
2	Zhenganli				

With rotten wood and loose bricks, this dilapidated Shikumen building was later gut renovated into an upscale store on the north side of the fountain plaza.

CHAPTER 2

THE DEBATE ON RESTORATION

Dreams don't work unless you take action.

There was no shortage of great ideas in China nowadays. Without action, all great ideas are useless. The key that turns dreams into reality is a good plan of action. People who act on their ideas are in the minority. An individual may birth the dream, but to make the dream a reality requires collective efforts of people who have come to believe in the individual's dream. With an ideal team committed to a particular dream over a period of time, the realization of the dream is inevitable.

It has not been easy to integrate a modern leisure lifestyle into the rundown *Shikumen* alleys. With an intended life span of 50 years estimated by the real estate developers in 1914, the *Shikumen* houses started to decay due to around 80 years of overuse and lack of maintenance. It was during the relocation that the rotten wood pillar bases in the decrepit houses were found to have failed to support the weight of the house at any imminent risk of collapse. Water could also enter through vapor condensation and penetrate the structure as a result of the loose flakes and deterioration on the surface of the gray brick walls in times of torrential rainfall.

Shikumen houses were stumbling into devastating disappearance.

Many developers tried in vain to salvage the dilapidated *Shikumen* alleys due to cultural challenges instead of technical hurdles. Since most residents welcomed the demolition of their old homes and the promise of relocation to new high-rise apartments on the city's outskirts, the old brick blocks were razed and replaced by modern high-rises. On the other hand, with *Shikumen* falling out of the category of cultural relics, government-funded restoration and redevelopment projects would be financially unfeasible.

Since the site of the first National Congress of the CPC was a "Major Historical and Cultural Site Protected at the National Level", Shanghai Municipal Administration of Culture Heritage (SMACH) was involved to evaluate and supervise the redevelopment project of the site's adjacent two blocks.

Xintiandi and the CPC site are largely complementary to each other: The success of the Xintiandi project would cast a direct impact on the reputation and political influence of the CPC site.

There had been heated debates over the renewal of the two blocks among cultural heritage professionals, Xintiandi developer and architecture professionals who were given free rein to express diverse cultural perspectives, signifying the rebirth of Xintiandi in an innovative atmosphere.

The debate promoted cultural heritage awareness that cast a far-reaching positive impact on the urban construction of Shanghai in the next decade when distinct approaches were adopted to the restoration of historic sites such as *Tianzifang*, the Bridge 8, Sinan Mansion, and *Bugaoli*.

The ultimate confrontation fell on the renovation plan proposed by Benjamin Wood, the principal architect, who championed the idea of restoring and repurposing the houses for a spacious and trendy entertainment hub, while seamlessly blending new architectural elements with original brick and tiles, stone gates and window shades.

Some local architecture and cultural heritage professionals, however, held a different opinion: conservation of historic *Shikumen* houses around the CPC site could not be limited to preservation of their visual and aesthetic character but should also include consideration of the underlying physical, social, and economic structures, as well as the lifestyle of the residents and the culture of the *Shikumen* alleys. They believed the urban redevelopment was to improve the living conditions of residents in the shanties and dilapidated areas by installing modern amenities.

Mr. Wood further explained his design philosophy: restoring the *Shikumen* houses to improve its housing conditions would turn them into museums where tourists would simply come in, take a picture and leave. Our development proposal was to rejuvenate the old downtown housing quarters into a mixed-use community.

His proposal met with diverse responses.

The notion felt radical to some *Shikumen* conservation experts who were convinced that simply preserving the exteriors would cause the inauthentic to drive out the authentic altogether in time and the incompatibility with the traditional context would generate cultural fault lines. As a result, emphasis should be placed upon retaining the historical fabric of *Shikumen* architecture in its original form.

Some professionals were, on the other hand, more concerned about the financial feasibility for the developer since the estimated renovation cost of the two blocks amounted to 1.4 billion yuan, meaning the cost per square meter would stand at as much as 20,000 yuan, three times more than that of a newly constructed apartment at that time. With drastic lifestyle changes as compared to last century, transformation of the residential function of *Shikumen* houses was inevitable.

The debate over whether to retain the historical context of *Shikumen* houses in the original form or reshape them to suit modern needs placed much pressure on Shui On who, as the capital provider amid the Asian financial crisis, had to stake all its HKD 800 million to foot the bill for the relocation of 2,300 households only to be granted land parcels reduced to a mass of rubble. Usually, developers would be granted a vacant piece of land during the transfer of land use rights according to the relocation regulation. However, as a contribution to the nostalgic narrative of one of Chinese communism's most revered shrines, the two neighborhoods adjacent to the CPC site were preserved for the experts and architects to decide what to keep. Should the final decision be a wholesale demolition of the old brick blocks to be replaced by residential quarters with *Shikumen* architectural features rather than a hybrid mixture of historic richness and commercial development, Mr. Lo's dream would never have been realized.

All the players involved were trying to walk a fine line between preserving a core of low-rise, courtyard-style buildings around the party's founding site to maintain the atmosphere of the original neighborhood and driving long-term growth underpinned by profitable operations. Encompassing a national historic shrine where the Chinese Communist Party originally met, this project, extremely challenging and error-prone, was too important to fail.

None of the commercial establishments where people felt overwhelmed by garish commercialism would be permitted beside the CPC site. Nor would the project survive if it was transformed into an iconic residence doubling as a museum where visitors came only for picture-taking or reconstructed as nostalgic ornamentation like a movie studio.

The future of the project appeared in doubt in the wake of the debate.

After over a decade of friendly relations with local government in Mainland China, Mr. Lo, with a clear perception of the intersection of economy and politics, had discerned that the understanding and support from the decision makers would be the backbone of shifting people's mindset to embrace the new project.

In 1997, Mr. Lo addressed the 8th Shanghai Mayor International Entrepreneur Consultation Conference on the importance of developing leisure business in Shanghai to encourage public interaction and how this new lifestyle and an international metropolis intersected: "Shanghai should become a magnet to attract, train and retain top global talents through creating an amicable and livable environment...As an international financial and trade center, well-designed public spaces, including trendy restaurants, cafés, bars and art galleries, should be built in city center to facilitate the gathering of professionals from home and abroad."

At that time in Shanghai, people's mindset hadn't yet been redirected from "work before life" to "work-life balance". Thus, it was hard for the local residents to appreciate the global talents who were in pursuit of a high quality of life and frequent social gatherings.

Seeing the inadequacy of an urban environment with open space, international vision, cultural competence and vitality, Vincent Lo was convinced of this business opportunity and committed to the creation and design of Xintiandi. It remained, however, mysterious how the *Shikumen* experts would grasp its concept.

Since most of the buildings neighboring the CPC site were in poor shape, it would take painstakingly tremendous effort to restore or even rebuild them to give the area its unique character of leisure and culture. Shui On was deeply concerned about preserving everything, as suggested by some experts, which was not financially feasible.

Having realized that wholesale destruction of the dilapidated *Shikumen* houses was against the sustainable urban planning which should take into account the preservation, protection and promotion of the rich cultural heritage, Luwan District, composed of a group of middle-aged officials with open-mindedness and willingness to take in new concept, was inclined to back up Shui On's design plan.

The preservation plan will involve a high level of funding. *Shikumen* experts believed that the government should foot the bill and profit-driven enterprises should be denied involvement in the project to avoid commercial exploitation of cultural heritage projects. The government, however, had limited financial resources and was under huge pressure to complete the redevelopment project, a contribution the city of Shanghai was making to the Communist Party on its 80th anniversary, by July 1st 2001. Having voted in support of Shui On's proposal, the authorities were convinced that the success of Xintiandi would set a new benchmark for future urban developments.

Meanwhile, the district planning department put forward a prerequisite for the project implementation that convinced the experts to reconsider their stance: Xintiandi should be constructed to meet modern seismic building codes, achievable only by gut renovating the houses to insert reinforced concrete structures while the traditional brick-stone structure wouldn't survive high-intensity earthquake.

Mr. Lo was lucky enough to gain support from several historical architecture experts in Shanghai. Professor Luo Xiaowei from Tongji University was one of them.

Prof. Luo addressed the importance of preserving the historical context and cultural climate of a city to directly and effectively

One of the oldest surviving public buildings built during the Victorian era, Murray House was transplanted in 1990 from its original location in Central as officers' quarters of the Murray Barracks to where it resides today in Stanley, the south of Hong Kong Island.

Reconstructed Murray House at Stanley's waterfront

Murray House has found a good home in Stanley and today is fully restored and open to the public housing shops and restaurants.

reflect its characteristics, individuality and identifiability.

Heritage preservation and urban redevelopment seem in tension, as historical buildings fail to conform to modern urban lifestyles.

Punctilious historic preservation which maintain all of the things in their original places resemble a museum disconnected from the modern world.

The very notion of juxtaposing innovation with preservation provides not only a challenge, but also a great opportunity for the historic site and the local residents as a whole. Examples have shown that different approaches to the treatment of historic properties could be adopted based on a variety of factors.

According to the historical, scientific and artistic value of an excellent historical building and its conditions, the requirements for protecting the historical building in Shanghai are divided into five categories. The first and the strictest one stipulates that "The façade, structural system, plane layout and internal decoration of the building shall not be changed". The last and the least stringent one, on the other hand, only requires the character-defining features remain intact.

Although the neighboring blocks were designated as a historical conservation area according to the master plan, they were not included in the "Historic and Cultural District of

Shanghai", as defined by the urban planning and municipal administrative department of cultural relics, that prohibited the CPC site and its adjacent buildings from being demolished. The two blocks were instead allowed to be altered as long as the exterior architectural features remained compatible with the traditional context in the area.

With the business model underpinned by the philosophy that its development projects should dovetail with the development plan of the city, Shui On identified the cultural values of *Shikumen* alleys and incorporated them into the commercial values of the redevelopment project without compromising the social richness or the historical narratives of original *Shikumen* settlements. Rather than development-oriented preservation, Xintiandi project adopted a preservation-oriented development concept.

Serving as the honorary president of Architectural Society of Shanghai and awarded honorary academician by American Institute of Architects, Prof. Luo spoke with authority. As a result, voters' opinions began to tilt toward Shui On's proposal. Yet they remained justifiably concerned about this unprecedented project to be carried out by a relatively small Hong Kong developer.

Shui On's boldness and confidence was derived from the reconstruction project of the Murray House it was responsible for.

One of the oldest Victorian-era buildings in Hong Kong, Murray House was built as officers' quarters of the military barracks during the early years of British rule. After World War II, several government departments used the building as offices. In 1982, the historical landmark was dismantled to yield to the new Bank of China Tower. Over 3,000 building blocks were labeled and cataloged for future restoration. In 1990, the Housing Department proposed the resurrection of the building in Stanley, a seaside community with a relaxed vibe on the southern side of Hong Kong Island. Shui On started to re-erect this historical monument at Stanley in 1998.

Despite the project's high complexity and excessive difficulty,

Shui On and its mastermind Vincent Lo spearheaded the redevelopment on an unprecedented scale.

The reconstruction of Murray House was based on the development-oriented preservation concept: preserving the authentic architectural features and historical context, corresponding to the modern commercial use as a new landmark of tourism and leisure consumption, and complying with modern building codes.

The Shui On team had to meet not only the structural requirements of the Housing Department, but also the artistic requirements of the historians specialized in the restoration of historical monuments. Special attention had to be paid to every detail during all stages of the project with repeated testing and multiple trials.

Each original stone of the Murray House was numbered indicating its original position before it was dismantled. Shui On engineers had to re-install each of the 3,000 plus stones into its original position with computer aid, just like putting a 3000-piece puzzle back together.

The reconstruction aimed to develop its commercial functions. In order to restore the uniqueness of the Murray House and fulfill special requirements demanded by historians, Shui On imported a special kind of lime from Britain to seal the stones instead of the usual plaster normally used for the purpose. Shui On engineers went to great lengths to search for stone components in Fujian Province that could replicate the original ones. In order to comply with the structural design, Shui On had to build an inner concrete structure to support the building before the original stones were re-installed as exterior walls of the Murray House. The historical monument, having been restored for a trendy hub of restaurants and shops while maintaining its original character, became a new landmark in Hong Kong.

Shui On team was thrilled about the opportunity to be constructing another landmark in Shanghai and firmly grasped the opportunity to build its own corporate brand.

It wasn't easy to convince the experts who voted down Shui On's proposal based on their own patterns of thought and standards of value unless they, as the gatekeepers of the city's historical and cultural sites, witness a finely wrought balance between modern and old.

All experience showed that people's way of thinking was essential to urban development. Hence the company constructed a model house in one of the *Shikumen* buildings in the north neighborhood to showcase the preservation-oriented development concept and collect feedback from the public.

The general contractor, Shanghai Meida Decoration and Construction Co., Ltd., which excelled in refurbishing historical buildings, was dismayed at the request to keep only the gray brick walls, stone door frames and black roof tiles and discard the rest. Meida was doubtful about incorporating a sense of romance into the project proposed by the architects.

Experienced in restoring outstanding historical sites such as Former Residence of Dr. Sun Yat-sen and Former Residence of Zhou Enlai, Meida was unquestionably the contractor of incomparable qualifications.

Suffice it to say that the regeneration of *Yongqingfang* opened a new chapter in historic preservation in Shanghai through repairing the old buildings to be as historically authentic as possible.

The regeneration would transform the once run-down city core areas into two contrasting types and mix them together seamlessly: one to suit modern needs and the other to maintain the original appearance. But what *Shikumen* buildings originally looked like baffled the experts since the remaining ones had changed beyond recognition after several vicissitudes.

In an attempt to locate the original materials of this century-old architectural style, Shui On visited the Urban Planning & Design Institute and many architectural research centers, consulted professionals in the College of Architecture of Tongji University, and searched high and low in the libraries and museums. Just when they were about to give up, the autographed drawings of the original architectural design of these neighborhoods were discovered in Shanghai Municipal Archives.

Great gratitude should be paid to the dedicated archivists as much as to the committed developer.

While the developer and architects opted to retain only those architectural features that gave the area its unique character, almost all the interiors had to be gut-renovated. The infrastructure indispensable to modern amenities had to be installed including air conditioning, gas, tap water, lighting, Internet, sewage, and fire protection.

In order for a *Shikumen* building to house restaurants or cafés, the sewage pipe had to be much bigger in diameter than that of a residential establishment. While the water storage tanks would be too heavy to be placed on the roof, they had to be positioned at the basement as deep as 9 meters underground or over the height of a two-story house. The costs amounted to 700 million yuan.

Internal structural alterations were done through opening up the roof and hollowing out the entire interiors. The outer walls, similar to the Ruins of St Paul's in Macau, a stone façade left off of a burned down church, threatened to crumble at any time, if not supported by a dozen of iron scaffoldings.

The tremendously challenging project involved excavation over 3 meters in depth, with the walls intact, to install underground piping system including electrical cables, water and gas pipes, telecommunications cables and firefighting pipes. As the vibration caused by excavators would put the walls at risk of crumbling, all the digging work and transportation of construction materials had to be performed manually, highly time-consuming and labor-intensive. The attention to detail was also drilled into the construction workers who were bewildered by the value surge of these old broken bricks and tiles overnight.

As the most distinctive residential house, *Shikumen* buildings, featuring wooden frame and load-bearing brick construction, had originally been built with moderately sized rooms to offer

A row of **Shikumen** *houses in Yongqingfang was transformed into a model house in 1999. With a sharp contrast between the restored historical exterior and refurbished modern interior, the model house now accommodates "Ye Shanghai" restaurant.*

The glass curtain blurs the boundaries between the inside and outside space.

more privacy. Because Xintiandi had a variety of entertainment options that required an excessive amount of open space with stricter structural requirements, Shui On opted for the framed structure system which comprised a network of columns and connecting beams that formed the structural 'skeleton' of a building. The restored outer walls that merely served as ornamental façades to reflect the original historical context of this site didn't come cheap: costly protection products for waterproofing and restoring historical buildings, such as Aida Kiesol, Funcosil Facade Cream, and Funcosil Stone Strengthener System, were imported from Remmers Germany. The buildings were handled the way cultural relics would be treated: high-performance water repellent was injected to protect the walls from penetrating damp and water damage and to strengthen historical renders and joints to withstand seismic shock.

Historical context cost money to retain, a huge amount.

Complexity of the undertaking on a hitherto unprecedented scale often resulted in onsite changes, errors and omissions that required rework.

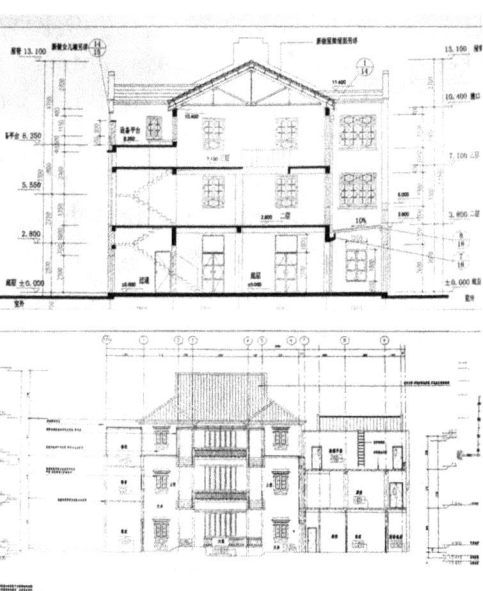

Preserving the Shikumen *alleys greatly altered by the residents over time requires respect and appreciation for history and culture. It took Shui On much effort to locate the drawings of the original architectural design of these neighborhoods in Shanghai Municipal Archives.*

EAST MEETS WEST

Internal structural alterations were done through hollowing out the entire interiors, while the outer walls were preserved to reflect the historical context and cultural climate through architectural conservation.

This row of Shikumen *buildings, with walls between the adjoining houses knocked down and reinforced concrete frames installed inside the outer brick walls, has become a new house but preserves its original visual character.*

Windows had evolved through time to help define the houses the residents accompanied: while less wealthy families would keep the wooden windows, affluent residents replaced them with metal ones—first in steel and later aluminum alloy—for their aesthetically-appealing look and durability.

Painstaking efforts were made to nail down the windows that would best showcase the cultural identity of Shanghai: the initially installed steel windows that looked too modern to reflect the historical narratives of original *Shikumen* settlements had to be replaced with wooden shutters popular in the '20s.

Another significant feature of the *Shikumen* houses was the doors that were coated with black lacquer and fitted with a pair of bronze knockers. While doors had to be left open to welcome the customers, it would be a waste of energy with the air conditioning running. The architects came up with a brilliant idea that solved the dilemma: the wooden doors that embodied the preservation of visual character would be wide

The outer walls threatened to crumble at any time, if not supported by a dozen of iron scaffoldings. Extra care had to be taken to avoid destruction of the ancient walls.

Workers are undertaking the excavation over 3 meters in depth to install underground piping system including electrical cables, water and gas pipes, telecommunications cables and firefighting pipes.

open, meanwhile a glass door would be installed to save energy and encourage a seamless indoor-outdoor interaction.

Striving to achieve nothing short of perfection, Shui On performed construction rework no less than a dozen times. Daily meetings at 8:30 were held to improve communication and collaboration between the developer and the construction company throughout the year. While the entire regeneration project was completed within 12 months, it took the same amount of time to accomplish a single model house with all the efforts and money devoted.

When the model house opened to the public, it was an immediate success, winning much praise even of the experts that once objected to it. The cross-century project, with construction commencing shortly thereafter, then started to go full steam ahead at the end of the 20th century.

According to the master plan, the reconfiguration would create new outdoor pedestrian streets and plazas where a dozen *Shikumen* houses were to be demolished. More than twenty old

The original roof tiles are being taken down and treated with special chemical components before being put together to retain the old-time vibe.

Windows have evolved through time. Painstaking efforts were made to decide on the wooden shutters that would best showcase the cultural identity of Shanghai

buildings would be gut renovated with protection products injected to strengthen the outer walls, coupled with a few houses to be dismantled and rebuilt.

Instead of using bulldozers or hammers, Shui On decided to take the houses down manually brick by brick, an approach under the guidance of overseas cultural heritage conservation professionals. Each brick was carefully labelled and stacked alphabetically. Special sandpaper was used to remove the residual stains on the bricks—no shovels or hammers were allowed either. The construction workers were almost driven crazy with the relentlessness of the foreign architects' demands, grumbling and moaning behind their backs.

A total of 140,000 old bricks were carefully taken down, labelled and sanded before being put back together as "new" building materials. The grand project lasted 15 months, during which 5 batches of workers quit their jobs who failed to meet the demanding requirements. The cost of labor far exceeded the cost of 140,000 new bricks, showing Shui On's determination and commitment to the restoration.

The reason behind was revealed by the experts: new bricks served as a snapshot of contemporary urban development, while old ones represented cultural narratives of the past. To exude the feel of Shanghai in 1920s, everything had to be as historically authentic as possible. Sanding the old bricks, as carefully as one would wipe away the cobweb on a genuine antique to reveal its true glory, was expressive of reminiscence about the old days when Shanghai was the financial hub of Asia.

The original roof tiles were taken down and treated with special chemical components before being put together, to retain the old-time vibe. Another two layers of thermal insulation and waterproofing were laid between the roof and the tiles.

Scuff marks were intentionally left on the walls to underline the aesthetic appeal of incomplete beauty. Gray bricks were laid on top of the concrete pavement with a whole set of underground piping system buried below. Recessed grouting encouraged the growth of moss for a charming weathered feel. A sharp contrast was the inner modern designs and facilities of the *Shikumen* buildings housing upscale stores and restaurants, including elevators, central air conditioning systems and internet access. The result was a magical cornucopia recalling this city's former reputation for fusion, of East and West, old and new.

One might find the resemblance of Xintiandi to a human being: the new underground piping system was like the blood vessels and the reinforced concrete structure was similar to the skeleton. With a century-old appearance and a pounding

EAST MEETS WEST

Old stone gates decorated with Western style ornamental motifs

Adaptively reused stone-gated facades of a trendy landmark

This stately, European-style mansion was refurbished with reinforced structures to incorporate modern designs into its original character.

THE DEBATE ON RESTORATION

The mansion, suited for private dining events and small meetings, now serves as a world-renowned clubhouse, One Xintiandi.

commercial heart, Xintiandi was revitalized into a pioneering initiative in urban heritage.

Here, the old historical fabric of *Shikumen* was used as a component in the creation of a completely modern space to revive the forms of a lost vernacular.

The preservation-oriented development, after much of Shui On's practice and exploration, could be summarized in three categories:

1. **Minor renovation with reinforced structures**

An example is One Xintiandi, among the best preserved of the original houses in the neighborhood. Originally built in 1925, this stately, European-style mansion was refurbished with reinforced structures and stronger beams to incorporate modern designs into its original character. One Xintiandi now serves as a world-renowned clubhouse visited by politicians and celebrities.

2. **Preservation of the roof and outer walls with gut renovation of the interior**

An example is Lawry's The Prime Rib (formerly French restaurant La Maison). Built in 1920s with a Dutch style roof, the house was renovated, in compliance with the standard of commercial establishments, with reinforced concrete structures after a complete demolition of the interior. The outer walls were retained while the wooden roof frame was replaced with a steel one. The space between the third floor and the second floor was left empty to accommodate a performing stage and a glass ceiling was installed in the courtyard to bring in natural lights.

3. **Preservation of the stone gates and outer walls with complete demolition of the rest**

An example is the three buildings that now house the Mediterranean restaurant, Luna. Built in 1930s, the severely deteriorated buildings were taken down, retaining only the outer walls with three doors on the north and those with seven doors on the south. The three buildings were combined into one during the renovation, with adoption of glass curtain wall design on the north-west side, standing in vivid contrast to the encompassing traditional *Shikumen* architecture. The glass provides expansive views of the neighborhood for the diners, allowing a glimpse of the activities taking place within and blurring the boundaries between the inside and outside space.

Xintiandi pioneered three modes of preservation-oriented development, incorporating but ultimately transcending the logic and stipulations of historic preservation.

A row of Shikumen *houses in Dunheli, of which roofs and outer walls are preserved with gut renovation of the interior*

The residential houses in Dunheli have been transformed into a commercial hub where La Maison, a French restaurant, used to stand.

This row of Shikumen *buildings were almost entirely taken down, retaining only the outer walls with three doors, as a display of* Shikumen *cultural context.*

The curved glass structure currently houses Luna Café where customers enjoy dinners in an epic portrayal of decades past

EAST MEETS WEST

An alley before renovation

THE DEBATE ON RESTORATION

An alley after renovation

Murray House, the iconic landmark in Stanley restored and reopened in 2000, quickly garnered much recognition in Hong Kong. One year later, Xintiandi, another redevelopment project that exquisitely preserved century-old buildings in Shanghai, drew immediate international attention to the city upon its opening.

Xintiandi introduced a form of architecture that synthesizes within itself both modes of preservation and development. Amidst the popular sentiment of Shanghai Nostalgia as well as the government's own active endorsement of heritage preservation, Xintiandi was conceived of as an urban redevelopment project involving the partial preservation and adaptive reuse of *Shikumen* structures. However, it has been heavily criticized by conservators for its commercialization rather than preservation.

Prof. Luo Xiaowei responded wittily, "the criticism revealed the conflict between preservation and development which is a long-established misunderstanding. It was heartbreaking to see bulldozers ruthlessly knock down some well-preserved old houses one after another, simply because the developers couldn't wisely conjoin preservation and development. But Xintiandi did. Furthermore, it painstakingly salvaged the social richness and historical narrative of Shanghai's indigenous culture. Xintiandi should, instead, be lauded for its successful combination of conservation and entrepreneurialism."

Interestingly, Xintiandi has received unanimous praise in the international community, winning the Urban Land Institute's Award for Excellence at its 2002 annual meeting, a recognition of the powerful impact of thoughtful urban design that has contributed to the greater community.

Having invited Benjamin Wood and senior executives of Shui On to give a lecture in the campus introducing the Xintiandi project which was subsequently selected as a case study, Harvard University also organized summer programs for its students to visit the site in person.

As we look back at the debate, the project reinforced the idea of preservation that has made a significant contribution to the urban development in Shanghai. The truth was found through diverse perspectives that inspired insightful discussions about the core issues. Multiple opinions of different parties have agreeably refreshed the materialized views of the city in two aspects:

First, culture was recognized as an integral part of urban development linked with acknowledging diversity in cultural heritages, a bridge from the past to a better future.

Second, local cultural resources were used to inspire, catalyze, and drive social and economic change, enhancing local resiliency and development potential.

he role of cultural practices and values in sustainable urban development has been consequently explicitly recognized, supported, and integrated into planning and policy in a systematic and comprehensive way.

EAST MEETS WEST

Xintiandi has given the century-old Shikumen a new lease of life.

THE DEBATE ON RESTORATION

CHAPTER 3
TURNING DUST TO GOLD

Long before the rebirth of Xintiandi, investment in converting historical buildings into commercial properties had already been made. A street imitating late Qing Dynasty style and one harboring the former residences of celebrities only lasted one year or two before they faded into anonymity.

The development and renovation of historical buildings in China at that time usually went to extremes: either historical buildings were turned into museums or modern buildings were designed to imitate the historic period of architectural excellence.

Although genuinely historical, the former failed to cater to modern comforts. The latter, however, showed ambiguous and coarse simulation of historical design and structures, lacking in true historic and architectural character and flavor.

Rejuvenating the historical buildings was an ambitious goal to achieve. But Shui On did it. As a Hong Kong based company unacquainted with *Shikumen* culture, Shui On managed to incorporate and ultimately transcend the logic and stipulations of historic preservation. The success of Xintiandi, favored by both locals and foreigners, made the local competitors green with envy and yet curious about its secrets behind.

Although initially ignorant of a proper design to exude the feel of Shanghai with its *Shikumen* culture, Vincent Lo and his team possessed pioneering thinking, global vision and financial soundness that distinguished Shui On from the local developers, which was exactly why Luwan District chose it.

A holistic and integrated approach to development needs to

take creativity, heritage, knowledge and diversity into account. After Shui On had been granted the land parcels, it assembled a team of architects—experts in restoration of archaeological sites, landscape design and modern architecture for collaborative brainstorming. Since urban design and infrastructure must have cultural relevance and resonance both in design and in use, this preservation-oriented redevelopment project aimed at integrating cultural assets into urban development strategies. Consequently, Vincent Lo invited experts who were highly experienced and influential in their respective fields—Benjamin Wood, a famed American architect who authored master plans for revitalization of many famous historical sites, the Singapore Office Nikken Sekkei International Ltd, and Prof. Luo Xiaowei from the school of Architecture and Urban Planning of Tongji University.

The division of labor was clear-cut, each one being charged with specific responsibilities: Mr. Wood and his firm were responsible for the space design, Nikken was in charge of the project expansion design and construction drawings, and Prof. Luo and the other experts from the Department of Architecture from Tongji University served as consultants to ensure the authenticity. Other parties included structural engineers, electromechanical engineers and lighting designers. Moreover, Albert Chan, an architect registered in the U.S. and Design Director from the Shui On Group, actively participated in the planning and development of Xintiandi. Having worked at the New York City Department of Design and Construction prior to joining Shui On, Albert Chan leads the conceptualization, site feasibility and design management of large mixed-use developments and manages challenges associated with rapid urbanization.

It was the team composition that had the right combination of skills to contribute to Xintiandi's success.

As the investor, Shui On preserved cultural memories and provided the project with a source of inspiration through forming the right mix of cultural values: Mr. Wood represented Western culture, Nikken offered an Asian perspective while professor Luo presented an indigenous outlook.

Having a clear vision for the project, the mastermind manages architectural concerns to ensure more productive and effective outcomes and plays an instrumental role in understanding the bigger picture in terms of operating. In the construction of a theater, for example, the sole attention given to its visual appearance will lead to revenue loss due to a mere capacity of 500 seats. In order to find a balance between seating capacity and profitability, the theater has to accommodate at least 1,000 patrons. The major responsibility of a good architect is to add value to the operational lifetime of the building.

Shui On put these architects with different cultural backgrounds to work together on the same floor, turning cultural

The old Shikumen *neighborhood before Xintiandi was completed*

collisions into sparks. Truth has been found through diverse experience and views that inspired insightful discussions about the core issues from macro vision to micro design.

From the large glass window on the top floor overlooking Shui On Plaza, architects enjoyed an aerial view of crisscrossing *Shikumen* alleys. The two blocks with 22 alleys covered an area of three hectares, comprising 2,300 residential neighborhoods. Built in 1911 by different developers, these old houses and alleys were poorly interconnected.

After 1950, increasing population pressures and discontinuance of public housing policy resulted in residents' creative ways to build add-ons and lean-tos in the courtyards and on the terraces. The crowded and disorderly alleys were so heavily patched that the original characters failed to show.

Good architects have the ability to capture intricate details that are often overlooked. Crumbling and outdated, the two old blocks nevertheless possessed rich cultural connotation and extremely great value as either historical site, art pieces or cultural heritage. Determination to revive the form of a lost vernacular shows the burgeoning desire of the city to protect its built heritage.

"We must look beyond the filthy, rotten, crowded and unhygienic living conditions to a cultural artifact that could for generations to come symbolize the meeting of East and West in the Yangtze River Delta," said Mr. Wood.

He also believed that the *Shikumen* houses no longer matched the living conditions of the rest of Shanghai and few people were nostalgic for the suffocating conditions in most of the lanes. He foresaw wholesale destruction of *Shikumen* buildings in the wave of urbanization that could be a threat to urban cultural heritage and a loss of urban identity. Therefore, Mr. Wood predicted that Xintiandi, an area that exudes a stronger sense of Chinese culture and a display of domesticity, would undoubtedly receive overwhelming popularity and tourist spending in the 21st century. He suggested that Shui On complete the project within this limited time frame of two to three years to set a new benchmark for style in the new century.

Excited about the new challenge outside his home ground, Mr. Wood mobilized all his cultural resources in an attempt to accomplish one of his best works. His team had to be extremely cognizant of the historical significance of the neighborhood and the cultural memory behind and stay mindful of the city's authentic history through its bricks.

In addition to the written documentation and precious cultural relics, visual illustration of a city's history also includes its buildings. Albeit in a decrepit state, historical buildings exhibit, through the visual appearance and spatial structures, dreams and lifestyle of old times.

Prof. Luo Xiaowei and the other *Shikumen* experts in her team, Sha Yongjie, Qian Zonghao, Zhang Xiaochun and Lin Weihang, played a dominant and irreplaceable role in this regard. Whenever the foreign architects ran out of creative juice, Prof. Luo, well versed in both Chinese and Western architecture, would introduce them to the historical context and cultural climate of Shanghai.

The *Shikumen* neighborhood at Xintiandi was built in 1914 during the expansion of the French Concession. The neighborhood culture of *Shikumen* buildings in the French Concession had distinct characters that marked it off from the British Concession. *Shikumen* experts told the foreign architects that the former French Concession introduced from France London planes as roadside trees on Huaihai Road, a well-known shopping area featuring elegance and romance that was hailed as Avenue des Champs Elysees in Paris. This French connection contributed to the trees' popular, albeit misleading, name, in Chinese, French plane. The plane tree is a large deciduous tree that has thick and broad leaves. People love the cool canopy it provides during summer. There is also the charming scenery of its leaves turning gold and falling to the ground in autumn.

The British Concession, on the other hand, planted no trees

on Nanjing Road, the main thoroughfare through the Concession and Shanghai's equivalent to London's Oxford Street, to ensure that the storefronts and business signs wouldn't be blocked.

At the early stage of the reform and opening up, the picturesque plane trees lining Huaihai Road were cut down to give way to clearer visibility of the shop signs in pursuit of mercantilism which attracted strong objections from the residents. The authorities had to replant the plane trees and resume its sense of romance.

In addition, the British Concession used a voltage of 220V, efficient but enough to deliver a fatal electric shock, while the French Concession used 110V, which was less likely to electrocute people, to prevent electrical injuries especially for young children.

The people-oriented approach, adopted in the French Concession with an impact on multiple generations, was recognized as the distinguishing cultural identity of the Huaihai Road *Shikumen* neighborhood.

Design requires a progressive, craftsperson-like ingenuity and judgment, which translates into a commitment to lifelong learning.

In an attempt to rejuvenate the historical fabric of *Shikumen* into a characteristic mix of modern and old, we should make the regeneration solutions more people-oriented where they can lead a harmonized life with a more livable environment. To render the city a marvelous work of art, according to Mr. Wood, traditional structures shouldn't be measured by their size or glamor, but by how much value they would add to their residents' daily lives.

Therefore, the architects placed themselves in the local residents' shoes and tried to feel the joy and happiness in their quotidian life, be it a family reunion dinner, a social gathering, a high society gala, or a chance encounter with a celebrity, all of which were the richest sources of inspiration for the redevelopment to transform the scores of historic brick buildings into Shanghai's most popular lifestyle complex, with a range of restaurants, cafes, boutiques, clubhouses, beauty salons, even galleries and museums. The ultimate goal was to attract visitors and their spending.

Henry Cheng Bing Chark, Managing Director of Shui On, was in charge of business planning and creative solutions. A challenging role representing the investor, Mr. Cheng was the one to tell the architects the concept and idea that they wanted to bring to life.

More often than not, Chinese cities have seen awkward buildings that didn't evoke anything remotely indigenous, with one of the reasons being that the domestic investors were unaware of what they really wanted and left it at the hand of a foreign architect.

Mr. Cheng told the architects at a regular work meeting that Xintiandi should not be limited to dining and leisure but also had to embody visual and aesthetic character as part of its business innovation. He foresaw a shift in consumption patterns where consumers' participation in the shopping experience would not be limited to the malls and other brick and mortar retail markets but instead spending some time strolling along the narrow pathways to get a feel for the beauty of traditional *Shikumen* architecture.

As a historic landmark and cultural corridor, Xintiandi would become a delightful maze of pedestrian-friendly streets with scores of trendy outlets and a concentration of culture and innovation. Resembling a majestic art gallery, it encourages the visitors to wander through and explore the "Chinese ink-wash paintings" and "Western oil paintings", emblematic of the buildings in the complex, that showcase the mix of West and East, old and modern, classical and abstract. In addition to appreciating the three-dimensional artworks, the cultural hub also invites visitors to come to socialize, have a bite to eat, and enjoy a great cup of coffee.

Mr. Wood shared the same sentiment. He agreed that the future of Xintiandi would have to reflect the diversity of urban

EAST MEETS WEST

The Shikumen *alleys photographed by the architects*

Architects envision Shanghai's characteristic mix of modern and old on their computer

space and architectural forms to facilitate a seamless blend of modern and old, reflecting the exquisitely-preserved twists and turns of an evolving neighborhood over the century.

The clarification of goals sent a ripple of excitement through the architects who strived to reinterpret the material history of *Shikumen* houses to suit the new development goal of adaptive mixed reuse by creating a virtual time tunnel through a century of history and heritage that would take visitors back in time, from the entrepreneurship spirit in the 20s, to the Great Leap Forward movement in the 50s, to the Cultural Revolution in the 60s, to the reform and opening up in the 80s, to the rapid urbanization in the 90s, and back to present, where they discover the lost vernacular, reminisce about old times and contemplate historical consciousness.

It took the architects almost one year to observe each building and find out when and by whom they were built so that the architects could determine which house to keep and which to demolish, which would best showcase the culture of certain

The glass structure is a magical cornucopia of exchange of ideas among architects.

period, which could be transformed into a Chinese restaurant, which would best house a Western-style bar or a gallery, and which to pay tribute to the great development of history of *Shikumen*.

The architects found it most difficult to decide which old building to remove and which to keep, endeavoring to carefully preserve the city's cultural elements that could not be restored once erased.

There had been a heated debate over the demolition of the three adjoining old buildings where Luna Restaurant and Bar now stands. The architects unanimously agreed to keep the one on the south with gorgeous gates as well as the one on the east. The one on the north, however, provoked a spirited debate: some were in favor of keeping the traditional house while some suggested replacing it with a new one that would look as historically authentic as possible.

Mr. Wood was thinking out of the box. He insisted on introducing a modern glass structure, just like Louvre's Glass Pyramid, that would represent a careful balance of the cutting edge and the conservative.

The glass structure is located between two **Shikumen** *buildings, a finely wrought balance of old and new.*

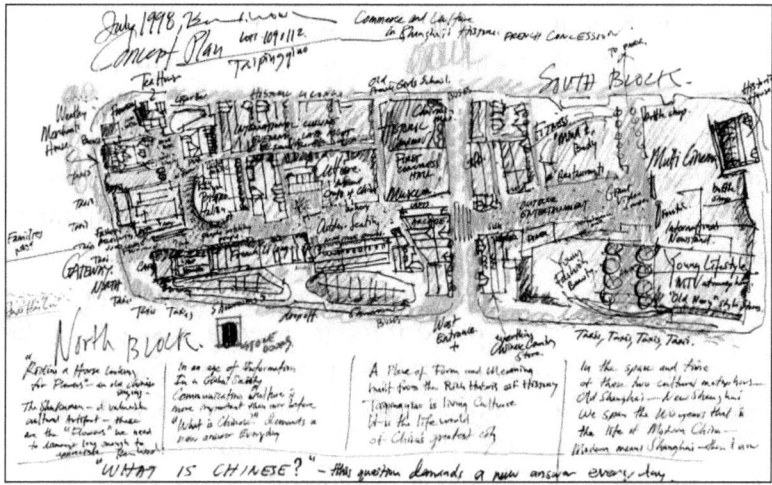

This precious manuscript shows the architect's conceptual plans for Xintiandi.

His bold, modern presentation was met with resistance from the planning team and design department. Most pointed to the alien nature of modern architecture and its incompatibility with the traditional context. Mr. Wood explained that as architecture reflected cultural heritage, the characteristic mix of modern and old would offer rich pickings for the visitors exploring on foot. He stated uncompromisingly that a simple replication of the past would result in loss of future distinctiveness, indicating inability to express oneself in a contemporary and creative manner.

While it was understandable that most architects wished to retain as much of the original charm of *Shikumen* as possible, Xintiandi is representative of the city in the future as a preeminent symbol of modernity.

After much discussion, they reached a consensus on building the glass structure there which later proved a commercial hit.

Spatial integration and connectivity of Xintiandi that stretches over two city blocks were of utmost importance. Mr. Wood wanted to incorporate a sense of the romance into the project: remove several rows of old houses and lean-tos on both blocks and retain the north-south axial promenade as the spine of the project that diverges off into smaller winding side alleyways.

When building the main street, workers accidentally found Dunheli alley, a row of *Shikumen* houses with nine well-preserved gates, a handsome façade and beautiful Dutch-style roofs, after knocking down a wall. Architects were thrilled with the discovery. Moreover, the buildings were facing east instead of south, a perfect site to house stores in the pedestrianized complex.

Rather than finalized at the beginning of the design process, the architects' ideas evolved through a series of steps that led from initial concept to realization. They enjoyed embracing the uncertainty in the design of Xintiandi that had propelled the seed of creativity to form tiny shoots that grew upward with enough force to defy gravity and break through the ground.

The main street and the sub alleys, lined with restaurants, bars, and shops converted from the historical residential buildings, exemplified the first development in the city to prove that historical architecture made big commercial sense.

When it came to decide the width of the pedestrian streets, there was a substantial divergence of opinion within the

Several old houses and lean-tos have been removed to make room for a pedestrian street in the North Block.

A broad alleyway was retained as the spine of the project, serving as the main street that connects the two blocks and blends old and modern. The old houses to the east of Xintiandi have been knocked down in preparation for the artificial lake project.

TURNING DUST TO GOLD

Architects were thrilled with the discovery of Dunheli, the beautiful Dutch-style roofs of which were under renovation with the wooden frame replaced with a steel one to retain the historical authenticity.

The old buildings photographed by the architect

The plaza in the North Block visualized by the architect

architects. Some suggested on maintaining the original width to assert a faithful historicity and showcase the city's cultural memory.

Some, from the business perspective, proposed that the alleys should be widened to properly handle the potential volumes of pedestrian traffic.

The two different viewpoints, one based on historical preservation and the other on commercial development, created a more expansive and objective look at the topic. However, Mr. Wood had a different vision. The alley width should provide adequate flexibility to encourage public interaction and promote return patronage. His people-oriented input struck a balance between the two opinions and the alleys were therefore determined to go so wide that people could have eye contact.

The architects also sliced away large section of space previously allotted to a residential building in the North Block to create a plaza that resembled Western piazzas for outdoor dining and public interaction since public space could help build community pride and become central to the cultural identity of a place.

It is a bold design to remove most of the Shikumen buildings and insert modern establishments in the South Block.

The architects had their own justification for why a European style plaza befitted the *Shikumen* complex: while the alleys still held much of their unique agricultural civilization character, the architects aimed at subtly shifting it away to an open-air living room that would improve not only the livability of a city, but also its lovability. The result was a harmonious blend of an outdoor plaza with traditional *Shikumen* alleys that resembled mingling a Western fireplace with intricately carved Chinese hardwood table and chairs, perking up the otherwise mundane cityscape and attracting visitors and their spending.

Mr. Wood had an even bolder design: most of the *Shikumen* buildings would be removed with only a few outstanding historical buildings left intact for the simple reason that they had to be torn down to make way for an underground garage which would allow Xintiandi to outperform its competition with Hengshan Road, the biggest and the oldest bar street of Shanghai.

The proposal that evidently shocked and stumped the experts from Shanghai Municipal Administration of Cultural Heritage who strived to retain the neighborhood south to the CPC site touched their bottom line which was to preserve a core of low-rise, courtyard-style buildings around the party's founding site to maintain the atmosphere of the original neighborhood and obscure the view of the modern structures springing up around it.

Mr. Wood elaborated on his idea from both cultural and marketing perspectives: the middle-stage *Shikumen* buildings in Xintiandi were less attractive to foreigners than those on Hengshan Road bar street which evolved into garden villas under the influence of Western architectural styles at later stage. But inadequate on-street parking and impossibility of building an underground parking lot to protect the villas above ground were the fatal flaws of the bar street.

Mr. Wood said that the only way for Xintiandi to outshine its competitors was to use their weaknesses to its best advantage. As far as the master plan was concerned, functionality outweighed

Architect's manuscript of the main entrance on Xingye Road

Architect's manuscript of the outdoor plaza at the entrance. (at the crossroad of Taicang Road and Madang Road)

aesthetics in that a parking lot would be essential for the customers who come from afar since cars would be future's dominant modes of urban mobility. Unfortunately, Xintiandi neighborhood couldn't either stay intact with the excavation for underground parking, leaving no other option but to remove the entire block.

Mr. Wood further explained that a blend of the seemingly contradictory architectural styles would epitomize the soul of the project—yesterday meets tomorrow at present, and the massive shopping complex housing ritzy glass contemporary buildings in the South Block would complement the *Shikumen* houses with limited shopping area in the South Block. Moreover, these modern buildings would ensure a smooth transition between the historical architecture in the North Block and the planned residential district featuring commercial high-rises and luxury apartments.

The Committee eventually accepted these innovative ideas on condition that the two rows of old houses opposite the CPC site would be retained and the height of modern construction on the south would be limited so that the window on the second floor would provide an unobstructed view of the blue sky.

While one of the most distinctive architectural features of *Shikumen* is the stone-framed gate, the architects went out of their way to come up with the best design of the entrance to Xintiandi. The planned entrance to the North Block on Huaihai Road, where an old building was situated on Taicang Road, brought heated discussion on whether to retain it with the result that visitors would have to access Xintiandi via the building, an unfriendly and uninviting gate to the complex, or remove it to give the residents of Shanghai free access to experiencing the public realm as something pleasant.

Integrating cultural heritage into urban landscape has differentiated Xintiandi from most other tourist attractions.

Some of the historical landmarks, cultural attractions, and leisure streets in Shanghai that feature a giant arch to attract visitors from a distance, are fenced off to collect admission fees upon entrance. On the contrary, Xintiandi, one of Shanghai's favorite complexes with a concentration of culture and lifestyle, is not walled off, offering free entry from any side at any time.

To create a more open composition, the architects decided to remove the building. The active and vibrant public space, studded with outdoor seating and umbrellas for visitors to kick back with a cup of coffee, resembles a piazza commonly found in European cities.

EAST MEETS WEST

The busy crossroad of Xintiandi and Xingye Road makes few people wonder how many entrances Xintiandi has and why. In fact, this is a sensitively designed approach to integrating the new development into the city's existing fabric through providing 15 freely accessible entrances. The idea is to celebrate the significance and the history of the site and revitalize it, turning it into a vibrant, diverse open space for all kinds of people—for leisure, culture, activity and public events.

The significance of this approach to today's urbanization and cultural construction is that a good public space stimulates interaction between people and the environment, generates a positive use of space and increases urban vitality. However, many of the grand theaters, stadiums, swimming pools and concert halls under construction as well as the newly built residential quarters are walled off, discouraging and limiting neighborhood social interactions. The spaces created by humans are in turn shaping community ties in neighborhoods. Enclosed spaces isolate the city from the outside world, harming the quality, diversity and vitality of its urban public culture.

Unlike the traditional practices of domestic architects, the Xintiandi team developed advanced concepts and techniques.

Construction workers are filling the gaps of the bricks with lime.

Details define architecture. Throughout history and all across the Eastern world, embellishment with precious metals like gold and silver has been used to stunning effect in both exterior and interior architecture and design. However, the ultimate sophistication is expressing beauty through simple, natural forms and designs.

A customary practice for the exterior work of historical buildings was to coat the old bricks with a redwash and then carefully

TURNING DUST TO GOLD

The alley's entrance before renovation

The alley's entrance after renovation

paint the mortar joints with thin white lines. Xintiandi team took a completely different approach: the architects utilized all the mansion's original bricks in the restoration with real lime as the bedding material, showcasing the traditional sensibilities in the '20s.

The primary color of Xintiandi is gray, a thought-to-be bare and neutral visual effect unacceptable to people of Shanghai who, just lifted out of poverty, were fascinated by bright colors that represent celebration, vitality, and fertility in traditional Chinese color symbolism. But Mr. Wood considered gray as a color to turn to for its ability to add instant style and a timeless elegance to designs simply with a combination of its different shades.

It is the simple, straightforward, unpretentious emotions that touch people's heart the most. Simplicity reveals the pure beauty of life. It is always the simple that produces the marvelous.

Throughout history, architecture has stood as a representation of society, reflecting its values and cultures over time. From the monumental structures to the residences and buildings that make up the fabric of a city, we can learn a lot about the people who inhabited them long before our time.

Two traditional Chinese architectural arches, Dunheli Paifang, inscribed with historical imprint "Songshan Packaging and Shipping Station" on the main street, and Changxingli, with red inscriptions on the stone pillar which reads "Great Chairman Mao steers the country through revolution" located in the back alley, that witnessed the Great Cultural Revolution, were preserved after having resolved the cross-cultural conflict among foreign architects, Chinese experts and local government officials: Chinese architects proposed to remove the embarrassing past of the Revolution while their Western counterparts offered an opposite view that if it had happened in Europe it would have been constantly discussed and reflected on to prevent it from happening again. Reflection is the core of "cultural self-consciousness" that contributes to creating a more innovative culture of a nation.

The 10-story-high Augarten Flak Towers, located in the Augarten Park in Vienna, Austria, were built during the Second World War to protect Vienna against allied bombings. The towers remain as concrete witnesses to the country's shameful history and as unforgettable reminders and warnings of Austria's culpability. Today a huge graffiti in the plinth area with the words 'Never Again' greets visitors to the park, serving as a warning to present and future generations never again to allow such a tragedy to happen.

The Western architects argued that the relics of the Revolution were extremely valuable for cultural reflection and history should not be buried or removed. The two memorial archways, located in the downtown area, would warn future generations much more effectively than being left out on the outskirts.

The open-minded government officials and local architects were receptive to the new ideas and decided to keep the relics.

With a different cultural background and varied lens of looking at the world, Mr. Wood managed to perceive details locals were unaware of. Shui On hired a professional consulting firm to conduct research on the potential of casual dining market in Shanghai. The survey concluded that the idea of outdoor dining was a bet not worth taking as Shanghai residents were not willing to eat al fresco, let alone throw a banquet for the rich and powerful.

Mr. Wood held a different opinion. He observed that the residents preferred eating outdoors and chatting with their neighbors when the weather permitted. He said with certainty that the future of outdoor malls was very bright. Traditional enclosed malls would experience a decline in popularity as people flocked to outdoor retail establishments which would often include an emphasis on innovations and customer experience.

The consulting firm saw banquets in ritzy restaurants and private dining rooms which was in sharp contrast to the filthy and messy roadside eateries. But Mr. Wood has discovered that it was the lack of upscale outdoor dining facilities that curbed local people's desire to dine al fresco.

Xintiandi takes strides to revolutionize the dining style in Shanghai and cater to the consumers' potential dining needs and preferences early and often, setting a benchmark for dining in a pleasant and relaxing natural environment.

Identifying potential markets and shaping new market trends deliver insights for innovation.

Shanghai experienced the biggest building boom the world had ever seen in 1999. One-fifth of the world's construction cranes, according to CNN, were in intensive service in Shanghai alone. Meanwhile, the Xintiandi team was concentrating on developing a unique new model for urban regeneration in Shanghai. The low-rise houses in the charming *Shikumen* neighborhood in Xintiandi are decidedly favored by both domestic and foreign visitors, and far outperform the skyscrapers, in terms of popularity and aesthetics, that have sprung up all over the city in the following years.

The once run-down city core area now flourishes as a vibrant lifestyle complex and modern, livable community.

TURNING DUST TO GOLD

A magnificent night view of Xintiandi

CHAPTER 4

SHANGHAI'S URBAN FABRIC IN THE NEXT STAGE

The Chairman and Chief Executive Officer of Louis Vuitton, the world's leading luxury products group, has visited Xintiandi many times. To him, London, New York City, Paris, and Tokyo were considered the global "Big Four" fashion capitals. However, Xintiandi, with unique character and charm, has promoted Shanghai as the fifth fashion capital among other global cities on his list.

How does Xintiandi incorporate the traditional *Shikumen* neighborhood into the contemporary fashion scene that seems remotely related?

Benjamin Wood, the principal architect of Xintiandi redevelopment, shared his philosophy when he took on the project: "*Shikumen* architecture is easy for me to understand, which is like the lines on a piece of paper. It is understanding the spirit and culture of the city, life of the people, and what they want in the future that is most challenging."

Having arrived in Shanghai at the turn of the century, Mr. Wood felt he had a responsibility to give the people of Shanghai a good urban design rather than a simple architectural design.

Space is a basic concept in architecture. The spatial forms and dimensions that reflect a generation's aspiration for a trendy lifestyle constitute urban culture. The essence of urban design is that the architects focus on thoughtfully creating a cohesive composition that accommodates people's indescribable aspiration.

A good architect touches the heart and nourishes the soul.

Most people have experienced the same awkward moment during a photoshoot: their eyes blink and their smiles look forced and unnatural with every snap of the camera. To capture the most expressive moments, a good photographer has to stay alert—camera in hand—way beyond the posed pictures and obvious events.

A good architect is equally visionary, while a mediocre architect only focuses on the existing urban fabric and follows the latest trend.

Foreign architects flooded into China in recent years, viewing the country as both a new source of revenue and a loosely-regulated tabula rasa on which to test bold new ideas. There were countless opportunities for ridicule. They have designed oversized, xenocentric, weird buildings that are devoid of cultural tradition and identity of the city. Even famed architects have created truly outlandish proposals.

Tadao Ando, one of the most internationally famous and popular Japanese architects, shared his top piece of advice to the young architects: architecture is responsible for performing the attitude of the site and makes it visible. As an architect, he believes that architecture can change society, that "to change the dwelling is to change the city and to reform society".

When a building is disconnected from its essential context, the compatibility between the building and the city will be lost. It is therefore crucial for the architects to be humble enough when working on buildings to let the city take preference.

Prof. N. Voronin, an architectural historian of the former Soviet Union, pointed out in his book *Reconstruction of the Reoccupied Soviet Union Areas Formerly Occupied by the German Invaders* that urban planners must be able to achieve a city's unique vision of the future by aligning new developments with city goals.

So, what is Shanghai's urban fabric in the next stage? Mr. Wood flew to Shanghai 32 times in 6 months, at the expense of Shui On, to experience the quotidian life in *Shikumen* alleys.

Meanwhile, Vincent Lo demonstrated extraordinary patience and support to ensure that compelling, truthful, and empathetic insights were provided.

Mr. Wood simply rented a unit in the *Shikumen* alley to live with the local residents, observing their life—what they ate, drank, wore, played, listened to, said, thought about, and why they laughed, cried, fought—and embracing the local.

With a bike and a camera, Mr. Wood himself conducted an extensive photo study of the existing neighborhood, *Shikumen* structures, and their inhabitants. Although he couldn't understand a word of Chinese, he was fond of striking up a conversation with the older adults in the alleys by gesture.

Having had several dozen bowls of Chinese soy milk and Yang Chun noodles, taken tens of thousands of photos and hundreds of hours of video clips, Mr. Wood discovered that the *Shikumen* residents were happy and content despite a lower income level. With a limited wardrobe, *Shikumen* residents make sure they are always well-groomed. Their pursuit of trendy fashion is persistent: from short sleeve dress to sleeveless, from slim pant legs to wide and back to slim again. When it comes to fashion, they never fall behind.

Mr. Wood came to the conclusion that people of Shanghai wished to look stylish and chic in the sleepless city of romance which means Xintiandi has to look polished to be successful.

He also noticed that Shanghai people were leading a fast-paced life in all aspects at the end of the 20th century: young people were talking on the phone while striding; girls were wearing headphones and listening to music while walking; business meeting was held in a restaurant; inspiring talks took place in a teahouse. Multitasking seemed to be the only way to get ahead in today's fast-paced, 24/7 society. If the speed of the world continued to increase, as Mr. Wood predicted, people would want to embrace a slower pace of life.

Common values have been epitomized in the preferred gifts in Shanghai. Imported Nestle coffee, bottled Coca-Cola and Fanta, were among the most decent gifts in *Shikumen* neighborhoods. It took Mr. Wood some time to realize that it was not the beverage the residents were fond of, but the trendy flavor and the lifestyle it symbolized. Instant coffee, teabags, and bottled juice helped people keep up with the fast pace of the modern world.

However, local residents didn't realize that standardized convenience food tasted the same, bottled juice and bubble tea were made from chemical compounds, chemical preservatives were added in instant foods for longer shelf life. Once they become aware that processed foods could be harmful if consumed in excess, they will switch to a healthy eating lifestyle.

Located on the eastern fringe of the Huangpu River, Pudong was dominated by a forest of skyscrapers that looked like New York, and was defining the city's landscape to a new level in the late 20th century. While on the other side of the river, Puxi, the historic center of Shanghai, was home to narrow streets and crowded alleys where many homes were in various stages of dilapidation. The residents in the *Shikumen* neighborhoods saw a rapidly modernizing city at the other side of river and were eager to move into new apartment towers and own a private car.

This American architect, however, had a totally different interpretation of modernization. The 1940s saw the emergence of skyscrapers made of glass and steel in the United States. Successful urbanism must recognize the inherent social, economic and environmental benefits of preservation, adaptive reuse and repositioning in activating our urban fabric, providing continuity between the past, present and future. But bulldozers were ruthlessly knocking down one decaying neighborhood after another, burying the city's history under new layers of civilization.

Mr. Wood said that Pudong was filled with new skyscrapers but was hardly left with any historic fabric, and Puxi should not follow suit. He offered this analogy: there were family pictures on the wall of his mother's house, including those of his great grandfather, grandfather, his late father, him and his children.

They were taken at different times, showing varied states of mind of everyone that shared family history in a rich context. If the pictures were of his family members only in their childhood, no one would recognize who was who. A city as a concrete jungle would provoke the same ridicule.

Mr. Wood believed the ancient *Shikumen* neighborhoods were of varying quality: Some only looked dilapidated due to overuse and lack of maintenance and could be rejuvenated to extend life spans over the next 100 years, while some were results of shoddy construction and should have been replaced by contemporary buildings as an inevitable progression towards modernity. He had a clearer picture in mind of how to revibrate *Shikumen* on an unprecedented scale: changing people's stereotype of historical buildings and helping them recognize the city's distinct history and culture with urban design that would transcend the boundaries of culture and nationality as well as reflect the city's indigenous culture.

With his architectural acumen, Mr. Wood made two major discoveries during the six-month observation and contemplation. He found the old alleys in *Shikumen* were a semi-private space, or essentially the "gray space" of the city—the transitional space between the internal space of the building and the external environment space, an area in between the public and private realm.

Mr. Wood was intrigued to find out why many of the residents that moved into new apartments seemed happiest when reminiscing about the old days. He noticed it was the gray space in *Shikumen* neighborhood that they were nostalgic for, something that was missing in the newly built apartments and residential communities. Walled-off residential areas, office buildings and public cultural facilities were void of gray space, interrupting community interaction and bonding.

The concept of "gray space" was first proposed by the Japanese architect Kisho Kurokawa, with the core idea that the buffer zone blurs the boundary between interior and exterior of the space. Just like vitamins are necessary for the body to stay healthy, gray space serves as the most important breathing spaces in the community.

Mr. Wood also discovered that Shanghai men had a reputation for being "henpecked". What many people view as 'henpecking' is just a more equal, less patriarchal relationship between the husband and wife. Hauling two plastic bags full of fresh vegetables and meat from a neighborhood market after work, Shanghai men regard cooking and doing housework as part of their "family tradition". Evening was the liveliest moment in *Shikumen* neighborhood when residents would move their dining tables in the spacious alleyways to eat, chat, and exchange information about the outside world.

According to Mr. Wood's observations, British men love to go to pubs after work to relax, have a drink and talk about all sorts of different topics. They enjoy success and manage stress at work which has become part of their life. They unwind at the pubs after work to socialize with their colleagues which is regarded as continuation of work.

The Japanese Izakaya is famed as a heavenly post-work stop-off for Japanese men craving some much-needed and much-earned refreshment. It is a place for the office workers to melt away mental stress from the workplace before heading back home. A very interesting cultural phenomenon in Tokyo is that a man who goes home straight after work indicates that he has no friends or social connections. Sometimes a Japanese man would rather while away an evening alone in the Izakaya until 11 o'clock before the subway shuts down at midnight.

Lan Kwai Fong, once a garbage collection area in Hong Kong, became home to Central's major party complexes and caused a ripple effect as other bars and restaurants moved in. It is now a popular haunt for expatriates and local white collars alike for drinking, clubbing and dining.

The cultural differences sparked off the idea that Xintiandi would enliven *Shikumen* alleys through fostering "gray space" that would accommodate the culture of "dinner in the alley". Mr. Wood even dubbed this innovative idea "let people of Shanghai come home for dinner".

Some, however, raised skeptical doubts concerning *Shikumen*'s relation to fashion since wealthy families resided in fancy apartments while *Shikumen* residents were still struggling with crushing poverty and waiting to be relocated. Moreover, the residents would rather entertain their guests in a restaurant's private dining room than throw a dinner party at home with all the stress and hassle.

Talented architects often have an extraordinary sixth sense and design thinking ideology that echoes Taoist philosophy: Being and non-being create each other. Difficult and easy support each other. Long and short define each other. High and low depend on each other. Before and after follow each other. Early Chinese philosophy of logic has contributed toward greater opportunities for innovative thinking of today. Eating at home and dining on the street are taking turns to lead the fashion trend.

As one of China's top cities in terms of comprehensive competitiveness, Shanghai has become a city of contrasts. Despite the extraordinary growth and achievements of the Chinese economy, a gulf still exists between Shanghai's richest and poorest residents. Competition may cause stress and anxiety, a person's enemy in decision making which can greatly impact the ability to make quality decisions. So, relax and let go of any remaining stress and simply perform at your uninhibited best. When people talk to friends and engage in leisure activities, they have lower stress levels, better mood, more experience and strength.

Leisure was already a very common lifestyle in developed countries such as the UK and Japan but still an emerging trend in Shanghai at the end of the 20th century. This is the fundamental reason why Xintiandi has been so well received among the upper class since its completion.

The ultimate purpose of innovation should be much more far

reaching, helping create a smart future where people can enjoy the best quality of life possible. The spiraling trend in future innovation highlights the importance of creating great public spaces that are accessible to people, engage the public with activities, and foster a sense of community. With a rich history of *Shikumen*, elaborate gardens, and vibrant street life behind the glamour, no place bridges the past, present and future better than Xintiandi.

Xintiandi, where yesterday meets tomorrow at present, displays a stunning futuristic skyline, shaping the evolutionary trajectories of the universe. The team of architects has transformed it into a pioneering initiative to spark a trend of leisure-oriented lifestyle, widely recognized as a landmark of the city's urban development.

Yet, the architects must identify the technique that will allow them to make the idea materialize in the best possible way. The whole process can be overwhelming, and the risk to get disoriented is high. In order to bridge the conceptual level of intended experience to the validation of the final solution, materialization requires strong focus and much attention to detail.

In reality, innovation isn't the goal; it's everything that gets you there. It's what and how to eat, drink, wear, play, watch, listen and write every day. The idiom "The Devil is in the details" connotes a word of caution to pay attention to minor details.

Interestingly, spending time in a tea house, a pottery studio, a book club, or rural settings has been an emerging popular culture in Shanghai when the society is still dominated by a fast-paced lifestyle, indicating a new fast-rising consumer trend of slow living in the city.

The Industrial Revolution marked the change from producing materials by hand to producing materials with machinery. While in the post-industrial era, the society is facing movements against this mass production and encourages more hands-on manufacturing and craftsmanship.

Pottery allows people to produce a piece that has their own unique creative style. Rural tourism let them enjoy picking fresh fruits and other produce, which perfectly suits the trend of travelers seeking authentic, unique experiences and local lifestyles. Although the bustling energy of the city is part of the urbanites' identity, they are fascinated by the idea of a more balanced and unhurried way of living without having to be swallowed by the hustle and bustle of life.

Pump noise and vibration come from the construction sites of the skyscrapers and high-rise condos that keep springing up around the *Shikumen* neighborhoods in astonishing numbers.

Living in high rise buildings adversely affects people's satisfaction level and social relations. Residents in condominiums have fewer friendships and help each other less. Moreover, the relationships between high rise residents are likely to become more estranged with many people in modern cities experiencing a feeling of isolation and loneliness. Accordingly, this isolation in such upper floors and lack of social interactions are reasons for many physiological and social issues in condominiums. Subsequently, social interactions are the main component that highlights and enriches social sustainability. Many people lament the demise of the intimacy and sociability of *Shikumen* life.

In the 21st century when shiny newness once reigned large, and when historic buildings were regularly razed, there now appears to be more appetite for restoration projects. People have started to love historic buildings because they trigger a certain nostalgia and are the physical embodiment of a different era. In the rapidly modernized city, a traditional townscape evokes fascination from the young, and nostalgia from the old. In the case of Xintiandi, the *Shikumen* neighborhoods would have to inspire imaginations as well as recollections of the Old Shanghai days.

The team of architects therefore aimed to evoke nostalgia through a display of domesticity within a recreated historical architectural setting. Appreciation of an enduring legacy takes time. Cafes provide spaces for people to linger, bond and interact, and restaurants are perfect for a cozy meal or to relaxed conversations over drinks.

People usually patronize cafes and restaurants to eat or to socialize. Xintiandi places the emphasis on social interaction. Whether meeting a friend for coffee, having lunch with co-workers, or taking a date out for an intimate candlelit meal, restaurants in this *Shikumen* neighborhood provide a spot for social interaction and connection.

The architects encourage a slower approach to aspects of everyday life in Xintiandi. Tea ceremony performances are held in the teahouse, freshly squeezed juice offers so many health benefits, and freshly ground coffee is what makes the difference between the worst cup of coffee you've ever had, and the best.

The central tenet of the slow philosophy is taking the time to do things properly, and thereby enjoy them more.

In the '80s, local residents used to invite guests for a simple dinner in their *Shikumen* home—a bowl of braised pork, a plate of stir-fried vegetables, and an assorted casserole. In the '90s, dining became complex and lavish, with a tableful of dishes, in upscale restaurants and star hotels that boasted exquisite

Most of the cafes and restaurants in Xintiandi feature outdoor seating, leaving a wide passage in between that resembles the runway of a fashion show. Al fresco dining offers a nice vantage point to people-watch, creating space for interaction and the circulation of ideas in the air.

T8 restaurant in Xintiandi chose to move the cooking range closer to the dining room, with modern design open kitchens on view to all. In this way, customers can satisfy their curiosity and find out what's cooking in professional kitchens, as well as being reassured as to the hygiene conditions. Customers are firsthand witness to a cooking show that offers theatricality, intimacy and authenticity.

interiors with banquet tables and crystal chandeliers. In the 21st century, Xintiandi has revolutionized dining in *Shikumen* by offering homemade culinary delights, differentiating itself from its competitors on Huaihai Road and Nanjing Road commercial streets.

Restaurants on the commercial streets strive to maximize their turnover rates. The more guests served in a given time period, the more sales a restaurant will have. Customers who linger and remain at their tables longer contribute to decreased revenue and are likely to be rushed off by the waiters. They are asked to pay the bill, finish their food as soon as possible, and leave well ahead of closing time. Some restaurants use a passive-aggressive approach of nonverbal cues to get guests up: wiping the table, sweeping and mopping other areas, turning off the lights, water glasses or coffee cups and so on.

Xintiandi, however, features high quality food and outstanding service in an attractive and comfortable atmosphere. Bilingual staff greet incoming and departing guests with a genuine smile and eye contact. Highly trained staff offer slow-paced dining experience in the case of a gathering of friends, and they speed up the service when the diner is in a hurry. They are also knowledgeable about all of the food and beverage menu offerings, have the ability to recognize and greet repeat customers by their names, and enthusiastically help guests with menu selections.

Restaurants and pubs will never make the customers feel rushed even if they are lingering well after closing. The bar manager will ingeniously offer the guests a free drink as a hint. Smart guests will get it and encourage their party to leave immediately.

Traditional open-air market lost ground to the department stores on the commercial streets that blossomed for a century. But the social function of this retail model has largely retreated behind shelves of products promising unlimited choice and simple convenience as commerce becomes more diversified and specialized.

As a real estate developer that makes cross-border commercial property investments, Xintiandi has renewed the true spirit of the physical marketplace and brought back the social vibrancy, creating space and vitality for authentic interaction.

As the famous quote from the German poet and philosopher J.W. Goethe goes, all theory, dear friend, is gray, but the golden tree of actual life springs evergreen. Just trust yourself and you'll learn the art of living. Unlike the traditional architectural practice that was dominated by the sight, Xintiandi has engaged the visitors in such a way that their five basic senses, namely sight, sound, touch, smell, and taste, are activated: the combination of gray brick walls, tiled roofs, stone gates, window shutters, flickering candles, dim street lamps, fashion icons, senior scholars, African singers, Caucasian dancers, sweet wine, aromatic coffee, indigenous music, art galleries and mini museums stimulate holistic experience from all the senses. A comprehensive and cohesive sensory experience can ignite the imagination and endow spaces with a sense of peaceful calm or vibrant energy.

SHANGHAI'S URBAN FABRIC IN THE NEXT STAGE

The past is the foundation for our future heritage in commercial use. The tangible fabric of the historical architecture and the intangible aspects that give it meaning are inseparable. An upmarket dining, entertainment and shopping complex modelled on traditional *Shikumen* houses, Xintiandi was the first development in the city to prove that historical architecture makes big commercial sense.

Well-established as one of the Chinese Mainland's most visionary and innovative property developers, Shui On Land continues consolidating its leadership as a commercially focused property developer, owner and asset manager in China. With a clear vision, an innovative mindset and ample international experience, Shui On manages to capture fully in its projects local historic and cultural characteristics and blend the "live-work-learn-play" communities harmoniously and seamlessly into Shanghai's indigenous cosmopolitan culture.

CHAPTER 5

THE SUCCESS OF A WORD-OF-MOUTH MARKETING STRATEGY

While the architects of Xintiandi were excited to create a new cultural paradigm in Shanghai, people remained skeptical about the "experiment": *Shikumen* alleys were considered as the ultimate examples of dilapidated, crowded and wretched urban living. It was not uncommon to see multiple generations squeezed into cramped rooms and garrets, and living spaces for individuals and families shrank dramatically. Weighed down by overcrowding and worsening infrastructure, many Shanghainese families had been eager to move to newer and more spacious residential homes.

Shaping consumption patterns went beyond traditional methods of modeling consumer behavior. The developer had to change people's perception of *Shikumen* and let them realize that the once run-down city core area would be reinterpreted to suit the new development goal of making Shanghai into a global city.

Creative marketing campaigns is a proven way to showcase brand personality and charm. Most of the global marketing consulting firms proposed to penetrate the market by investing substantial amounts of capital in boosting marketing capabilities and bombarding consumers across all platforms. Shui On management was, however, attracted to the word-of-mouth marketing strategy, an organic way of spreading information by more natural channels, proposed by Hong Kong-based A-World Consulting Company. The strategy aimed at offering consumers new ways to seamlessly share information and creating breakthrough customer experiences.

Conventional consumption patterns reflected people's emphasis on deliciousness, ampleness and affordability of the food rather than a pleasant environment or a thoughtful presentation.

In the era of customer experience, restaurants can no longer excel simply by providing good food, at fair prices, in a clean venue. Now that environment and service are table stakes — requirements that every restaurant should meet for guests to consider it — the ability to deliver consistently engaging, memorable experiences so that guests feel engaged, empowered, heard, and delighted is more critical than ever.

From the color scheme and background music to the furniture choices and lighting, the establishment's ambience and aesthetic are an extension of its brand and a powerful way to generate interest in and drive traffic to the restaurant.

Restaurants and marketers alike have seen the marketplace undergo an epochal shift.

With overseas work or study experience, the emerging affluents in Shanghai were a rising consumer class willing to pay more for a great customer experience. Nevertheless, most people continued to follow traditional consumption patterns.

Launching a big marketing campaign would no doubt grab consumers' attention. Customers who prioritized experiences above all else would be willing to pay a sizable sum for a nice selection of food in *Shikumen*, while those who preferred drinking at a luxury hotel bar to an open-air pub would be appalled at the menu prices and complain that customers were charged exorbitant prices for drinks. It was challenging to create an experience that truly fulfilled the varied demands of customer expectations when most people were still following conventional consumption patterns. The news media would be much likely to label Xintiandi as "blatantly ripping their customers off".

As one of the most effective forms of marketing, word-of-mouth strategy should be initially encouraged among the

customer group that prioritized customer experience. Similar to this method of spreading information, six degrees of separation, originally devised by a Harvard psychologist, is the idea that all people on average are six, or fewer, social connections away from each other.

Survey showed that Shanghai, as an elite dominated society, witnessed the influence of lifestyle a minority of elites had on the mass population. It was therefore crucial to consolidate their spending, patronage and loyalty behavior and leverage the influencers to make referrals among friends and acquaintances to create further value.

A shortlist of elites that Xintiandi would approach was made accordingly, spanning such fields as politics, finance, architecture, law, marketing, diplomacy, trading, news media, and entertainment business.

Government officials topped the list as the ruling-class, in charge of most social resources, has predominant power in the society. Engaging the decision maker would be the core of the word-of-mouth strategy.

The construction had to be completed by June 2001 with the intent of opening Xintiandi to the public in time for the 80th anniversary of Communism in China as well as the October convention in Shanghai of the APEC. The economic and political aspirations for this large and costly project were evident from the beginning.

An important factor for success was the involvement of the local government in the process of updating the plans to facilitate a collaborative dialogue between the decision makers and the developer. It significantly shortened the approval cycles and fit into the leanings of the local government.

The model houses that turned the *Shikumen* old buildings into a restaurant, gallery and café filled hub started the word-of-mouth campaign that lasted 18 months upon its completion at the end of 1999.

The campaign was considered inconceivable and far-fetched

to invite the then president Jiang Zemin to visit the Memorial Site of the First National Congress of CPC, Xintiandi and Taipingqiao Lake and Park, and showcasing Xintiandi as a symbol of the new China when the U.S. President and the Russian President were attending APEC meeting in Shanghai.

Much less well-known than it is now, Shui On had to devise a concrete plan to engage the local government.

Establishing a connection with the foreign consulates in Shanghai, who are responsible for organizing itinerary for the visiting leaders, would be a key to inviting country leaders to Xintiandi during the APEC meeting. However, the invitations to some celebrity exhibitions and parties initially sent to the 36 consulates in Shanghai met with no response—most probably tossed into the trash bin upon receipt.

Xintiandi had to find a way out.

When Shui On's public relations department learned from the Shanghai People's Association for Friendship with Foreign Countries that a famous Russian female artist had been invited to exhibit her artwork in the city, Shui On promptly offered to fully sponsor the exhibit. Captivated by the unique character

Art exhibit by the famous Russian female artist held at Xintiandi model houses. On the stage are the artist (second from right), Russian consul general (third from right) and the representatives of the Shanghai cultural community at the opening ceremony.

and charm of *Shikumen* houses, the artist agreed on the locale as soon as she visited Xintiandi to inspect the venue.

When drawing up the guest list of the opening ceremony, Shui On suggested that all 36 consulates in Shanghai be invited. The company would also host an upscale party with about 200 guests from local artists, entrepreneurs and bankers, with full sponsorship of a magnificent banquet.

The artist was so pleased that she agreed to ask the Russian Consulate for a favor. Thanks to her fame, the Consulate not only had its consul general attend the event, but also invited consuls general or consuls for Cultural Affairs of other countries.

In addition to the gathering of foreign diplomats on such a large scale, Zhou Muyao, the then Vice Mayor of Shanghai and Director of Shanghai Foreign Affairs Office, attended the ceremony in person. Mr. Zhou, also in charge of local tourism administration, was equally impressed with the refined cluster of traditionally styled *Shikumen* houses that he had heard about from his colleagues.

Mr. Zhou congratulated Shui On chairman Vincent Lo and affirmed Xintiandi's contribution to Shanghai's urban regeneration efforts at the opening ceremony. Mr. Lo took the opportunity to introduce the concepts of Xintiandi development which garnered attention also from the diplomats in attendance.

The exhibit was a huge success and the artist's artworks sold quickly. But the biggest winner was Xintiandi, whose reputation promptly spread across the consulates. Since then, French consuls have made Xintiandi cafés and restaurants their regular haunts. The Consul General of Italy even held the Italian National Day Gala there. On his recommendation, the Prime Minister of Italy stopped by Xintiandi during his visit in Shanghai, amazed and impressed by its characteristic mix of East and West, issued an instruction on the spot to set up a "National New Achievement Exhibition Hall" at Xintiandi, under the firm belief that it would gain global popularity and become the best platform to promote Italian products.

Shui On pulled out all the stops to invite domestic political leaders, business heads, and leading figures in the fields of media and culture through personal connections with the help of its expertise in public relations that gave it a knack for finding the right person who organized the leaders' itinerary for official visits to the city.

Government officials, general manager assistants, news reporters and editors, and secretaries-general of various organizations were the first to start the word-of-mouth chain that triggered positive buzz for Xintiandi.

All the promotional events were held in the Xintiandi model houses, where a restaurant, a café and a gallery were built to showcase how the old downtown housing quarters would be rejuvenated into a mixed-use community with residential, office, retail, entertainment and cultural functions. The model houses ran daily shows and banquets, held weekly parties and exhibit monthly art collections, inviting all kinds of influencers to witness the revitalization of the *Shikumen* houses.

The marketing cost eventually topped 70 million yuan, a staggering amount in that era. Yet the campaign proved cost-

The Artist gives Shui On chairman Vincent Lo a painting called "Seagulls" as a gift at the opening ceremony of the Masterpiece Art Exhibition.

effective, evolving from a word-of-mouth strategy to a citywide event that reached and engaged various elite groups.

Xintiandi encouraged the audience to participate in and share, just like the message in its advertising slogans: Come to enjoy or to create.

The Masterpiece Art Exhibition held on Nov 3rd 1999 started the first marketing activity at Xintiandi. Credit goes to Yao Rongquan, President of the Shanghai-Hong Kong Cultural Exchange Association. Originally a senior reporter in the art department of the Xinmin Evening News, Mr. Yao has a strong social network in the culture industry and works hard to promote cultural exchanges between Shanghai and Hong Kong. When he was attending the 3-day-long Masterpiece Art Exhibition held during the first Shanghai International Art Festival in October 1999, it suddenly occurred to him that presenting the Masterpiece Art Exhibition at Xintiandi *Shikumen* houses would be an exceptional experience. Mr. Yao approached the secretary-general of the Festival Organizing Committee with the plan, jointly devised by Shui On and himself, that the new concept exhibition center of Xintiandi in the vicinity of the CPC site could house the exhibition for a month or longer.

Accompanied by Mr. Yao to the site, the secretary-general was inspired and convinced that the artists would love the venue where the exhibition would be extended for free.

Immediately following the conclusion of the Art Festival, some of the selected artworks were displayed at Xintiandi, including works by Zao Wou-ki, a Chinese-French painter, Chen Yifei and Ding Shaoguang, Chinese-American artists, as well as Shi Hu and Shi Dawei, established modern Chinese artists.

The exhibition was meant to take advantage of the celebrity effect to attract the target audience. On the second day of the exhibition, unsurprisingly, Mr. Yao brought two special guests — Mr. Qian Weichang, renowned Chinese scientist and President of Shanghai University, and a senior official from the Ministry of Culture.

Renowned Chinese scientist Qian Weichang (front row, second from right) at the Xintiandi model houses, accompanied by Vincent Lo (front row right).

It was the refurbished historical building that really caught their attention. As they walked around in the house, they gasped in admiration at the magical cornucopia recalling this city's former reputation for fusion, of East and West, old and new.

Once a Vice Chairman of the National Committee of the Chinese People's Political Consultative Conference, Mr. Qian has developed and promoted a strategic vision. He recommended to the senior official that Shui On be the right candidate if Beijing Municipal Government was considering redeveloping Si He Yuan, the historical type of residence commonly found in Beijing.

When Mr. Qian expressed his appreciation for the mixed cultural ambience of the house at lunch, Mr. Lo added that *Shikumen* was indeed initially a combination of Chinese and Western influences. Mr Qian then shared his insights: "Strictly speaking, Xintiandi is not the combination of East and West, but the fusion of both. Cultural combination is a joining of different qualities in which the cultures are still individually distinct, while cultural fusion is a merging of separate cultures into a unified whole. Xintiandi is in essence a fusion of East and West, old and new. I expect that Xintiandi will have multiple impacts

THE SUCCESS OF A WORD-OF-MOUTH MARKETING STRATEGY

A rickshaw with a passenger in qipao for the marketing promotion of Xintiandi against the backdrop of Shikumen *alleys*

on the city of Shanghai."

Indeed farsighted, the scientist put forward the term "cultural fusion" in late autumn of 1999, when the rising trend of "fusion" started to stretch into the new century. Since then, Xintiandi changed its marketing slogan from "combining East and West" to "a cultural fusion".

The next guest on the list was Fang Zengxian, the chairman of the Shanghai Artists Association and Curator of the Shanghai Art Museum. Mr. Fang was so busy dealing with all sorts of invitations that he couldn't spare any time for Xintiandi which he instinctively thought would be a mundane result of *Shikumen* redevelopment.

Communication takes great patience and sincerity of effort. The office director and exhibition director of the museum were first invited for tea in the newly built glass structure bathed in sunshine, encompassed by oil paintings on the walls in the innovative art space. Now that the directors were enamored with the place, Shui On awaited the right moment to approach Mr. Fang, which would be the Masterpiece Art Exhibition. Nudged by his colleagues, Mr. Fang finally made his first steps in the model houses, astonished by the revolutionary and artistic renovation where art and innovation intertwined at the exhibition space. Xintiandi has since become a favored hang-out for him and his friends.

Luwan District authorities and Xintiandi received a notice from the Municipal Party Committee office at noon on Nov 13th that its Deputy Secretary was coming to inspect the site in the afternoon. Having repeatedly heard compliments from the painters on the "*Shikumen* Gallery" at Xintiandi, the Deputy Secretary was quite curious himself.

Thrilled at the unexpected good news, Shui On management was nervous with excitement. Walking around the construction site in a safety helmet, the Deputy Secretary kept asking questions but offered no affirmative responses when the district Party secretary, district Mayor and Mr. Lo briefed him about the site, leaving the management feeling anxious and uncertain.

The project was left in abeyance pending the outcome of the debate on the preservation of *Shikumen* buildings among the experts from the Municipal Cultural Heritage Management Committee at the beginning stage when residents had been relocated yet the construction could not kick off. In retrospect, the Company still felt apprehensive about the enormous operating expenses incurred on a daily basis. If the project had been voted down by the Committee that served as the guardian of the city's cultural heritage, all Shui On's efforts would have gone in vain. As the Director of the Committee, the Deputy Secretary played a key role in the final decision-making process.

Thirty minutes before the next scheduled meeting, the Deputy Secretary surprisingly called it off and suggested further discussion with Shui On management and the district officials who were caught off guard and felt even more restless. But they were soon relieved at the sight of his smile when he was seated and finally shared his thoughts, "When I saw many historical buildings in Europe—old factories repurposed into restaurants, pubs, hotels and art galleries—I was wondering how we should revive the old fabric of our city. I'm glad I've found the answer here today." He added, "Shui On's development projects have dovetailed with the development plan of the city, covered our shortage of funds, and contributed to its prosperity. Xintiandi is indeed a pioneering initiative in urban heritage revitalization in Shanghai."

The Deputy Secretary spoke highly of Shui On's insight in preserving the traditional aspect of the city and offered a cornucopia of good ideas: assign good-looking and English-speaking police officers in the nearest police station to match Shanghai's global reputation as an international cultural metropolis; borrow the idea from Disneyland by hiring college students to work as janitors-cum-tour guides dressed in traditional costumes from the '30s; relive the past by offering rickshaws plying the streets of historic, street vendors selling souvenirs, and street artists drawing portraits of the tourists. Xintiandi was designed to incorporate global perspectives as emblematic of the city's identity as well as of the nation.

The deputy Secretary inadvertently changed his role from a city leader to a participant in the development of Xintiandi.

During the two-and-half-year construction, valuable insight and constructive input were provided by distinguished guests from the government and all walks of the industry. These "opinion leaders" wished to contribute to shaping the urban development towards sustainable and prosperous futures they had been longing for. The word-of-mouth marketing campaign drew more engagement than expected and fostered the participants' expectations, recognition and sense of belonging.

The Deputy Secretary soon put his words into practice—the Xintiandi police station was officially established, with handsome police officers capable of holding a conversation in English.

The second phase of the marketing campaign aimed at attracting global attention.

In 2000, the press officer of the Municipal Foreign Affairs Office was proudly and excitedly introducing the Lujiazui

Financial District of Shanghai Pudong to a group of Western journalists, only to draw a lukewarm response. They admitted that the Manhattan-like district of gleaming skyscrapers sprouting across the Huangpu River, a typical urban design paradigm in the West, was not special enough to be televised. Meanwhile, a Dutch journalist asked the press officer if there was any indigenous historical architecture they could visit. First place that came to his mind was Xintiandi, a construction in progress with newly built model houses in a refurbished alley, where all the foreign journalists were, upon arrival, so captivated by the enchanting neighborhood of old *Shikumen* that they climbed up high and got down low to capture its unique character and charm with utter magnificence. Surprised at the awe-inspiring heritage restoration that transcended the logic and stipulations of historic preservation, the Dutch journalist told the officer that he was exhilarated to have found such good news material that it would definitely achieve a high rating.

On another occasion, an editor-in-chief of a famous French magazine was taking a tour in the Shanghai Urban Planning Exhibition Center accompanied by an official from Shanghai Municipal Tourism Administrative Commission. A young female guide proudly introduced the French lady to the focus of the exhibit—a visually stunning model showing the entirety of urban Shanghai, including existing buildings and approved future buildings. Dismayed to hear that all of the dilapidated buildings had been torn down to make way for a brand-new cityscape, the editor expressed her extreme disappointment. The official explained that local government had been attempting to preserve the important historic landmarks and further elaborated on Xintiandi project, a notable example, that immediately intrigued the editor. She was so fascinated by the model houses when she paid a visit to Xintiandi that she was going to write about the city's desire to stake a claim for the preservation, protection and promotion of its rich cultural heritage.

Positive Western media coverage of Xintiandi attracted

attention from political leaders in Shanghai who realized that Xintiandi had become a visual representation of the city's urban development. Xintiandi has since served as a window to the foreign journalists to provide the rest of the world with a glimpse of Shanghai's development under the guidance and recommendation of local authorities.

What began as a local event promoting preservation of the built heritage has become overwhelmingly popular among foreign visitors. Sometimes the local coordinators were even embarrassed to find that Xintiandi, a place they had never heard of, was a must-see for the visiting international delegations.

Following deputy mayors' unanimous support for the project, Xu Kuangdi, the then Shanghai Mayor, decided to lead a delegation of officials to Xintiandi to collect studies on urban regeneration practice. After hearing the briefing by Mr. Lo, inspecting the construction site and scrutinizing the model houses, the mayor, who had been trying to find a balance between demolition and preservation of *Shikumen* buildings critical to preserving viable neighborhoods and restoring vitality to the city, was enlightened by Xintiandi's holistic and integrated approach that prompted him to make two critical decisions on the spot.

Firstly, he said: "From now on, when the leaders of the central government, foreign heads of state, ministers and provincial mayors come to Shanghai, we will show them Xintiandi's preservation-oriented redevelopment approach that can later be expanded throughout the country and share with the world a glimpse of our urbanization progress."

Successive mayors maintained the continuity and consistency of his instruction for another decade. On-site inspections have been conducted by government officials from 31 provinces, cities, and autonomous regions, including Long Yongtu, Vice Minister of the Foreign Economic Cooperation, Shi Guangsheng, Minister of Foreign Trade and Economic Cooperation, Vice Premier and former Foreign Minister Qian Qichen, Vice Premier Li Lanqing,

The grand dinner party of the International Business Leaders' Advisory Council for the Mayor of Shanghai at Xintiandi in 2001.

Premier Wen Jiabao, and President Jiang Zemin.

Secondly, the dinner party of International Business Leaders' Advisory Council for the Mayor of Shanghai 2001 would be held at Xintiandi upon its completion, allowing industry leaders across a wide range of sectors to experience the urban redevelopment and contribute their expertise and ideas to the future direction of business development in Shanghai.

The project went more smoothly with the mayor's endorsement. On November 4th, 2001, the dinner party was successfully held in the atrium of Xintiandi South Block which

THE SUCCESS OF A WORD-OF-MOUTH MARKETING STRATEGY

was completed in fall.

In early 2001, consular officers of the APEC's member economies, such as the U.S., Russia, Canada and Japan, that confirmed to attend the APEC meeting were all impressed by the evolution of Xintiandi with concentration of culture and leisure and therefore recommended that Xintiandi be included in the schedule of the heads of state. The officers believed that Xintiandi, as the latest symbol of Shanghai's urban development and a re-imagining of Shanghai's old streetscape as consumer experience, would serve as a unique new model for urban redevelopment worth recommending to the heads of state.

The Speaker of the Canadian House of Commons and his delegation visiting Xintiandi, accompanied and briefed by Shui On Deputy Marketing General Manager David Ng (front row, second from right)

On the other hand, most of the local government officials preparing for the APEC meeting had either visited or heard of Xintiandi and thus unanimously included it in a shortlist of must-see attractions for the foreign heads of state, in an attempt to showcase Shanghai's achievement in urban development.

Preparation leads to readiness.

During the APEC Summit in Shanghai, Russian President Vladimir Putin had his first dinner of authentic Shanghai homestyle cooking at One Xintiandi upon arrival. Other foreign heads of state, including Prime Ministers of Canada, Singapore and Thailand also dined at Xintiandi *Shikumen* restaurants organized by local government.

The places that Chinese and foreign politicians, celebrities, the gold-collar and white-collar workers frequented have attracted a great deal of attention and will shape the future of consumption.

Having enjoyed a ripple of popularity by the time of the APEC meeting, Xintiandi garnered a strong and highly loyal following during the summit.

Sometimes the train of plans derails. But with the help of some resourceful people, the results can turn out to be much

THE SUCCESS OF A WORD-OF-MOUTH MARKETING STRATEGY

Christopher Francis Patten (front row middle), the then European Commissioner for External Relations, touring Xintiandi, accompanied and briefed by Shui On Executive Director Henry Cheng Bing Chark (front row left)

more gratifying than expected.

The initial word-of-mouth marketing strategy evolved into a platform of sharing and engagement where different cultures blended: grasstops met grassroots, foreign overlapped with indigenous, and historical encountered contemporary. The result is a commercial hit beyond expectations that echoes a famous saying of the Chinese Taoist philosopher Zhuangzi: What was simple in the beginning acquires monstrous proportions in the end.

CHAPTER 6

Passion, the key to success

Shui On Group took a chance on the future of Xintiandi at its own risk. The idea for the project emerged at the beginning of the Asian economic crisis in 1998. The entire Asian real estate market slumped. The banks in Hong Kong were doubtful about the economic return on the project and declined to grant it a loan.

The uncertainty of this development model also caused Shui On's board of directors to view the project with skepticism. However, against objections raised by his advisory board about the risk, Vincent Lo insisted on undertaking the investment.

Since Shui On was not a listed company and Vincent Lo owned 90% stake in the company, even though the entire board voted down the project, Mr. Lo had the final say to go forward with the plan. In fact, he had confirmed with the financial director prior to the board meeting that even if the project failed, the company wouldn't go bankrupt.

Successful innovation strategies include forward-thinking mindset that helps the company move beyond the status quo. Regularly measuring and evaluating the plans helps the company address the unknowns as they arise and identify where tactics need to be adjusted to improve the results. Timing is key. Having a good idea is not enough. More important is having the right idea at the right time.

Banks imposed tighter lending standards on borrowers due to the economic uncertainty. Yet Vincent Lo was willing to take and embrace the risk with his commitment to making his dream come true, prediction of future trend and years of solid investment experience. Since he started his own business in the '70s, Vincent Lo has weathered plenty of ups and downs, developed strong business acumen and always been ready to seize opportunities.

Economic cycles demonstrate alternate intervals of high and low growth. When economy hits a low point, real estate investment costs are at extremely deep discounts, signaling strong opportunities for new development or re-development. When the construction is completed, growth might begin to recover and the property achieves a higher market value.

Back in the mid-1980s, many of Hong Kong's moneyed elite were cashing in their chips and moving abroad before the transfer of sovereignty over Hong Kong in 1997. But Vincent Lo didn't budge. Indeed, he decided the time was ripe to bet on the mainland. He purchased a parcel of land in Victoria Harbor, where Shui On Center now stands, for only HK$300 million. When Hong Kong's economy gradually recovered from a low base, the offering price of the Center soared to HK$7 billion.

Truth always rests with the minority. While discovering truth is hard, efforts and commitment to preserving the truth are even more precious. Both persistence and discovery need innovative ideas with a wide array of inherent risks that depend on attempting to predict the unknown. The larger the organization the more risk averse it becomes. Fear of risk is the biggest factor holding large companies back from innovating. On the flip-side most startups and small companies embrace risk and innovation. It is their lifeblood and their competitive advantage.

As a young startup founder, Vincent Lo had the luxury of trial and error. One risk taken by a startup has the potential to kill the organization as has happened with numerous startups, but those risks are required in order for startups to grow and flourish. Being a small-sized construction firm, Shui On was geared for agile as it had small teams that operated in rapid learning and fast decision cycles.

During the Asian financial crisis, many large Hong Kong enterprises significantly reduced their real estate investments

PASSION, THE KEY TO SUCCESS

Vincent Lo is well on his way to becoming China's best-known developer.

in Mainland China. However, Shui On adopted the opposite approach. Due to the difficulty in finding investors, Vincent Lo financed most of the HK$800 million through personal investment and loans. Shui On took out 670 million yuan to foot the bill for the relocation in the first phase of construction in order to get a three-hectare land parcel of dilapidated blocks.

People thought he was crazy.

China is a large country that houses lots of great talent, creative ideas and a booming market. What it needs are ambitious entrepreneurs that are willing to take risks even if they are big ones that can jeopardize the venture.

Attitudes arise out of core values and beliefs held internally. Vincent Lo would not be in the position he enjoys today without the acts of courage and foresight he displayed as a young entrepreneur.

Benjamin Wood, the principal architect of Xintiandi, spoke of him with admiration that Lo's most important contribution to the project was not how much he invested, but his unremitting continuance in spite of opposition.

In the late '90s, the trend toward a more active lifestyle increased the demand for leisure venues.

Some businesses in Shanghai started to consider transforming *Shikumen* buildings into an iconic leisure area, but hesitated to act due to the substantial possibility of failure from a risky strategy. None had succeeded in bringing the idea to a fruitful conclusion until the young Lo, with innovation and his readiness to take a calculated risk, decided to move forward quickly.

Xintiandi has established itself as the leading entertainment district in Shanghai, if not China, after the economic crash of 1997. People were keen to find out more about the chairman that headed the Shui On construction and property empire.

Although dressed simply in perfectly cut clothes, Vincent Lo is an explorer who shifts his focus from the routine projects and venture outside his comfort zone. Indeed, the scale of Lo's ambitions ranked him as a visionary, rather than just an entrepreneur.

The spur of Lo's innovative streak can be found in his personal background. Vincent Lo grew up in a typical Chinese family where the father was the figure of authority and mother was nurturing and protective of the children. His father, Lo Ying Shek, founder of Great Eagle Holdings Limited which has developed into one of the largest real estate developers in Hong Kong since its establishment in 1963, raised his seven children in a stringent regime.

Vincent Lo recalled that his father required the family sit together for dinner every evening and listen to his review of the hustle-bustle of everyday life. Dinnertime was the toughest part of the day for the children who just wanted to finish eating and leave the table. Now that he was a father of two children, he has realized that his father was trying to introduce them to a wider variety of methods of dealing with life and give them insight into the real world.

Lo had no recollection of his father taking them to the park in his childhood. Instead, the children spent every Sunday at the construction site with their father who attempted to set an example for the children. Consequently, Lo has gained market exposure and established awareness about market opportunities since he was a child.

But his father wanted them to additionally learn ways to face their failures head-on. In traditional Chinese cultures, shame and anxiety are intricately tied to failure and setbacks. While in the West, teachers increase a student's resilience by telling them that failing isn't a problem with learning, but it is just another feature. It isn't something that needs to be eliminated.

Fully aware that kids who endured hardship would take setbacks in their stride, Lo's father decided to send him to study in Australia when he was 15 years old. When his mother wanted to buy him a plane ticket, his father stopped her and said, "I send him overseas to experience hardship, not to enjoy life! Let him take the ship!"

The ship waiting at the harbor was not a cruise ship, but a cargo vessel where young Lo had to live with the sailors on the orlop deck with poor air circulation. He suffered from seasickness during the entire voyage that lasted 13 days. Lo remained concerned about traveling by ship in the aftermath of the voyage.

At the approach of the summer vacation, when Lo received his father's reply that turned down his request for money to go back to Hong Kong in summer and asked him to find a job to pay for his own college and living expenses, he was so upset over his father's decision that he didn't go out for three days. Soon money was running out, and he was forced to work during his study to support himself. He had washed dishes, sold ice cream, made hamburgers, been a hotel busboy and even sung in a pub. The broad diversity of social experiences equipped him with living skills and rid himself of the temperament and personality of a rich second generation.

Children from less affluent families tend to be more motivated to work hard and devise creative ways to manage their limited financial resources, while rich children are less likely to become fiscally and socially responsible. As the ancient Chinese saying goes: "To be bestowed with great responsibility, one must be crucified with ordeal and tribulation so as to break one's will; subdue one's spirit; exhaust one's muscles; starve one's flesh." Mr. Lo Ying Shek had apparently fully captured the essence of Chinese parenting.

When Vincent Lo joined family business following graduation, he received most reprimands among all siblings. Having endured two mainly frustrating years, he secretly found another job.

But his mother forbade him to work for anybody else and talked to his father for three days about his future. Lo still remembered the hurt feelings when he overheard his father shouting to his mother that he was a disgrace to this family and it would be a waste of money, while he was waiting for the result under the stairs. Becoming an entrepreneur was the only way to go. Lo started a construction and building materials company, helped by a small loan of HK$100,000, which had to be repaid with interest, from his father. Vincent Lo couldn't understand why his father was so frugal to the point of stinginess despite his great wealth until decades later when he realized that his father wanted to teach him that "there's no such thing as a free lunch".

Lo understood there was no turning back once he left the family business. He knew little about construction when he started his business, so he worked 16-hour days for several years without a break to close the gap. Desperate to prove himself to his father, Vincent Lo started by studying the fundamentals of construction materials and methods. Seven years of hard work paid off when the team was finally winning successful bids.

Lo's vision and passion for excellence, alongside a desire for learning are the key ingredients to his success, just like the seagull, the symbol of Shui On Group, that represents its spirit to strive for excellence.

Shortly after Shui On was founded, the Hong Kong stock market saw a boom. Lo's friends tried to persuade him to invest in stock markets where they made more money simply by making a phone call than he could earn in a year. Yet he was committed to building a company, as opposed to making a fast buck. His farsightedness came to the fore when he decided to make steady money in the long run.

In December 1984, the Chinese and British governments signed a Joint Declaration on Hong Kong to affirm that China would resume exercise of sovereignty over Hong Kong on July 1, 1997. The handover sent shockwaves through many sectors including real estate and construction in Hong Kong. Concerns over social unrest and the region's political autonomy pushed Hong Kong migrants and businesses to flee overseas.

Vincent Lo decided to stay. He had had the bitter taste of second-class citizens in Australia. Once on his bus ride to work, Lo was told to vacate his seat for a white woman while there were plenty of empty seats on the bus. The woman arrogantly told him that she just wanted the seat and he, as an Asian, should give it up to her. While all the other passengers remained silent to the racial discrimination, he got off the bus in humiliation.

That experience triggered his appreciation for Chinese cultural identity and kept him motivated and committed to his goals. As a Chinese national, he expected to see pockets of strategic opportunities in Mainland China emerging from its reform and opening up in the coming years.

By actively contributing to the region's continued growth, Lo has built contact with mainland officials in the Liaison Office of the Central People's Government in Hong Kong in an attempt to play an active part in the development of the region (as well as himself) and understand the working style and customs in the Mainland.

Convener of the Business and Professional Group of the Basic Law Consultative Committee from 1985 to 1990, Lo spent 80% of his time in community services in addition to his business capacity. The rewards were a broader view on the challenges and opportunities and an elevated level of economic perspectives.

Economic and political matters are intertwined. Growth and expansion of local businesses have to be supported through political channels to achieve economic growth. Lo's community engagement prepared him for demonstrating, over the next decades, that he is a master of context in the rapidly changing Chinese environment.

The ever-rising land prices in the mature market of Hong Kong forced Vincent Lo to switch to the mainland market. The top ten tycoons who dominated Hong Kong made much of their money in the Pearl River Delta during the reform and opening up of China's economy.

But Vincent Lo took a greater China view and decided to spread his wings in the Yangtze River Delta, centered around Shanghai, that plays a significant role in China's economy. Shanghai was bidding to regain the glory it once enjoyed as a center of international finance and trade during the first half of the 20th century. The atmosphere of rejuvenation aroused the capitalistic spirits for which Shanghai used to be famous, fueling one of the most spectacular boons in China's reform era.

Lo entered the Shanghai market in 1985. His first project there was a joint venture with the city's Communist Youth League for the building of the City Hotel, a project which lay the foundations of his future influence.

It was through this collaboration that Vincent Lo started building his political capital in Shanghai. He believed these capable, aspiring young government officials would be a key lever to ensure inclusive and sustainable urban development. Indeed, he decided the time was ripe to bet on the mainland and started his ongoing and increasing investment in Shanghai.

Lo was right. Many of the mid-level officials in the 1980s were promoted to high-rank positions years later—Governor of Zhejiang province, Mayor of Shanghai, minister of the central government, to name a few. With a competitive edge over his rivals, Lo strengthened his company's position further by building a top-notch commercial and office building, Shui On Plaza, in Shanghai.

In 1995, the then Governor of Shanghai Luwan District, Han Zheng, who had been the Secretary of the city's Communist Youth League, was working on the ground improvement project to prepare for Shanghai's first subway line that runs under Huaihai Road, relocation of residents, residential demolitions, and building a new central business district on the eastern section of Middle Huaihai Road.

By then, Hong Kong's property giants Sun Hung Kai, New World and The Wharf Group had acquired land parcels in the CBD, all gearing up to build office towers and shopping malls. But they suspended the projects due to the depressed property market in Shanghai in 1995.

Shui On was a latecomer, and the land parcels in the CBD had already been snapped up. But every cloud has a silver

EAST MEETS WEST

Shui On Land is headquartered in Shanghai and sits in Shui On Plaza on the prosperous Huaihai Road. Construction of Shui On Plaza launched in 1995 when the real estate market fell into a deep decline.

lining. Shanghai Jiuhai Limeng, a state-owned enterprise located in Luwan District, had obtained the best site in the CBD—just above the current subway station South Huangpi Road. Jiuhai was seeking funding while Shui On was looking for businesses to get involved with. Strategic partnership was consequently formed to enable both parties to lean into each other's strengths on condition that Shui On take the lead to build the office tower that would drive the CBD development during the economic downturn.

The property market outlook was uncertain at that time when many were fighting shy of investing in the city's future. Undeterred, Lo noticed a strange phenomenon after careful research: on the one hand, there was a significant oversupply of commercial floor space, while on the other hand many multinational corporations were renting rooms for daytime office use in five-star hotels. It turned out the existing office buildings were in a worse condition than the hotels, reflecting a shortage of Grade A office space in Shanghai.

In a market where real estate opportunities changed every minute, Vincent Lo acted swiftly on the well-timed real estate opportunity. The investment topped 300 million yuan. Shui On Plaza was built with premium-grade quality outfitted with top-of-the-line fixtures and amenities. Construction was proceeding at full speed.

Effective advertising didn't need to cost a fortune. Office building brochures were delivered to the corporations situated in the hotels and a 70% occupancy was soon achieved, with tenants consisting mainly of major multinational corporations—PricewaterhouseCoopers, IBM, DuPont to name a few. The other developers who had been rather reserved quickly followed suit and resumed their projects with an eye to tapping its burgeoning markets.

The result was enduring trust and respect from the government that later entrusted him with developing 52 hectares of prime cityscape

Over the first decade after its founding, Shui On has been constantly employing a clear vision, an innovative mindset and ample experience to pave the way for its brand and reputation.

The glitzy Xintiandi project is Vincent Lo's crown jewel. He summarized his experience in retrospect, "With hard work and effort, you can lead a good life. But if you want to become a successful entrepreneur, you need vision and a little bit of luck." Luck is what happens when preparation meets opportunity. By then Lo was already a master at adapting to changing circumstances in Mainland China.

Every adversity brings with it the seed of an equivalent advantage. For some businesses, an economic recession is not a setback. It's an opportunity to thrive and grow.

Strong economic developments send ripples to the farthest reaches of the planet—creating opportunities but also significant risks. Transformative change can expect opposition from those with interests vested in the status quo, and such opposition can be overcome for the broader public good during an economic crisis.

Every recession creates opportunities for innovative entrepreneurs who not only cope with the current conditions, but also learn and adapt from them, propelling them to greater heights.

Xintiandi project was launched at the height of the Asian financial crisis. A strong team is the foundation of a high-performing business. A team exists to allow an endeavor to grow, scale, and thrive in a way that would be literally impossible for one person to do.

A successful team starts with hiring the right people—those who value working toward a common goal. Vincent Lo managed to assemble a strong team with technical expertise and years of experience.

Henry Cheng: Managing Director of Shui On Land Limited, Hong Kong passport holders in Australia. He once ran a newspaper, taught Chinese literature in Hong Kong, is familiar with European culture and once served as the head of

Marketing and Communications of the Hong Kong Tourism Association. With over a decade of experience in construction industry, he is in charge of overseeing the development of the Xintiandi project.

Tony Wong: First General Manager of Shanghai Xintiandi, Hong Kong resident. Former Financial Director of Kerry Properties, he provides marketing expertise in commercial real estate leasing with a strong sense of innovation.

David Wong: Chief Economist of Shui On Land Limited, Hong Kong resident. Decades of experience in business strategy, macroeconomic analysis, and property policy research.

Hei Ming Chang: Chief Financial Officer of Shui On Land Limited, Hong Kong resident. Former assistant loan manager of Standard Chartered Bank with extensive finance experience to the organization.

Albert Chan: Senior Planning and Design Manager of Shui On Land Limited, Chinese American. Former Project Director at the New York City Department of Design and Construction.

SS Hui: Deputy Engineering General Manager of Shui On Land Limited, Hong Kong resident. He started his career at Shui On after graduation and has had over 30 years of experience in the construction industry.

David Ng: Deputy General Manager of Marketing Department of Shui On Land Limited, Hong Kong passport holders in Canada. Extensive experience in food and beverages industry marketing.

Alfa Cheung: Deputy General Manager of Operation Department of Shui On Land Limited, Hong Kong resident. Over 20 years of experience in the property management industry.

Allan Tian: Senior manager of Human Resources Department of Shui On Land Limited, Hong Kong resident. Over 20 years of HR-related experience.

Zhou Yongping (author of this book): Senior Manager of Public Relations Department of Shui On Land Limited, resident of Shanghai. Assistant to Vincent Lo since 2002. Former Deputy Director of Information Office of the Shanghai Municipality.

The diverse global team and Shui On's inclusive company culture have enabled the team members, despite their different backgrounds, motivations and values, to leverage their creativity and innovative culture.

In countries such as the United States, migrants have contributed to creativity, innovation, and invention thanks to its inclusive immigration policy. The presence of large numbers of talented immigrants has pushed American institutions to be more meritocratic and open to innovation than they would be otherwise. (In the UK, on the contrary, only British citizens have the automatic right to live and work there.)

Successive waves of talented immigrants have brought innovative ideas and entrepreneurial spirit to the U.S. and enriched its culture. Their mixed culture and unique position gave the country more possibilities for innovation.

In addition to the abovementioned team, external parties were invited in support of the project including American architect Benjamin Wood, Nikken Seikkei International from Singapore, Prof. Luo Xiaowei from the School of Architecture and Urban Planning of Tongji University, and Sam Lam from Hong Kong

Mr. Lo (third from right) and his team brainstorming at the construction site of Xintiandi.

A-World Consulting.

Knowledge and practice are substantial to the interpretation of culture as well as memory. Benjamin Wood is a former Air Force pilot who enjoyed aerial views from the cockpit. This experience made him always keep the big picture in sight after he had started his career in architecture. He was consequently able to zoom out to see the big picture of the distinctly disheveled, dilapidated and run down *Shikumen* neighborhood and came up with the overall symbolic portrayal of Xintiandi, in which his cultural background played a key role.

Xintiandi project was given free rein to develop into a most dominating symbol of the city that exemplifies the fusion of East and West, contemporary and traditional, conventional and unique.

Innovation helped the Company to upend its status quo. The management and operation personnel were experiencing an adrenaline rush at all times—alternating between the excitement of innovation and deadline pressure.

Each of the team members had a protective helmet and leather safety shoes. At 8:30 every morning, architects went on field inspection of the construction site where long stretches of decades-old *Shikumen* houses were in ruins and bricked up with shattered tiles, damaged walls, and nails on board wood inside. The architects conducted extensive photo and video studies of the site, sharing ideas, planning and brainstorming together. These images became the raw material for their subsequent photomontage designs, which served as an imaginative and conceptual drawing board for experimentation with images—an artistic creation Shui On had never done before.

Breakthrough ideas hatched overnight and architects knocked down the newly refurbished house and started all over again. Innovation may take longer than expected to get off the ground. Lo was facing ongoing cost pressure since the architects charged on an hourly basis. On the other hand, the architects and management team were also under stress to achieve project success. Nevertheless, they believed work-life integration was the key to boosting productivity in a holistic and flexible manner. They dined at different restaurants where innovative concepts got their creative juices flowing.

Innovation hurts. Working "out of the comfort zone" is "working through pain" in reality. Everywhere the architects went, they saw the world through the lens of design. When seized by a sudden inspiration—whether they were walking, sitting, or even in bed, they would write or sketch out their ideas straight away. It was very much a 24/7 way of thinking, a mix of pain and pleasure, anxiety and excitement.

Thinking and behaving influence the world in ways obvious and not so apparent, but the effect is real, nonetheless. There are four basic kinds of people in business today. They can be best characterized by their attitudes:

The doer
This person is a safe pair of hands who is reliable and trustworthy and gets the job finished. They meet deadlines and they hit targets, but only within their job responsibilities.

The lover
They tend to be generous and open and they share their ideas. They finish their assignments on time and can persuade people to get involved in their projects.

The leader
They have a vision of what they want to achieve, and this is usually in alignment with the vision and mission statement of the organization they work for.

The dreamer
This person is unconventional. They think outside the box and they are very good at borrowing ideas

from unconventional sources. They're often struck by inspiration at strange times. They're hungry for new ideas and information and they're great at tracking them down. They continually ask themselves if there's a better way to do things.

Wang Xizhi, one of the most celebrated Chinese calligraphers, was a typical dreamer. One of his most famous pieces of writing is *Lanting Xu* (Preface to the Poems Composed at the Orchid Pavilion) written in the semi-cursive style. Wang wrote *Lanting Xu* in one go when he was drunk. It is said that he rewrote *Lanting Xu* a few times after he sobered up, but none could compare to the original.

Being dreamers imparted in Xintiandi team the ability to truly champion their ideas and work together in an engaging way with a vision of incorporating a sense of romance into the project, coupled with a striving for perfection.

Because dreamers tend to feel so much ownership over a project, they need to keep their micromanaging tendencies in check. Frustration can arise if the dreamer's vision becomes lost in translation as the general and the workhorse drive the project toward fruition. Consistent communication and a well-mapped plan for that vision are key.

One of the subconsultants for Xintiandi project, Nikken Sekkei International out of Singapore, invented new possibilities by combining the right mix of experience, creativity and passion to bring innovative ideas to life.

Unlike mediocre design firms that usually try to be strategic about how they deploy their resources by only producing a dozen conceptual drawings of a house to be renovated due to shortage of talented architects and tight budget and shifting the responsibility to the construction team, Nikken Sekkei has formalized processes and mechanisms that allow designers to integrate their skills, knowledge and experience, and provide hundreds of drawings of the same house.

Working for a project has a lot in common with endurance running in that they both need the right mindset and a disciplined approach to cross the finish line. The runner might not be in the best of his physical fitness levels but if he has the will to endure and has a strong will to run, he can do it. Running is about mind over body. Similarly, self-motivated employees will give their 100% and have conviction to do what they are intending to do.

Between 1999 and 2001, employees put in long days, responded to their emails at all hours, and willingly donated their off-hours—nights, weekends, vacation—without complaining. Overwork cascaded from the top of the organizational pyramid to the bottom.

Parents who were worried about their children, young females in particular, working until midnight for months went to confirm with the managers of Shui On. When they learnt how the project stimulated the spirit of initiative and creative potential of the employees, they were fully supportive of their children being part of the great effort.

Department heads, among the most hardworking, had to lead by example, show guidance and strength to inspire those around them.

During the project period, one of the department heads of Shui On suffered from cholecystitis and pancreatitis due to overwork. After he had registered at the hospital in the morning, he went to the office and returned to the hospital at noon time when there were fewer patients. When the results from a blood test and an ultrasound came back, he was immediately admitted to the hospital and a notification of imminent death was subsequently issued. His wife burst into tears, sobbing, "is your job worth sacrificing your own life for?"

In the first month of treatment, the patient was not allowed to eat and drink after surgery and nutrition was given as a liquid solution through the vein. He didn't stop working though. While the catheter was inserted in his left arm, he used his right one to call the office and deliver remote instructions. Sometimes a meeting was held in the ward until doctors and nurses put an end to it.

With such strong work ethic and dedication, nothing could stop the company from achieving its goals.

Sensitively integrating the new development into the city's existing fabric was a key goal. Juxtaposing new and old materials allowed Xintiandi to retain its original charm and authentic flair with a stylish modern spin.

With collaboration as a shared value in the company, working towards the same goal instilled the team members with a strong sense of purpose. It took the team's combined ideas and work to pull off the complex project, to innovate, and to come up with quality products that would beat the competition.

Ten years have passed since Xintiandi was completed, and it is still standing in good shape—no wall cracks, collapsed structures, leaking pipes, sewer overflows, or falling bricks and tiles.

With properly-designed and well-maintained grease exhaust and ventilation systems, visitors enjoy dining at a smoke-free restaurant and strolling through the alleys surrounded by the smell of freshly brewed coffee and the yeasty aroma of the bakery.

It was the hard work, commitment and invaluable contribution of every dependable team player that helped make the company's collective dream a reality. The constant need to strive for excellence sowed the seeds for the "Shui On spirit"—Integrity • Dedication • Innovation • Excellence.

It is indispensable to cultivate motivation in the team as motivation is a vital business resource with a direct influence on performance.

With a tight budget at the early stage of the project, delivering trust and respect was the most straightforward way to keep the team engaged and motivated. Each team member knew the company believed in their smarts and skills, and trusted that they would act responsibly and be effective. They were given a chance to create opportunities for themselves and maintain real control over projects. Employees were motivated to build authentic relationships and felt committed to their leadership through a sense of ownership and pride in the work they were doing. They felt empowered to work from the heart and contribute to the company's shared vision.

When the marketing department proposed to host an Asian theme masquerade ball, other departments were also involved to offer ideas based on their perspectives and duties — Public Relations to reach the target audience, Leasing to manage client reception and handle clients' inquiries and Operations to offer logistics support. When there were not enough ladies in the ball, employees asked their girlfriends or wives for help. Even tenants, partners and suppliers were invited to join the brainstorming sessions.

Everyone liked it when their hard work paid off and ideas came to fruition.

While Xintiandi project was in full swing, Peregrine Investments, an investment company based in Hong Kong, lost all liquidity during the Asian financial crisis. Its collapse, triggered by the failure of a single large loan, struck many in the financial community and spread panic through all Hong Kong companies.

Shui On, however, continued to transfer its capital assets to Shanghai. Shui On Hong Kong slashed executive salaries as a way to avoid layoffs, while Shui On Shanghai committed to no pay cuts or layoffs, and bonus and promotion programs remained unchanged. The decision boosted morale and kept the employees motivated to take on new, challenging work.

Patience and perseverance have a magical effect before which difficulties disappear and obstacles vanish. The year 2000 marks a turning point in urban development of Shanghai, when efforts of Vincent Lo and his team eventually came to fruition.

As Shanghai's booming population moves into new apartment towers, the city's historic *Shikumen* houses are struggling to survive. People have finally realized that these historical buildings are the memory of the city, and the overall landscape they constitute displays the typical scene of Shanghai in a certain historical period. Thus, they are of value for protection.

The focus on urban regeneration efforts has seen the renovation of *Shikumen* houses in Xintiandi, which demonstrates how contemporary spaces are imagined in ways that conjure up "Old Shanghai".

Being in the right place at the right time with the right team is what truly helps make Xintiandi a Shanghai icon.

When Vincent Lo responded to the compliment from a senior government official by saying "A lot of people thought I was crazy last year", the official replied, "Genius is often just one step away from madness. And you are apparently a genius!"

Henry Cheng, the Managing Director, said emotionally, "Vincent is indeed crazy. And he drove us crazy, too. We are a bunch of crazy people working to produce innovative solutions for Xintiandi." Lo once joked that if the project couldn't be completed by the end of June 2001, all employees would jump into Huangpu River.

Banks that had been initially wary of the project approached Shui On with proactive loan offers at the beginning of 2001 when Xintiandi had received considerable recognition in Hong Kong and Taiwan.

Xintiandi has a powerful allure for visitors including politicians, entrepreneurs, bankers and cultural icons from Hong Kong and Taiwan. After having paid a visit to Xintiandi, a Hong Kong freelance journalist wrote an article lamenting Hong Kong's economic downturn that made entrepreneurs like Vincent Lo pivot their businesses away from the region.

The then Chief Executive Tung Chee-hwa once asked Lo at a dinner party why he hadn't done the same in Hong Kong. The reason was simple. Vincent Lo hadn't planned a major heritage tourism enclave in the region because it couldn't be done. Hong Kong does not have a glowing track record in cultural heritage preservation or much success in integrating it with visionary

Mr. Lo was made an Honorary Citizen of Shanghai in 2001. Xu Kuangdi, the then Mayor of Shanghai, presented him with a certificate of honor.

urban development due to lack of conservation foresight in the 1970s.

In Shanghai, on the contrary, Lo enjoyed swift approval and total support from the municipal government. Furthermore, the government immediately devised a plan to preserve another *Shikumen* neighborhood spanning 20 million square meters when Shanghai had gained an expertise and a successful model that Hong Kong has failed to acquire.

The risk of investing in Xintiandi in the 1997 Asian financial crisis was substantial, but Shui On was capable of discovering and exploiting new and emerging opportunities by, among other things, encouraging employees to broaden their horizons of thought and pitch innovative ideas.

Shui On has been facing a myriad of challenges in the course of its development, from conflicting expert opinions to varied approaches to heritage conservation. It encouraged architects with different cultural backgrounds to generate unique ideas and share diverse perspectives by fostering open channels of communication and a collaborative company culture.

PASSION, THE KEY TO SUCCESS

Shui On has created a culture where Xintiandi concept was conceived and innovation continued to thrive.

Nothing brings people together like a crisis. The economic downturn increases employees' commitment and productivity that money cannot buy. In the face of the 1997 Asian financial crisis, Shui On, bolstered by the strength of a resilient workforce, emerged stronger.

Team members who were involved in and committed to the Xintiandi project considered the experience a once in a lifetime, memory making, life changing adventure. They found great joy in creating throughout each step of the process rather than only in the outcome.

The Xintiandi initiative sparked a series of "Tiandi" revitalizations, and it has set a new benchmark for style that is fast being imitated around China, but never surpassed.

Lack of passion is the core issue. Passion needs to ooze from every pore of the entrepreneur. This passion translates into infectious enthusiasm that ultimately feeds the energy and drive of every employee in the office. And, most importantly, this passion is the glue that holds the company together and gets it through its most difficult times. Without this powerful edge, the company will be hard-pressed to overcome what it's up against.

Shui On is no exception. Passion cultivated in the financial crisis will not be duplicated, just like the improvisation of *Lanting Xu*.

CHAPTER 7

INNOVATION IS THE ADMISSION TICKET

When Xintiandi opened to the public, it was an immediate success. Many people attributed its success to a mere stroke of luck.

Indeed, luck depends largely on fate: being at the right place, at the right time. Yet success is a balance of preparation and opportunity. One needs to be prepared to respond when luck comes his way.

At the early stage of Xintiandi project, a market research company concluded that the idea to "invite people of Shanghai to *Shikumen* for dinner" wouldn't work. Consulting firms suggested that each *Shikumen* building house a luxury brand store: Louis Vuitton, Hermes, Gucci and Zegna, to name a few, to deliver an exclusive trendy experience. As a matter of fact, this trend didn't shape the retail landscape until ten years later, much longer than the investors could wait.

People typically predict the future based on relevant information gleaned from prior experiences, albeit uncertain. Whether Xintiandi would stand out in the uncertain market depended on Shui On's creative thinking and imaginative approach.

Managing Director Henry Cheng shared his perspective on the positioning of Xintiandi: Xintiandi will be an upscale and trendy entertainment hub that outperforms the bustling Huaihai Road Commercial Street situated nearby in terms of branding and shopping experience. Veering away from the typical mall set-up, Xintiandi will be the perfect launchpad to explore modern marvels and historic attractions.

Leisure concepts were not introduced in the city back then.

The commercialization of leisure took the initial form of shopping centers that offered the possibility to linger and enjoy the welcoming space. Unlike the traditional commercial business model that focuses on the financial results, leisure business aims at enriching the customer experience in every possible interaction.

Leisure is inextricably bound to Shanghai's urban development. At the early urban development stage, work, residence and shopping became dissociated from one another. Affluent residents gave up old *Shikumen* houses for new suburban apartments, and the rest were waiting to be relocated. The result was a decline in consumption, and the once prosperous Nanjing Road and Huaihai Road started to wither.

For those households that moved to the suburban area, downtown shopping centers were only accessible by vehicles. However, the lack of parking is one of the reasons for the declining vitality of the downtown business district. No matter how attractive a shopping center or a restaurant may be, it will not attract the customer who uses a motor car for shopping unless adequate parking facilities are provided. With the growing use of cars, this problem is becoming increasingly acute.

So where should the people of Shanghai go shopping in the 21st century?

When God closes one door, he opens another.

Shopping malls, hypermarkets and chain restaurants began springing up in the suburban residential areas, unleashing the community-based business model designed to fulfill the basic necessities of life.

Nevertheless, the newly rising Chinese urbanites began craving a new lifestyle for their leisure time — the pursuit of a certain type of lifestyle through shopping and entertainment emerged.

The conventional retailing business model that prevailed in Shanghai at the turn of the century includes department stores, supermarkets, grocery stores, etc. that were isolated from one another.

Despite the European charm and open courtyards of the lavish villas on both sides of the street, Hengshan Road pub street lacks a holistic planning process to shape active and well-connected public spaces.

The retail landscape is evolving. Success at the shelf is no longer about the depth and breadth of inventory, but rather creating welcoming environment, personalized services, ample choices and engaging experiences for customers.

With a strong business acumen, the developer was quick to adapt its operating model and capture the emerging market growth opportunity by creating a commercial complex with dining, retail, entertainment and cultural functions, on top of a large underground parking lot.

An integrated and holistic dining, shopping, entertainment and leisure complex injects fresh vitality into urban settlements and provides customers with a remarkable and individual experience that does not feel like a transaction. The complex fosters a living urban environment where customers feel welcome, want to spend their time, and ultimately want to make their purchase.

With a stylish tenant mix, the complex boasts a concentration of culture and lifestyle, and a range of restaurants, cafes, book stores, shops, and boutiques. Customers are privileged with a wide range of shopping and dining choices and seamless personalized and individual experiences.

One of the reasons the retail industry is so large and powerful is its diversity. Malls and shopping centers are successful because they provide customers with a wide assortment of products across many stores. Most popular lifestyle complexes cater to the tastes of a wide customer base in order to provide a unique shopping encounter.

The opening ceremony of the first Vidal Sassoon Academy in China, situated in the heart of Xintiandi

Shopping complexes are a witness to a new lifestyle where entertainment has become crucial and indispensable to shopping practices. Its customer-centric business model is key to success in today's marketplace and has revolutionized the retail model in Shanghai.

How can Xintiandi stand out, despite its size, confident of the long-term sustainability of its retail model among other shopping centers such as Plaza 66, Citic Square and Westgate Mall on West Nanjing Road?

Tony Wong, the first General Manager of Shanghai Xintiandi, revealed the secret behind its success years later. Xintiandi offers a wide selection of bars and restaurants, but the food and beverage are merely a nice supplement for its cultural and creative industry. Through extraordinary creative pioneer cultural content, Xintiandi empowers diverse social experience and builds a community with resonance and sense of belonging.

Let's take a look at the California Gold Rush that radically transformed California, the United States and the world. the Gold Rush prompted one of the largest migrations in U.S. history, with hundreds of thousands of migrants across the United States and the globe coming to California. While the Gold Rush allowed some of the earlier prospectors to become rich, it was the ensuing economic development that sprang up around the industry that would prove most profitable; new businesses designed to satisfy the needs of gold prospectors and the mining industry would ultimately result in the establishment of boomtowns, rapid economic growth and prosperity.

What does "the new vitality to be injected into the old buildings of *Shikumen*" that Benjamin Wood shared with Vincent Lo upon Xintiandi's foundation refer to? It is the tenants. A successful selection of tenants plays a crucial role in enhancing Xintiandi's attractiveness among its patrons. The shop owners, chefs, bartenders, bakers, hairstylists, designers and artists constitute a favorable tenant mix which is the major determinant and dynamic of Xintiandi's long-run prosperity.

Industrial design and cultural design, categorized as the upstream portion of the global industry chain with considerably higher value, are usually tightly controlled by developed countries. At the end of last century, "Made in China" was still lying among the low-end links of the global value chain for most industries, which carried out processing and manufacturing activities of lower added value.

In 1999, the cultural and creative industry in Shanghai was still considered in its infancy. Where should Xintiandi get the source of tenants in that industry to underpin its tenancy mix and vacancy profile?

The leasing team led by Mr. Wong had to turn to other Asian markets where creative economy has grown to become one of the great powerhouses of our times.

Xintiandi offers a platform for its tenants to showcase their creativity, just as the advertising slogan in its marketing booklet says: Come to enjoy or to create.

The collaboration of ideas resembles a talent show where the director (or developer) is responsible for the overall creative decisions of the production and the contestants (or tenants) demonstrate their talent and creativity to follow the written script and portray different characters.

The platform has its own tenant selection criteria:

1. Select the store that makes its Shanghai debut in Xintiandi
2. Select the brand with strong innovative capabilities and a high market share
3. The store needs to have a good capital structure as it will experience stagnant growth due to lower traffic in the early operation period. The tenant must assume a collaborative stand with Xintiandi through this time.
4. The tenant must be a mature brand with at least three to five years of experience in the industry.
5. The tenant must keep an engaged and loyal customer base ensuring customers will stick around upon the launch of a new store.
6. The tenant must honor the terms of the contract and follow property rules. It works together with the developer towards finding a solution to their differences that results in both sides being satisfied.

The tenant interview was special. Mr. Wong talked with potential tenants about the history and culture of *Shikumen*, the story of *Shikumen* being transformed into a retail destination, and innovative trends that would shape the future of the retail industry.

According to Mr. Wong, urban retail business model in the past employed complex division of labor where different establishments specialized in different industries, but the global retail and leisure landscape is undergoing fundamental change—lasting and structural—that fosters integration of leisure and dining. Spending of Shanghai people will shift from transactional to experiential. The variety of food concepts will increase dramatically as consumers have become much more adventurous, open to new experiences and familiar with global cuisines as a result of increased travel. In terms of fashion industry, as Chinese consumers have become increasingly sophisticated in their consumption patterns, their personal styles continue to evolve. Travelling, more than just movement, has become a chance to discover exciting cities, see fascinating sights, explore beautiful landscapes, and experience different cultures.

Sitting back in the sun-soaked model house and relaxing with a glass of hot-brewed tea or a cup of freshly ground coffee, Xintiandi leasing team and the prospective tenant representatives shared their insights into culture-based creativity. The decision was not made based on how creative a tenant's business plan was, but its innovation potential that could be unlocked.

"What is creativity?" Mr. Wong asked rhetorically, "Creativity is the act of turning new and imaginative ideas into reality. It is the ability to displace existing services or products and transcend your traditional ways of thinking."

Inspired and enlightened, the tenants were ready to spearhead a renaissance of innovation and potentially set the stage for a new era of sustained inventiveness and creativity.

In 1999, Liuli Gongfang from Taiwan was in the process of turning its artwork into products. Emboldened to rise to their highest potentialities, the founders Loretta H. Yang and Chang Yi decided to expand their brand footprint into Shanghai.

They boldly incorporated *liuli* into the food and beverages industry by opening the first hand-crafted *liuli* theme restaurant TMSK. With a dazzling interior as stunning as that of a crystal palace, the restaurant offered surprises around every corner: everything within sight and touch is made of, or partly of, *liuli*, including the bar, the tables and the chairs, the lamps and lanterns, the tableware and so on.

Founded by a Taiwanese couple and advertising's creative elites Kuo Cheng Feng and Wang Hsiao Hu, Shanghai Color retail store and Herbal Legend restaurant exemplify a new paradigm for business creativity. Having been two of the most important minds behind the excellent work on behalf of their clients for

Interiors of Herbal Legend restaurant, located in the South Block of Xintiandi

28 years before eventually gravitating to founding their own brands, the couple spearheaded innovation in retail and food industry through tapping Xintiandi's rich vein of resources.

Shanghai Color re-interprets Shanghai's unique intersection of cultures and influences in the past on the foundation of modern aesthetic color palette and showcases the city's characteristic mix of the traditional and the contemporary.

The Herbal Legend restaurant offers a wide range of Chinese dishes seasoned with the best traditional spices, coupled with a healthy food concept aimed at gourmets. The culinary masterminds at this herbal house draw upon thousands of years of Chinese traditional medicine expertise to brew over 30 kinds of nourishing herbal stews — tomato with Fo-ti, golden Chinese yam, stir-fried sliced pork with goji berries, duck with aweto, to name a few — offering a refreshing alternative for those searching for a healthy lifestyle.

La Maison French Cabaret, founded by the French brand of automobiles Peugeot, was the result of an even greater crossover investment. The general manager of La Maison is an artist who has never worked in the food industry, but he accepted the job offer out of fondness for Chinese food. The restaurant featured a combination of dinner with the spectacular Moulin Rouge musical dance entertainment, Paris' iconic not-to-miss night show.

Chen Yifei, a well-known Shanghainese contemporary artist, returned to his hometown after spending more than a decade immersed in study in the U.S. Pledging himself to the slogan of "Great Art, Great Vision," Chen Yifei's artistic revolution was manifest in multiple realms. In addition to oil painting, he transformed himself into a style entrepreneur, creating fashion brands, decorating hotels and selling high-end clothing and chic home furnishings. He created the Layefe Home label and situated his first retail outlet in the North Block.

Shui On pulled a few strings to invite Alan Zie Yongder, a multifaceted artist of Chinese descent, to bring his expertise and experience. He has been hailed as a legend in the Hong Kong publishing industry who opened 32 magazines in a month in the '70s and also introduced overseas publications to Hong Kong. He went on to become a founding member of the Hong Kong Designers Association and the Hong Kong Artists Alliance.

When the pony-tailed Yongder first came to visit Xintiandi model houses in ripped jeans, Hong Kong's latest trend in fashion, he was stopped by the guards who mistook him for a poor tramp in tattered clothes. Mr. Zie told the guard he was meeting Tony Wong, the General Manager and a good friend of his, the guard replied that Mr. Wong was not available. Mr. Zie then asked to meet David Ng, the Deputy General Manager and also a good friend of his, his request was denied again. He had no choice but to call Mr. Ng, who immediately ran to the entrance to welcome the long-awaited guest.

The participation of Alan Zie who was in charge of LifeZtore, a cultural and creative project backed by the Asian Development Bank, resulted in the opening of the first LifeZtore concept store in Shanghai. A total solution provider for home lifestyle products, LifeZtore offers inspirational design ideas, through a unique fusion of Oriental and Western styles, which are functional and with a twist of fun.

In addition to his role as the Art Director of LifeZtore Xintiandi, Mr. Zie was also the designer of Fu Lin Tang traditional Chinese medicine shop and participated in the art design of Shanghai Color and Herbal Legend restaurant.

Australian fashion designer Anthony Xavier Edwards displays his own form of Shanghai glamor in his Xintiandi Boutique, called X, where, alongside fabulously flamboyant fashions that guarantee no two outfits are identical, he offers fashion-forward designs that prominently feature elements of Chinese culture while other designers still place an emphasis on Western styles.

Today the creative industries represent an important mainstay of the local economy, and people are wondering where and when this concept came into existence. The answer, surprisingly, is the old *Shikumen* houses.

As a hub that houses creative practitioners and businesses from Asian regions and countries as well as the West, Xintiandi has placed the emerging concept in the antique *Shikumen* buildings in the belief that historical sites are capable of fostering creative openings, where memory and culture are not simply vibrant and alive, but also allow for transformation and renewal. The result is rapid and unprecedented growth in the creative economy and Xintiandi's commercial success: no visit to Shanghai is complete without exploring the bustling pedestrian street of Xintiandi.

Xintiandi has been promoting cross-industry collaborations for more than a decade, constantly merging the worlds of fashion, music, art, fitness, health, reading and so on, using food as the common denominator.

Creativity and innovation are the heart and soul of Xintiandi retail business that bring a diverse curation of tenants.

The pursuit of unique ambiance and feel of the cafes, pubs and restaurants keeps attracting customers, and most importantly, converting them into loyal patrons. The right atmosphere entices and engages customers who are craving more than just a jolt of caffeine or alcohol.

Already, Xintiandi has set a new benchmark for style that is fast being replicated around China.

On a national level, many replicas of this project have sprung up without a clear positioning strategy: the developers have no idea whether to adopt traditional retail or experiential retail model. Focus is primarily placed on the architectural replication rather than the commercial operations; thus, losses and risks are created by lack of retail focus within such a property. Poor tenant mix, including unreasonable levels of competition, will eventually jeopardize the shopping mall's own financial health.

Too often, great ideas don't materialize. Creative people are rarely lacking inspiration; rather, they lack effective processes and tools to make their ideas happen. Then how did Xintiandi

LifeZtore is situated at the end of the corridor on the top floor of the mall in the South Block. Three colorful doors are cleverly put up along the corridor with seating to draw customers in.

Fu Lin Tang traditional Chinese medicine shop boldly features bright pops of color to express its cross-cultural emotion.

EAST MEETS WEST

The architects, marketing and engineering departments, as well as shop tenants, are studying the renovation plans of the business premises.
The person standing in the photo is Tony Wong, the first General Manager of Xintiandi. The second on the left is Albert Chan who is responsible for the planning and design of Xintiandi.

validate its new design hypotheses?

The project documentation and records unraveled the secret behind: Xintiandi adopted a market-based development approach involving project construction and the negotiation of a lease simultaneously, rather than a widely used construction-based approach.

This is similar to the focus on how facility design impacts teaching and learning.

Addressing the needs and goals of the principals through school design planning before the actual construction phase begins provides better articulation of the vision and continuity in the educational delivery.

Wide participation in educational facility planning results in greater understanding of the educational program, more functional buildings, and a greater interest and pride on the part of school administrators.

Initially, Xintiandi architects found it hard to determine the location of the stairs, main entrance and rooms as the prospective tenant and its requirements were unknown. The space had to be carefully designed to allow as much flexibility as possible for any future tenants.

To solve this problem, the project team came up with an idea: engage early with the future tenants in designing that would be tailored to their exact needs.

The market-based approach allows for optimally efficient use of the building as the future tenants specify how they want it to be designed to meet their business needs—where to place the stairs and doors and how to arrange the piping system of the kitchen. The interiors of an upscale restaurant are well-furnished along with expensive carpets, delicately carved wall panels and wall dressing mirrors to compliment the furniture and add character and value to the restaurant. Unlike typical quick service restaurants, cafes and pubs, an upscale restaurant usually features a separate stairway for the circulation flow of the waitstaff to avoid stains on the carpets.

The tenants were involved in the *Shikumen* construction and able to incorporate their specific needs in the future space to optimize customer experience and create value.

Among the first tenants to settle in Xintiandi was a Japanese music restaurant Ark Livehouse, one of the few bastions of live music that displays Shanghai rock scene greeted with enthusiastic rock'n roll fans. Located on the second floor of a *Shikumen* building above Shanghai Color and Xavior that retain a quiet and elegant ambiance of style, the restaurant keeps the sound of live music and dance parties inside its own space by having a couple of extra layers of insulation under flooring and double pane windows for soundproofing so that all the stores can coexist harmoniously.

This unprecedented approach to building to suit the tenants' requirements is a result of bold, experienced leadership.

Being an essential cog in defining and communicating the vision of the project and how this aligns to business strategy, a competent project manager is thinking strategically and applying commercial common sense to the space planning along the way. Henry Cheng, Managing Director appointed by Vincent Lo, is such a person with incredible capability in development and tremendous expertise in marketing that drove the commercial success of Xintiandi.

Widely credited with his profound knowledge and insights, Mr. Cheng has shared his inspirational thoughts: the most successful retail business models are those that always remain half a step ahead of the consumer. There's little commercial point in getting too far ahead of the market, especially given the time cost of waiting for the market to mature.

It is extremely challenging to be half a step ahead of the rapidly changing retail market for once, let alone always. The immediate success of Xintiandi drives successive teams to steam ahead with solutions that will instill Xintiandi with a lasting vitality. It takes painstaking effort to keep moving; just like climbing up the mountain, the only way is up.

INNOVATION IS THE ADMISSION TICKET

Every business aims to grow sustainably. So does Shui On.

When businesses require a large financial investment, some choose to sell their innovative projects for funding while others partner with venture capital firms in the hope of going public to raise capital from public investors.

When Xintiandi has received considerable recognition, a European fund company offered to buy the project in order to cash out some or all of their shares at a later time. Vincent Lo declined the offer and said jokingly to its founder that he couldn't afford the price. "Just name your price." the founder took it seriously. "No matter how much you offer, I won't sell it." replied Vincent Lo firmly.

Despite Shui On's need to raise capital in 2001 in order to invest in subsequent projects of Taipingqiao Lake, the office and Lakeville residential developments, it was determined to keep hold of the Xintiandi project out of its full confidence in the city's economic prospects as the new land of opportunity and a place to settle down.

Shanghai's real estate market had dropped to an all-time low in 2001 before it started to rise two years later and continued to climb for ten straight years.

Shui On is fully aware that the prerequisite for unified marketing, leasing and operational strategies to adapt to the ever-changing market and stay attuned to the target customers' needs is retaining the ownership of the project. To succeed in the fast-paced world, it has to stay ahead of the innovation curve, keep abreast of market trends and quickly spice up its strategies.

There are also political factors behind. The row of houses opposite the site of the First National Congress of the CPC must accommodate cultural facilities such as galleries, postal museum, visitor center, etc. No food or entertainment businesses are allowed in those houses as a token of respect for the site. If a change of ownership occurs, the sacred place of solemnity might be jeopardized and trigger global attention.

A sustainable business follows a business philosophy based

on balancing business planning, financial feasibility, strategic rationale and legal considerations. The myopic pursuit of short-term gains has seen the drivers of long-term value creation sacrificed at the altar of short-term profitability.

In order to make a quick profit, the developer of an office building on Huaihai Road offered the option to lease or to buy the property. The result was a commercial property that blended residential and commercial uses into one space, creating uncomfortable encounters of both the residents and the office workers.

Residents complained about the indiscriminate commercial use of the residential building that would jeopardize the environment needed for housing. Office workers also felt degraded in such unpleasant work environment. High-performing companies and affluent residents gradually moved out of the building, leading to falling rents and smaller business tenants. Without ownership in severalty, the developer failed to adjust the tenant mix to upgrade the environment.

One of the ancient and most prosperous commercial streets in Shanghai saw empty storefronts after a makeover with wider sidewalks and taller buildings. The reason behind is that the establishments on the streets, sold to multiple individuals, corporations, and entities, now harbors diverse businesses without a coherent strategy which has imperiled the prospects of the entire area.

Despite its inadequate cash flow and access to capital, Shui On managed to keep its business afloat while holding onto Xintiandi project.

Listed on the Hong Kong Stock Exchange in 2006, Shui On Land saw a huge influx of capital that came with significant challenges. Before Shui On went public, Vincent Lo was the sole owner that made all business decisions. But in a publicly traded company, management has less freedom to make decisions as they have to get the majority of shareholder approval.

Innovations are always likely to have unintended

INNOVATION IS THE ADMISSION TICKET

The Postal Museum opposite the Memorial Hall of the First National Congress of the CPC.

consequences. Revenues can be huge, but highly uncertain, while the hit rates are low and the costs of failure are often very high.

Commercial yet artistic, Xintiandi is an enchanting neighborhood exuding the feel of Shanghai in 1920s with its old *Shikumen* buildings. The outstanding artistic endeavors take time, effort and money. The artistic expression of *Shikumen*'s original charm and authentic flair that utilized all the buildings' original bricks and tiles in the restoration seems to have marked the high point of Xintiandi's reputation.

Stockholders are impatient and risk averse. They are only interested in financial returns and focus on investing capital effectively to generate more cash flow with less risk. Investors prioritize quarterly earnings over long-term innovation and quickly shift their capital elsewhere for a more profitable investment.

The initial success of Xintiandi cannot be replicated because of Shui On's patience and commitment to help innovations go to scale in a booming market where businesses are prioritizing short-term returns over long-term investments.

Management has been facing increasing pressure from shareholders since Shui On went public, compelled to pursue growth and secure short-term gains.

"Sustainable growth fosters long-term success instead of rapid and reckless expansion", said Xu Jialu, a former Vice Chairman of the National People's Congress. Although profits determine the growth rate of a business, a rapidly growing one may end up risking its resources in the long haul.

Xintiandi represents, in many ways, the burgeoning cultural confidence that has witnessed and led the changing of Shanghai's commercial development as well as shaping the city's cultural memories. Whether it will continue to transcend the need for shopping and dining by remaining an expression of culture and lifestyle remains to be seen.

CHAPTER 8

PROTECTING CULTURE IN URBAN REGENERATION

Anyone in the property industry will tell you the key to property investment is "location, location, location". But Xintiandi has proved that creative space planning outweighs the advantage of a prime location. Developers may combine residential, commercial, cultural, institutional, and even entertainment functions to create a fully-blended multi-use setting.

Does creative space planning equate with outstanding architectural design? Xintiandi's success has always been a mystery. Other commercial real estate professionals came to visit Xintiandi to figure out the secret formula which, the developer generously shared, is, in addition to land development, the reinterpretation of the material history of *Shikumen* houses.

Modern buildings are usually of low cultural value. A newly constructed temple, for example, is in essence just a new building with no cultural identity. Once the temple captures the visitors' faith through the presentation of respected monk and combining Buddhist beliefs to the local faiths—devotees visit the temple with wishes that they hope will come true and will bring them good luck—the energy of the temple is recharged, cultural value formally recognized, and tourism landmark set up.

Land resources and architectural designs have long been acknowledged and highly valued in the real estate industry. In contrast, the cultural dimension of urban development is still too often misunderstood or undervalued, or seen as an optional extra to be added when the hard work of 'real' development is done.

Urban culture consists of traditional culture and modern culture and includes material and nonmaterial elements. Material culture can be found anywhere at any time, while nonmaterial culture is intangible and needs to be identified with perception.

Urban culture is a complex whole of collective human beliefs that have to be carefully selected and reinterpreted through a strong vision and long-term outlook to rejuvenate the commercial real estate project.

Xintiandi has rapidly enhanced its cultural values through developing urban cultural resources by strengthening the narrative of tradition and modernity.

Despite its lofty name, Xintiandi has more modest hopes, intending to painstakingly salvage the historical narratives of original *Shikumen* buildings but ultimately transcend the nostalgia of historic preservation.

Shikumen buildings, although historically valuable, have become so decrepit and grimy from decades of overcrowding, heavy communal usage and minimal infrastructural maintenance that its residents are eager to be relocated to new residential towers.

The reconfiguration of *Shikumen* neighborhoods created new outdoor pedestrian streets, providing visitors with their choice of restaurants, cafés, boutiques, galleries, and nightclubs. Will the visitors find it inviting, cosmopolitan and glamorous?

Should the role of *Shikumen* be reimagined to evoke greater appreciation for the antique buildings?

The primitive brick walls, tiled roofs, the dark-colored gates, and the gate lintel carved with coiled patterns are all telling old stories.

Xintiandi focuses on the interpretation of *Shikumen* that integrates cosmopolitanism, tradition and culture, considered as attributes of Shanghai's modernization during its heyday in the 1920s and 1930s. Not all histories are equally marketable. Only those with connections to the colonial period of Shanghai are actively preserved in an attempt to show that Shanghai was once

Artist Xu Yuanzhang (third from left), Shui On's Deputy Marketing General Manager David Ng (first from left) and foreign consular officers at the Xu Yuanzhang Recollections of the Old Shanghai Days Art Exhibition held at Xintiandi model houses.

an international metropolis.

Xintiandi has inspired imaginations as well as recollections of the Old Shanghai days.

On Jan 21 2000, Xu Yuanzhang Recollections of the Old Shanghai Days Art Exhibition was held at Xintiandi model houses. All of the watercolor paintings on display were old villas and houses in Shanghai that visually captured the historical and cultural essence of the city. Xu has dedicated himself to painting old villas and houses in Shanghai for almost 10 years to keep cultural memories fresh through his paintings since he witnessed the demolition of old villas in the process of urban regeneration in 1990s. Some of the buildings he has painted are no longer standing. They live on, however, in his colorful renderings.

Although Xu is not a prominent painter, the opening ceremony was surprisingly well received by foreign diplomats and consular officials. It turned out that Xu is the grandson of Zhou Zongliang, who was the general agent for German companies operating here in the 1920s. Xu's childhood home is a compound of five houses and a large garden, covering 5,000 square meters, where Xu hosts parties on Sundays and holidays. Finely dressed diplomats and consular officials come to socialize and dance waltzes as classical western music pours from a phonograph that harks back to a different age.

The exhibition has additionally garnered favorable attention from news media that ran Xu's story with the headline "The Last Aristocrat of Shanghai". The exhibition has further framed the public's understanding of these structures as emblematic of the city's identity as a hybrid fusion of Chinese and Western culture that was uniquely "Shanghai".

The art exhibition has evoked fascination from the young, and nostalgia from the old. In a city where shiny newness once reigned large, and where historic buildings were regularly razed, nostalgia has become a motivating force for historic preservation.

Antique Shanghai pop music in the 1930s and '40s, a true auditory feast of Old Shanghai, has an unparalleled glamour. *Rose, Rose, I Love You*, *Shanghai Nights* and *The Rose Blooms Everywhere* are among the popular songs composed by Chen Gexin, a famed and accomplished musician in the 1930s.

In memory of the late artist that no longer sounds familiar to the young generation of Shanghai, Shui On invited his son Chen Gang, a renowned pianist and one of the joint composers of the famous *Butterfly Lovers* Violin Concerto, as recommended by other artists, to hold a recital *My Father and I* at Xintiandi. The concert has captivated audiences of all ages while simultaneously telling the life stories and composing experiences of the two generations of musicians through melodious music.

Chen Gexin enjoyed equal popularity with Nie Er, musician and composer of the national anthem of People's Republic of China, and Xian Xinghai, one of the most prominent composers in the recent history of modern music best known for the *Yellow River Cantata*, in the first half of the 20th century. In 1938, Chen was appointed as the music professor of the Sino-French Drama Academy. He started a singing and conducting training class to rehearse and perform revolutionary Soviet songs. After the 1937 Japanese invasion of Shanghai, he began writing his own anti-Japanese resistance anthems, such as *No Trespassing for The Enemy*, *Through This Cold Winter*, in the foreign concessions which became an isolated parcel of territory since the war. His songs were a vital source of inspiration to the Chinese soldiers, but incurred hatred of the enemy.

The foreign concessions came to an abrupt end in 1941 when Japanese troops stormed in immediately following the attack on Pearl Harbor. During the Second Sino-Japanese War, Chen was imprisoned and tortured for three months in the notorious Shanghai Jisifeier Road 76 (now 435 Wanhangdu Road), by the Imperial Japanese Army for his patriotic songs. After his release, Chen continued to write songs including *Rose, Rose, I Love You* and *The Rose Blooms Everywhere* that became an instant hit and gave a glimmer of hope to the people of Shanghai in hard times.

With the wars ended, the country consolidated and the People's Republic founded in 1949, Chen returned to Shanghai and continued his songwriting for Kunlun Film Company.

Rose, Rose, I Love You became the 1951 Billboard top hit song but the 1-million-dollar royalties remained unclaimed with the announcement of "composer unknown, probably in China".

At that time, China was fighting the United States in the Korean War. "If the Americans call me over so I can collect my royalties, I'll donate them to the homeland to make airplanes!" said Chen Gexin.

In 1957, the patriotic musician got swept up in the "Anti-Rightist Campaign". He was labeled a "rightist" and sent to Baimaoling Farm—a re-education-through-labor camp a little over 100 miles from Shanghai in Anhui Province. In the early 1960s, China was going through the Great Famine when Chen Gexin died at 46 years old due to starvation and illness in Baimaoling. In 1979, his "rightist" label was removed and reputation was restored, but China lost a patriotic musician forever.

Chen Gang started to learn composition from his father Chen Ge Xin since he was 15 years old. From 1955 to 1959, he

Famous composer Chen Gang performing The Butterfly Lovers at Xintiandi

was a student at the Shanghai Conservatory of Music, studying composition. In 1959, Chen Gang, together with another student, He Zhanhao, composed the violin concerto *Butterfly Lovers*, one of the most well-known Chinese classical music works.

Meanwhile, Chen Gang had to distance himself from his father to stay out of trouble. This gave him great pain as his father was also his first music teacher and lifelong mentor.

When Chen Gexin managed to hear a recording of *The Butterfly Lovers* and that the composer was his son, he sent off a letter to his wife in Shanghai telling her to bring him a copy of the score. She didn't as she was afraid that any contact between the two could jeopardize their son's career, and this has become the most regrettable episode in Chen Gang's life.

At the recital, Chen Gang reminisced about old times and shared his feelings that the comeback of the old songs was a reflection of the city's history and its returning diversity.

A flurry of activities—art exhibitions, parties, social gatherings—with a hefty dose of nostalgia has been held at Xintiandi. Financial tycoons are recalling Shanghai's past glory as a center of international finance and trade; famous writers are chewing over the history of *Tingzijian Literature* produced by

Shanghai's canon of famous writers who lived in *Tingzijians* and the immense impact Eileen Chang, a Chinese-born American essayist, novelist, and screenwriter, has had on Chinese literature; renowned artists are discussing measures to protect and revive Kunqu Opera. These nostalgia themed activities have greatly contributed to the reinterpretation of *Shikumen* buildings and the awakening of the city's cultural memory.

Throughout human history, revisiting of the past has laid out the foundation for the great advancements of a nation, a country or a city. The Renaissance, for example, was a fervent period of European cultural, artistic, political and economic "rebirth" following the Middle Ages. It is about pushing the boundaries of what we know — and what we could achieve.

Locals are especially nostalgic about the 1920s and 1930s, when Shanghai established itself as the most renowned city in Asia. *Shikumen* buildings present a nostalgic narrative of Shanghai's modernization during that time in the hope that the city will revive its status as the world's financial and commercial center.

The city's rulers are endeavoring to build a glittering nexus of commerce on old Shanghai's faded ruins. They aim for the city to be the next global financial hub by 2030. Nostalgia, on the other hand, is the cultural support that reflects the city's determination to regain its past glory.

Shanghai, transformed from an international financial hub almost a century ago to a city of commercialism and consumerism, and then an important industrial center since 1949, was on its way to becoming the new gateway to global finance at the turn of the 21st century. This proves the theory regarding the spiral trajectory of social progress that goes ever onward and upward.

From a philosophical point of view, Xintiandi's reconfiguration of *Shikumen* alleys was in line with the abovementioned theory. Xintiandi exudes the feel of Shanghai in 1920s with its old stone *Shikumen* and pedestrian-only streets where you'll encounter some of the city's finest boutiques, restaurants, cafés, and bars, vividly showing the popular sentiment of Shanghai Nostalgia as well as a symbol that projects the city's bright global future. The cultural recognition of the sentiment and the sense of belonging that derives from it have encouraged customers' repeat patronage of Xintiandi for over a decade.

This opinion is well supported by the host city's exhibition theme "New Horizons Forever" which was selected from 40,000 submissions. Shanghai pavilion, with an exterior that evoked the glorious past of the city through the inclusion of a replica *Shikumen* doorway, made explicit reference to the sustainable urban development theme of the expo and showcased the unanimous voice of the city to realize this goal.

What we are today comes from our thoughts of yesterday, and our present thoughts build our life of tomorrow. Urban cultural heritage is not only the historical witness of urban development, but also the realistic carrier of urban civilization.

Xintiandi played an active role in shaping the city's cultural memories through empowering diverse social experiences.

In 2000, Shanghai was short of entrepreneurship—the mentality of pursuing stability was strong among graduates. Fresh grads were inclined to work for large corporations and young people got their money through a big fat inheritance. A startup campaign was therefore held at Xintiandi in March to unleash the entrepreneurial spirit that Shanghai had so cultivated during the colonial years.

The campaign, inspired by Vincent Lo's own experience, offered a prize of 100,000 yuan to the winner for a startup program. With a HK$100,000 loan from his father in 1970, Vincent Lo has built a multibillion-dollar property and construction empire within three decades.

Vincent Lo was inspired by the determination of the central character "Jonathan Livingston Seagull" in Richard Bach's book of the same name when he founded Shui On. The seagull Jonathan was not satisfied with the average flying skill like his fellow ordinary seagulls in the flock, and thus he continued to practice until he became a perfect aviator. But, unsatisfied with his new life, Jonathan returned to Earth to find others like himself to tell them what he'd learned and to spread his love for flight. The seagull remains the symbol of Shui On Group's today, representing its spirit to strive for excellence.

As an entrepreneurial role model, Vincent Lo wanted to help young people in Mainland China to turn big business ideas into business reality through the startup campaign—anyone who could come up with a business plan approved by the expert panel would be awarded a prize of 100,000 yuan, expert advice and work space at Xintiandi.

The news spread like wildfire and attracted hundreds of applicants, most of whom in lower social classes. This life-changing opportunity ignited young people's passion. When a young man, sitting on the train to Zhengzhou, Henan Province, saw the article about the campaign on *Southern Weekly*, a Chinese weekly newspaper, on the ground, he took another train down to Shanghai right after he arrived at the station.

The reform of the domestic household registration system in the new century signals a progressive relaxation of the control of domestic migration and a welcome effort of reducing the urban-rural barriers. Young people with career aspirations and life goals are flocking to metropolitan areas, working hard to realize the great Chinese Dream. Without a powerful or wealthy family background, they rely entirely upon the labor of their own hands in the hope of changing their fate.

The rise of China was in essence the collective effort of the hard work and persistence of Chinese people.

More than a real estate project, Xintiandi is also a platform that provides equal opportunities for everyone, regardless of their class, as long as they can contribute to society by finding innovative solutions to practical, financial or social issues.

The campaign would help potential entrepreneurs star in their own success stories and showcase Xintiandi as a splendid example to stimulate innovation and inspiration.

Jiang Qiong Er, a fresh grad who studied industrial design at Shanghai Tongji University, was among the hundreds of applicants. After rounds of expert panel review, she won the young entrepreneur award that came with a prize of 100,000 yuan and work space at Xintiandi to launch her own namesake jewelry label that features nuts and bolts industrial jewelry.

Xintiandi specially held an "graduation ceremony" for Jiang in the model houses with the attendance of artists, cultural figures, diplomats and corporate partners, coupled with a fashion show where, against the backdrop of the *Shikumen* houses, models sashayed wearing the industrial jewelry. Her 70-year-old grandma, wearing the industrial jewelry, was walking the runway that pushed the atmosphere of the fashion show to a climax. Jiang announced on the spot that her journey of designing started at Xintiandi and she would further her studies in furniture and interior design in France on the second day.

After she graduated in Paris, she started a company with Jean-Marie Charpentier, the famous French architect who designed the Shanghai Grand Theatre. Hermes China was one of her clients.

Understanding more and more Chinese craftsmanship and the deft skills of these craftsmen, Jiang Qiong Er was touched by the power and beauty of their work. This became the impetus of the dream to have the world appreciate the craftsmanship and design of China. Together with Hermes group, Jiang set up Shang Xia in 2008 and opened its first boutique in 2010. The brand started with four product ranges—garments, accessories, furniture, and homeware. The idea was to tap into the skillset of China's artisans to craft products imbued with quality, attention to detail, design sensibility and sophistication.

The name "Shang Xia" ("Up Down" in Mandarin) was chosen to express two opposing forces or sides—yin and yang, extraordinary and ordinary—that come together to strike a harmonious balance. With a mission to resurrect and nurture the sense of craftsmanship which was lost as China became a

Jiang Qiong Er (second from left), a fresh grad from Shanghai Tongji University, her father Xing Tonghe (first from right), a well-renowned architect, and Shui On executives on Jiang's Industrial Romance concept jewelry design and exhibition at Xintiandi model houses in July 2000

Jiang furthered her study in France after her Xintiandi debut in the art arena. She founded Shang Xia, a Chinese luxury brand, in partnership with the French luxury group Hermes. Walking into Shang Xia's flagship store at Xintiandi is like entering a grotto of clouds.

mass-production economy, Shang Xia's brand offerings are built on centuries of Chinese heritage with top-notch quality adding a contemporary twist on traditional Chinese aesthetics and crafts.

The brand has drawn Western attention and garnered extensive recognition. While Jiang's works received wide acclaim and distinguished design awards at national and international level, the appreciation for high-quality Made in China has spread among European fashion markets.

The little seagull soared high, with outspread wings.

Shanghai media soon became attached to the refurbished *Shikumen* buildings and the activities held at Xintiandi, the complexes that sprouted in the new century.

When the 108 contestants of the Miss World pageant were waving greetings to the public during their visit to Xintiandi in 2003, they immediately received wide media coverage. In spite of eager invitations from luxury hotels, the organizer of the pageant aimed at a unique landmark that would showcase the distinctive characteristics of the city. Harboring an impressive collection of *Shikumen* houses that are representative of Shanghai's indigenous cosmopolitan culture, Xintiandi realized that opportunity was knocking at its door.

To convince the organizer, Xintiandi presented its exquisitely designed event proposal themed "Miss World in Xintiandi — Shanghai through their beautiful eyes" with two major highlights.

Firstly, the contestants were expected to stroll along the *Shikumen* alleys, visit the courtyards opening on to the central bay featuring Chinese traditional tables and chairs, taste Chinese tea and appreciate Chinese paintings, creating a mix of vibrant cultures as a result of a modern beauty pageant and the historical narratives of original *Shikumen* settlements. A total of 108 professional photographers, many of whom were art editors of magazines and newspapers, would be invited to photograph these beautiful contestants to promote the publicity of Miss World in Shanghai.

Moreover, 108 pieces of red bricks would be made to carry

PROTECTING CULTURE IN URBAN REGENERATION

Contestants of the Miss World pageant are strolling the pedestrian-friendly alleyways at Xintiandi.

The girls are standing next to the 108 red bricks that were put together to build a Shikumen *shape, striking the most graceful and elegant pose, shouting in unison to the photographers "I love Shanghai, I love Xintiandi!"*

their autographs. The final competition of Miss World 2003 would be held in Hawaii. No matter who would be crowned, her autograph would have already been collected.

With such creative ideas that brought its vision to life, Xintiandi successfully impressed the organizer and took its brand to an entirely new level.

The surpassing charm of these beautiful contestants was a great ornament to Xintiandi alleys as well as the clubhouse One Xintiandi where their presence left a scented trail.

108 professional cameras pointing at the 108 contestants on the plaza at the North Block pushed the atmosphere of the event to a climax. The spectacular moment when the girls were standing next to the 108 red bricks that were put together to build a *Shikumen* shape, striking the most graceful and elegant pose, shouting in unison "I love Shanghai, I love Xintiandi!" was recorded by the photographers.

The soft clicks of the cameras, flashes of light and a moment in time were captured forever. The beauty of the girls is boundless, and the charm of Xintiandi is and will remain timeless.

Luciano Pavarotti, one of the most acclaimed and popular Italian tenors of all time, had his hugely successful Shanghai debut at the packed Shanghai Grand Theatre. Even more eye-catching was the news conference, held in Va Bene, an up-market Italian eatery at Xintiandi, to promote his round-the-world farewell tour concert.

The premiere of *The Road Home*, a Chinese-style implicit romance film directed by the distinguished director Zhang Yimou, was held at Xintiandi. Coincidentally, the premiere of *Breaking the Silence* that stars the internationally known Gong Li also took place at Xintiandi.

The currently popular Chinese genre of time travel TV series and fictions actually dates back to 2000, when the artist Chen Yifei held a fashion show in which models wearing white dresses traveled from the *Shikumen* alleys in the 20th century to the Xintiandi model houses in the 21st century. The show was eye-

PROTECTING CULTURE IN URBAN REGENERATION

The premiere of The Road Home, *a Chinese-style implicit romance film directed by the distinguished director Zhang Yimou, was held at the Xintiandi model house.*

opening yet sophisticated. Chen's appreciation for Xintiandi's slogan—yesterday meets tomorrow at present, epitomized his cultural nostalgia for old Shanghai.

Chen also incorporated the time travel genre into his movie *Old Dreams on the Sea* in which a girl appears like a dream and leads the painter out into the morning sun of the old city, transcending barriers of time and space.

The movie reflects both Chen's personal memories and his search for the Shanghai of the 1930s. What Chen portrayed in these figures, however, was not their personalities or life stories; instead, Chen used them as expressive tools, vehicles through which he addressed an attitude for respecting history while exploring the future. His views represented both a city and an era, shared by a growing number of young people a decade later.

Xintiandi drives an active program of fashion events and keeps some of them undisclosed to surprise the visitors that bump into celebrities unexpectedly. An entertainment journalist from *Xinmin Weekly* wrote: "Xintiandi, where local stars prepare to be outshone by global superstars, and beautiful women upstaged by even prettier faces."

Having developed into an iconic modern trendy landmark of the city, Xintiandi has become a favored hang-out for the white-collar workers, as, according to those in the office buildings along Huaihai Road, "the best way to rate your fashion sense is by the number of times you visit Xintiandi every month".

Xintiandi has inadvertently become Shanghai's showcase platform for various sectors ranging from automobile, electronics, cosmetics, fashion and film.

On its pathway to a global city, Shanghai stands for tolerance and embrace of people and culture from outside. In the past decade, Xintiandi has witnessed and led the changing of Shanghai's commercial development as well as reshaping the city's cultural memories.

In 2002, a European traveling artist conducted an interesting urban culture experiment "What's Art?" at Xintiandi. She had done similar experiments in various countries in Europe and Asia.

The artist put cardboard sheets printed with "Art" on an eight-meter-square space on Yifei Square (now Fountain Square), inviting bystanders and onlookers to write down their understanding of art.

The answers were varied: art is love; art stands for a beautiful dream; art represents a societal and personal progression from solely material to spiritual... There might be thousands of different answers. But the real purpose of this experiment was to test the citizen participation in civic life—attitude to life, community engagement, and social interaction—to demonstrate the characteristics of Shanghai's urban culture and level of globalization.

Nevertheless, most of the onlookers shied away from participating in the activity, epitomizing their attitude of standing aloof from things that they thought were irrelevant to their life. The majority of participants were foreign tourists and

PROTECTING CULTURE IN URBAN REGENERATION

A cultural exchange project between China and Japan, launched by Ondekoza, a Japanese troupe specializing in taiko drumming, is held at the Xintiandi model house.

Young Shanghai football fans meeting players from AC Milan, one of Europe's top football powers in front of the clubhouse One Xintiandi

The globally recognized singer Ricky Martin decided on Xintiandi after looking around several candidate concert venues.

Upon completion of Shanghai International Circuit, best known as the venue for the annual Formula 1 Chinese Grand Prix, the F1 organizing committee, in the hope of maximizing the publicity value of their entry, spent 700,000 yuan on a Formula One themed display using laser effects, giant screens and fireworks. A show car is on display among a cluster of trendy cafes.

Jackie Chan and other Hong Kong stars at the opening ceremony of the Star East restaurant

Two models dressed up in French costumes standing in the Shikumen alley in a magic show during the French Week, presenting a cross-cultural experience for the audience

local young people with overseas living experience. Some even encouraged their children to engage in the activity.

Countless performances, shows and commercial promotions from home and abroad are held in Shanghai, making it highly receptive to foreign cultures. However, without confluence of domestic and overseas influences, the notion of global city will cause Shanghai to lose the diversity and colorfulness of its indigenous culture.

The fact that indigenous cultural creativity is produced, deployed, used and enjoyed gives Shanghai its unique spirit as one of the country's most modern, diverse, and cosmopolitan cities. Thus, the particular patterns of interaction between the local and the global hold sway to form a local interpretation of the global as a potential vector of original creative process.

The citizens' indifferent attitude toward "What's Art" indicated room for improvement in urban cultural development. As the society progresses, citizen engagement will advance together with the globalization of the city.

At an early stage in Shanghai's urbanization process, greater emphasis was placed on the tangible urban buildings than the intangible urban culture, especially the community interaction and bonding fostered in public space which was missing in traditional Chinese culture.

The assistant of a European traveling artist is laying cardboard sheets on the plaza to conduct an urban culture experiment "What's Art?" at Xintiandi to test local citizens' attitude towards life, personal relationships and public interaction.

A pair of foreign tourists wrote down their understanding of art on the cardboard sheets.

There is a huge difference between the Chinese painters and their Italian counterparts. Chinese artists prefer working directly onto a piece of paper to be displayed on the wall upon completion, while Italian artists tend to create works of art on the outdoor piazzas, rocks, statues, and walls that are able to resist fading in sunlight and water and will be passed down over generations. The sharp contrast is a result of distinct cultural awareness of and behavior in public spaces.

Xintiandi is a splendid example of preserving architectural heritage, recasting the area as a consumer's paradise, activating the city's most dynamic public art gallery while inserting public space which has become central to the cultural identity of the city.

FLOWmarket, which was founded by Danish artist Mads Hagstrom and aiming to cater for the soul, made its China debut at Xintiandi.

The market that sells empty bottles, cartons and cans with labels that preach spiritual concepts and self-love for just a few yuan has proven a hit with locals and tourists.

People buy these as symbols, something to remind them of things they need to change or something that they would like to do differently, just like worshippers praying for good fortune in a temple—bottles of courage for men, cans of beauty for ladies, cartons of wisdom for children. Interestingly, local residents care more about their own selves when choosing the labels while foreigners and people with overseas experience tend to buy products that relate to the society or the environment.

The buying habits reflect people's inner world and thinking patterns. The self-serving traits of some residents, emblematic of the ancient agricultural civilization, are shown in all aspects of life: inconsiderate behavior on public transportation, pollution from factory waste water, and even incompatible building design to urban fabric.

The market and street performance arts are essential for the city to motivate its citizens to adopt new behaviors. Regular

EAST MEETS WEST

The award-winning American street-painter Kurt Wenner, sitting on the South Block plaza of Xintiandi to finish up his pavement art with special chalks, has excited people worldwide with his unique 3D street paintings. Sprawling over sidewalks, walls, and public spaces, Wenner enjoys creating interactive works and onlookers are encouraged to "walk" into the design.

Fishing in Old Shanghai *by Kurt Wenner, an alternative world that challenges perspectives and engages viewers*

Designed by French artist Virginie and photographer Tom Platzer, fluorescent canvas strips of different colors are pulled across Taipingqiao Lake to turn passive onlookers into active participants.

participation in cultural activities contributes to social inclusion and active citizenship. As the city encourages, recognizes, rewards and supports new behaviors, it will begin to see those behaviors become the accepted norms, customs and habits of a new culture.

The Corporate Avenue lined with office towers for multinational corporations and the Lakeville Regency residential development nestled around the Taipingqiao Lake upon its completion in 2002 have quickly become a landmark, contrasted with the nearby poor neighborhoods where bad habits and poor discipline were widespread –clotheslines between two trees by the lake, lakeside washing, trampled lawn littered with trash. It is crucial, therefore, that government cultivate positive citizenship compatible with the city's most celebrated vista.

Vincent Lo delivered a speech entitled "Improving the Quality of Shanghai Citizens as Quickly as Possible" at the 14th International Business Leaders' Advisory Council in 2002 and played a video which he took and produced himself, showing different types of uncivilized behavior of certain Shanghai citizens. He compared such unruly behavior of certain Shanghai residents with the civilized conduct of citizens in Tokyo and Paris. His short video created considerable stir not only at the forum, but across Shanghai as well. Reflective Shanghai citizens did not deny problems in their community. Recognition of these problems initiated animated public discussions on "How to be a lovable Shanghainese" which aimed to promote the quality of Shanghai citizens and the overall improvement of the level of Shanghai's urban management.

Moreover, Vincent Lo extended Xintiandi culture to the Taipingqiao area. On every New Year's Eve, Xintiandi would present a grand gala "the Xintiandi Countdown Party" at the Taipingqiao Lake to enhance the potential for social interaction in public spaces—attracting diverse nationalities, cultures, values—and thereby create a sense of inclusion and harmony with the rest of the city.

At that time, there was already an annual New Year's Eve celebration at Longhua Temple in Shanghai. Worshippers gather to watch as a grand bell is struck 108 times—a number believed to dispel evil and welcome an auspicious year at the stroke of midnight. The ceremony, organized by the city's tourism bureau under the deputy mayor's guidance, is a major tourist attraction where people pray for the prosperity, happiness, and good luck around the year.

If a similar event was to be held, support from the municipal government had to be obtained and seamless communications with the government had to be ensured.

The Public Relations Department ultimately produced a creative proposal to convince the authorities.

Determined to become a leading global financial capital, Shanghai is home to a number of international businesses, and its foreign population is continually growing. The foreign settlers are endeavoring to live in harmony and culturally integrated with the local residents, however, the possibility of integration in the local context is somewhat limited by the different cultural

PROTECTING CULTURE IN URBAN REGENERATION

When the clock strikes midnight, fireworks are lit across Xintiandi. People start cheering and exchanging hugs and wishes for the new year.

backgrounds and religious beliefs.

Both striking bell for luck at the Longhua Temple and the burning joss sticks on the first day of the Lunar New Year at Shanghai's Jade Buddha Temple are a big challenge for the foreigners to get locally integrated, which calls for an international New Year celebration.

Entirely convinced of the soundness of the proposal, the authorities approved of the brand new citywide New Year's Eve celebration.

Since then, the annual New Year countdown in Xintiandi has been Shanghai's most iconic celebration, while Longhua Temple and Jade Buddha Temple continued to hold traditional ceremonies to welcome the new year.

As the city's only official public countdown event for the new year, the celebration in Xintiandi, just like New York's annual midnight countdown where the famous New Year's Eve Ball descends atop One Times Square, has attracted local residents and foreign participants together with singers and pop idols. Coco Lee, the famous Chinese-American pop queen, performed for the crowds at the first Xintiandi New Year's Eve Countdown Party.

On the night of Dec 31, 2002, more than 10,000 people gathered on Hubin Road by the artificial lake, including consular officers from over 20 countries, representatives of the American and Italian chambers of commerce and big corporations such as IBM and Siemens, as well as successful entrepreneurs.

As midnight neared, the then Deputy Mayor Jiang Sixian who was wearing traditional Chinese suit, Vincent Lo, and the event organizer pulled the lever together to initiate the blasting-off fireworks from the lake when the clock struck 12 at midnight, with the vocals that counted from 5 to 1 and an impressive stone gate shaped light display. People started cheering, exchanging hugs, bidding collective farewell to the departing year and expressing joy and hope for the year ahead.

Following the first eight-million-yuan Xintiandi New Year's

On Dec 31, 2002, the then Deputy Mayor of Shanghai Jiang Sixian (fifth from left) and seven distinguished guests were counting down to the final seconds of the year and celebrating the beginning of a new year with tens of thousands of citizens.

Eve Countdown Party, Shui On spent over six million yuan on every annual celebration thereafter. Each year, an array of Asian super stars popped on stage and stirred a hot wave of the night.

2004: Andy Lau, a Hong Kong actor, singer and film producer
2005: David Tao, a Taiwanese Golden Melody Award-winning singer-songwriter and Elva Hsiao, a Taiwanese singer, songwriter, dancer, actress and businesswoman
2006: Alan Tam, a Hong Kong singer and actor and Hacken Lee, a Hong Kong singer, television host and actor
2007: Wakin Chau, Hong Kong-born Taiwanese singer, songwriter and actor and S.H.E., a Taiwanese girl group widely regarded as the most successful and enduring Mandopop group
2008: Leehom Wang, an American-born Chinese singer and Bibi Zhou, a singer, songwriter, and actress from Mainland China
2009: Eason Chan, a Hong Kong singer and actor and Sandy

> Lam, a Hong Kong singer, actress and album producer
> 2010: Aaron Kwok, a Hong Kong singer, dancer and actor and JJ Lin, a Singaporean singer, songwriter, record producer, and actor
> 2011: Wilber Pan, a Taiwanese-American singer, songwriter, rapper, actor and entrepreneur, Harlem Yu, a Taiwanese singer-songwriter, television host and businessman, Mavis Fan, a Taiwanese singer and actress and Tanya Chua, a Singaporean Pop diva and songwriter

However, the merger of Huangpu and Luwan Districts marked the last and 10th consecutive year of Xintiandi New Year's Eve Countdown Party. 2012 Shanghai New Year countdown party was held along Shanghai's historic Bund waterfront on the west bank of Huangpu River which is regarded as the symbol of Shanghai. As a result, the admission tickets and invitation cards of the 2012 countdown party have been greatly sought after and become a precious part of the city's cultural memory.

As Shanghai's new cultural landmark, Xintiandi continues to convey the narrative of urban development and the immersive experience to create a strong identity of cross-cultural interaction and integration recognized as the realization of "China Dream" and a new culture in a broader international context.

Overview of Xintiandi market promotion activities

1999

Aug 27	Opening of Xintiandi. Hong Kong Media Interview
Sep 24	Press Conference of *The Road Home* directed by Zhang Yimou
Oct 12	Mary Cheung's Shanghai Photography Exhibition
Nov 3	Opening Ceremony of the Masterpiece Art Exhibition
Nov 15	Star East Entertainment Center scheduled to open in Xintiandi
Nov 15	Magic Spot from France opened in Xintiandi
Dec 9	Endorsement Press Conference of luxury Watch featuring Kathy Chow
Dec 16	Chen Yifei's "Fashion 2000" fashion show

2000

Jan 20	Press Conference of *Sorry Baby* directed by Feng Xiaogang
Jan 21	Xu Yuanzhang Recollections of the Old Shanghai Days Art Exhibition
Mar 24	Exhibition of Poetry and Paintings by Salvatore, an Italian bank president and poet, and Rolf Kluenter, a German artist
Mar 31	Press conference of Zhang Feng's Solo Concert
Apr 3	Asia.com Marketing Campaign
Apr 7	"Wang Rending's Jiangnan" Photography Exhibition
Apr 8	Press Conference of *The Duel*

Apr 17	First Interview of Xintiandi's "100,000-yuan Startup Foundation"
Apr 21	Egyptian Female Painter (the Ambassador's Wife) Sharif's Exhibition "From the Nile to the Yangtze River"
Apr 23	Closing Reception of Shanghai International Airline Stewardess Contest
Apr 24	Press Conference of *Breaking the Silence* starring the famous actress Gong Li
Apr 24	Famous Painter Shi Hu's Art Appreciation Show
May 9	Press Conference and Welcome Reception of 2000 "RunYan Cup" Shanghai International Fashion Model Competition
May 12	Famous Painter Wu Changshuo's Art Appreciation Show of Four Generations of Calligraphy and Painting
May 17	Award Reception of "Top Ten Apparel Brands" of Shanghai International Fashion Culture Festival 2000
May 20	Special Performance of Cultural Exchange Between China and Japan Launched by Ondekoza
Jun 3	National and International Children's Art Exhibition
Jun 7	Opening Reception of "*Shikumen* Furniture Exhibition" in Wenhuali
Jun 9	Activity by Love Radio Station 103.7 MHz FM
Jun 21	Starbucks Coffee scheduled to open in Xintiandi
Jun 22	Italian club night "Architecture and Nature" Exhibition
Jun 28	Opening Reception of *Family Tie*
Jul 6	Exhibition of a Russian Female Painter's works of art (attended by 36 foreign consuls general in Shanghai)
Jul 15	"Towards the Future with You" by *Modern Weekly*
Jul 15	Second Interview of Xintiandi's "100,000-yuan Startup Foundation"

Jul 21	Jiang Qiong Er's "Industrial Romance" Jewelry Design Exhibition
Aug 11	ACNielsen Launch Event of Non-Durable Consumer Goods
Aug 18	Launch Event of Edongcity.com Interactive TV
Aug 29	Nepal Night—the 45th Anniversary Party of the Establishment of Diplomatic Relations between China and Nepal
Sep 7	Italian Banker China Carpet Exhibition
Sep 8	Opening of the Restaurant "Xinjishi"
Sep 14	Omega Press Conference
Sep 16	Exhibition of an Australian Painter's works of art
Oct 20	Press Conference of *Sigh*
Oct 28	Event by 2000 Riche Monde (China) Limited
Nov 4	Press Conference of "Poetic Space" Art Exhibition by Five Artists Including Xu Yanting
Nov 9	Pang Xun Art Seminar
Nov 11	Friends Gathering of Mr. Shi Mo's Art Exhibition
Nov 16	Launch Event of KOOKAI
Nov 20	Opening Ceremony of Han Binghua and Su Minyi's Design and Art Collection

2001

Jan 5	Groundbreaking Ceremony of the Public Green Space in Taipingqiao Area
Feb 13	Press Conference of the Open Audition for the TV series "Bright Future"
Feb 28	Grand Opening of Star East
Mar 3	Cosmopolitan Show
Mar 15	Announcement of the result of the Open Audition for the TV series "Bright Future"
Mar 20	Ports Fashion Show
May 3	Closing Ceremony of the 7th Shanghai International Fashion Culture Festival in 2001

May 16	Opening Ceremony of Vidal Sassoon Academy
May 29	Official Opening Ceremony of Star East
Jun 12	Launch Event of Virgin Atlantic Business Class Flights from Shanghai to London
Jun 24	Opening of the Japanese Music Restaurant "Ark"
Jul 2	Activity by Italian Chamber of Commerce
Jul 12	Fellowship Event jointly held by the Canadian Government and the Communist Youth League Central Committee
Jul 27	Cognac & Cigar Night Shanghai — Martell Elite Club Activities
Aug 25	Modern Art Exhibition "Existing Romance" by Jiang Qiong Er
Sep 8	Opening Ceremony of the French Restaurant "La Maison"
Sep 16	Performance Show by Warner Bros. Movie World, Queensland, Australia
Sep 20	Swiss Folk Music and Dance Performance at Shanghai International Travel Festival 2001
Sep 26	Launch Event of Tahitian Black Pearl
Sep 29	Opening Ceremony of "Layefe Home"
Sep 30	Interview and Report of Xintiandi by Yang Lan studio, Sun Media Group
Oct 12	YPO Fellowship Dinner Party
Oct 13	Famous Painter Shi Hu's Art Appreciation Show 2001
Oct 13	Traditional Bavarian Beer Promotion
Oct 21	APEC Business Advisory Council Farewell Dinner
Oct 24	A visit to the old residents of One Xintiandi
Oct 25	"Xintiandi Cup" Shanghai International Orienteering Championship 2001
Oct 26	Opening Ceremony of the Italian Restaurant "Vabene"

Nov 4	Dinner Party of Shanghai Mayor International Entrepreneur Consultation Conference 2001
Nov 16	2001 Shui On Employees Family Day
Nov 23	French Paper Gallery
Nov 30	North American Fur Association Fashion Show
Dec 9	Brigitte Lin, a Famous Taiwanese Actress, visited Xintiandi
Dec 13	Christmas light up
Dec 20	Opening Ceremony of the Restaurant "TMSK"
Dec 31	New Year's Eve Countdown Party 2002

2002

Jan 11	Opening Ceremony of Shanghai Trio
Jan 18	Opening Ceremony of the Restaurant "ZEN"
Jan 23	Signing Ceremony of partnership between the Taiwanese Restaurant YiChaYiZuo and Xintiandi
Jan 25	Zhu Ying Oil Painting Exhibition
Jan 26	Shooting of "Shanghai Weekend" Xintiandi by journalists from Taiwan and Mainland China
Jan 26	Opening Ceremony of Da Yi Art Museum
Feb 10	Signing ceremony of partnership between Xintiandi Branch of the Shanghai Postal Museum and Xintiandi
Feb 10	Opening ceremony of Shanghai Xintiandi Photography Competition " Everlasting Joy "
Feb 16	Hong Kong Singer Sandy Lam's New Album Press Conference
Mar 29	Awards Ceremony of Shanghai Xintiandi Photography Competition " Everlasting Joy " and Opening Ceremony of the Photo Exhibition
Apr 24	Opening Ceremony of the 8th Shanghai International Fashion Culture Festival in 2002
May 11	Opening ceremony of H&Z and first exhibition of H&Z Ink and Watercolor Paintings

EAST MEETS WEST

May 18	Opening Ceremony of C.J.W Pub
Jun 14	T8 was rated as one of the World's Best 50 Restaurants by *Traveler Magazine*
Jun 14	Opening Ceremony of Xintiandi Branch of the Shanghai Postal Museum and Xintiandi Post Office
Jun 30	Broadcasting 2002 FIFA World Cup Finals
Aug 30	"My Father and I" –recital by Chen Gang
Aug 31	"Light, Brightness and Song" — New Art Exhibition by Jiang Qiong Er
Sep 15	Performance of a Korean Ensemble
Sep 15	Performance of a Swiss Ensemble
Sep 19	Performance of Akram Khan, One of the Most Celebrated British Dancers
Sep 29	Exhibition by famous French Architect Jean-Marie Charpentier
Sep 30	Opening of Xintiandi UME International Cineplex
Sep 30	Evening Party of the Grand Opening of Xintiandi
Oct 2	Lakeside Symphony (130 cellos)
Nov 14	Shanghai World Travel Fair
Dec 3	Celebration of Shanghai's successful bid to hold the World Expo 2010
Dec 14	Opening Ceremony of Xintiandi New Year Photography Competition
Dec 14	Xintiandi New Year Lighting Ceremony 2003
Dec 14	Press conference of 2002 / 2003 "Shui On Cup" Real Estate Enterprises Football Championship
Dec 27	Exhibition by Mr. Pan Gongkai, a famous painter and President of Central Academy of Fine Art
Dec 29	Press conference of New Year's Eve Countdown Party 2003
Dec 31	New Year's Eve Countdown Party 2003

2003

Feb 18	Launch party of Shuion properties.com and Shuion Club
Mar 8	Awards ceremony of Xintiandi New Year Photography Competition
Mar 13	Certificate Awards Ceremony of "Xintiandi Primary Service Certificate"
Mar 18	Opening ceremony gala of Shanghai International Fashion Culture Festival 2003
Mar 21	Sheng Shanshan Art Exhibition
Mar 27	Gala ceremony of Laureus World Sports Awards
Apr 19	Xintiandi Charity Climbing Event
Jun 22	Mount Everest Photography Exhibition
Jun 28	Xintiandi Outdoor Sculpture Exhibition
Jul 4	"Bye Bye SARS" event held on the bank of Taipingqiao Lake
Aug 4	"New Shanghai, New Fashion" Ricky Martin Dance Party
Sep 13	"What's Art" held in the North Block
Sep 14	"Crazy Sedan" held at the South Block
Sep 19	"Man, Lotus and Nature" — Shi Mo's Art Exhibition
Sep 19	Xintiandi Beer Festival
Oct 22	Jerry and Snell Rock Concert
Nov 17	Miss World 2003 Contestants visited Xintiandi on their national tour
Dec 12	2004 Shanghai Xintiandi New Year Lighting Ceremony
Dec 31	New Year's Eve Countdown Party 2004

2004

Jan 10	Opening ceremony of " Deep love beneath the heaven, true feelings upon the Earth" — Charity Fundraising Event involving 10,000 people
Mar 18	Opening ceremony of Shanghai International Fashion Culture Festival 2004
Mar 30	Opening ceremony of Hong Kong Week
May 21	Shanghai Habitat Exhibit
May 29	Children's Day: traditional games of childhood at the old *Shikumen* alleys
Jun 1	AC Milan at Xintiandi — Paolo Cesare Maldini and His Little Fans
Jun 16	Delegation led by President of Harvard University visited Xintiandi
Jul 3	Sino French Cultural Year — Cultural Exchanges between China and France
Jul 24	Authentic Hawaiian Experience — Xintiandi Summer Tour
Aug 25	"HeineKen" Xintiandi Beer Festival
Sep 11	Wine Tasting Weekend
Sep 16	"Sharing Unlimited Glory" — Celebration of the F1 Team British and American Racing
Sep 28	2004 CCTV Mid-Autumn Festival Gala Xintiandi sub-venue
Oct 23	Shanghai Fashion Week Esprit Show in the air
Dec 17	2004 Shanghai Xintiandi Christmas Lighting Ceremony
Dec 29	Press Conference of New Year's Eve Countdown Party 2005
Dec 30	The Unveiling of National Cultural Industry Demonstration Base
Dec 31	New Year's Eve Countdown Party 2005

2005

Apr 3	Jazz Week
May 19	Global Luxury Brand Summit
Jun 8	2005 Xintiandi " Hawaiian Experience" Event
Aug 5	"A Star Is Born" held in the lobby of Corporate Avenue
Aug 11	"Harmony & Charm Creative Photography Competition" held at Xintiandi
Aug 19	"Tennis world" Midsummer Night Party
Sep 9	2005 International Chinese Male Model Competition
Sep 15	"Start Line of Today, Rostrum of Tomorrow " — Meeting between teenagers and sports stars
Sep 15	Press conference of "Love in A Fallen City" performed by Shanghai Dramatic Arts Centre
Sep 23	2005 Urban Remote Control Sailing Race held in Taipingqiao Artificial Lake
Oct 27	Shanghai Xintiandi held its first Fashion Show, featuring the latest Autumn/Winter styles from its tenants.
Oct 30	Exhibition of "Pop Pop" Art Action Plan
Nov 19	Hong Kong Wenhui Newspaper Group Annual Dinner
Dec 1	2005 Shanghai Xintiandi New Year Lighting Ceremony
Dec 2	Lakeville Regency Wine Tasting and Concert
Dec 31	New Year's Eve Countdown Party 2006

2006

Jan 22	The Charity Star Bridge completed in Taipingqiao Park to recognize generous citizens
Mar 27	Charity auction of celebrities' personal collection
Apr 12	British Musical Culture Exhibition
Apr 21	"Time Travel" — weekend Carnival Party

May 18	Launching ceremony of ticket sales for 2006 Tennis Masters Cup
Jun 2	Artemide showroom opening party
Jun 17	Talk on "when a monk meets a diamond" at Y + Yoga
Jun 20	Four internationally renowned artists were living in Xintiandi glass cabin for two weeks
Jun 28	Chinese International Photography Competition
Jul 12	Lion King party
Aug 1	"A Glimpse of Luwan in Eight Years" — 2006 Exhibition of award-winning works of Luwan's development Photography Competition
Sep 20	Fall-Winter 2006 Xintiandi Fashion Show
Oct 3	Exhibition of documentary photography by *Life Magazine*
Oct 21	The Eighth China Shanghai International Arts Festival — Week of Cultural Exchange
Oct 21	"Australian Style" event
Oct 27	Halloween party
Nov 4	Art exhibition by students from Luwan Special Needs School dedicated to the Special Olympics
Dec 1	Christmas performance by the famous Australian group "The Peppers, Manoeuvre & Aerial Angels"
Dec 2	2007 Shanghai Xintiandi New Year Lighting Ceremony
Dec 21	"Angel Dance" square art performance
Dec 31	New Year's Eve Countdown Party 2007

2007

Feb 14	Xintiandi Valentine's Day event
Feb 18	Lion Dance to celebrate Spring Festival
Mar 10	Promotion of the first "Irish Week" in Shanghai

Apr 22	"Bounded-Boundless" — Volkswagen Olympic Art Exhibition
May 24	"Life Defined by Inspiration" — an art movement expressing outstanding life experience through artistic ideals
Jul 1	Live broadcast of celebrating the 10th Anniversary of Hong Kong's Return to Motherland
Jul 6	2007 Xintiandi mid-summer games and entertainment
Aug 7	One Year countdown ceremony of Beijing 2008 Olympic Games
Sep 21	Promotional event of Huaihai Road Fashion Month
Sep 26	Launching ceremony of 2007 "Shui On Cup" Shanghai Civilization Etiquette Competition
Oct 12	Fall-Winter 2007 Xintiandi Fashion Show
Oct 27	"It's Snowing" — Halloween roadshow
Nov 19	Xintiandi Health & Fashion event
Dec 1	2008 Shanghai Xintiandi New Year Lighting Ceremony
Dec 7	"Model & Charity" Photography Competition by Wai Yin Xintiandi
Dec 30	"Chasing Dream in Shanghai" — 2008 Li Shoubai Art Exhibition
Dec 31	New Year's Eve Countdown Party 2008

2008

Feb 21	The 800-day countdown to the 2010 Shanghai World EXPO and celebration of the Lantern Festival
Mar 11	Opening ceremony of the second "Irish Week"
Mar 19	Shanghai debut of *Wai Yin* 25th Anniversary Commemorative Book
Jun 21	Launch ceremony of "Fu Lu Shou Fountain" or "Fountain of Blessings"
Sep 19	Fall-Winter 2008 Xintiandi Fashion Show

Oct 25	2008 Shanghai Xintiandi Halloween event
Dec 1	2009 Shanghai Xintiandi New Year Lighting Ceremony
Dec 5	2008 Christmas Stage Performance
Dec 31	New Year's Eve Countdown Party 2009

2009

Jan 26	Lion dance to celebrate 2009 Chinese Spring Festival
May 26	Event "Enlarge your life"
Jun 18	Asian Exhibition Tour of "Blue Whale", the largest animal on the planet
Jul 15	Launch ceremony of Xintiandi's creating standardized Cultural Tourism Destination
Oct 31	Xintiandi Halloween Costume party
Dec 31	New Year's Eve Countdown Party 2010

2010

Jan 8	Exhibition of Qingyang embroidery
Jan 25	"When Kunqu meets Tea" — Xintiandi Kunqu Opera Salon
Mar 27	Awarding ceremony of "Yangtze River Delta Expo themed Experience Tour Demonstration Base" and Shanghai Xintiandi *Shikumen* Cultural Week
Apr 30	"The Vogues of the World All Come to Xintiandi " themed Mini Expo
Nov 16	Grand Opening of Xintiandi Style shopping center
Nov 28	Opening Ceremony of The Langham, Shanghai, Xintiandi
Dec 1	2011 New Year Lighting Ceremony of Shanghai Xintiandi and Huaihailu Road Business District
Dec 31	New Year's Eve Countdown Party 2011

PROTECTING CULTURE IN URBAN REGENERATION

2011	
Feb 18	Joint event by Xintiandi and Haagen Dazs
Apr 8	"Love & Fanfan" — Christine Fan Album Signing
Apr 18	"Sketch 2011" Spring and Summer Collection Launch
Apr 28	Launch of Shanghai Fashion Week 2011 at Xintiandi
Apr 30	JJ Lin's first birthday party in Mainland China
May 7	Photo Exhibition of the 90th Anniversary of The Founding of the Communist Party of China
May 8	Exchange Exhibition of well-known calligraphers and painters
May 10	Signing ceremony of Shanghai Fashion Week Xintiandi Launch
Jun 8	Shanghai Reinvented — "Me and Xintiandi" Exhibition held as a celebration of the 10th Anniversary of the establishment of Shanghai Xintiandi
Jun 27	"Our Remembrance and Tribute" — the 46th Cultural Forum of *Jiefang Daily Press Group*
Aug 9	Launch ceremony of the "Ya Lu & Xintiandi" Cultural Development Fund
Sep 8	Xintiandi Style shopping center summer concert
Sep 11	2011 "Huaihai Tiandi Fashion Month" and VOGUE Fashion's Night Out
Sep 16	Opening ceremony of 2011 Korean Culture & Tourism Week
Sep 29	Urban Culture Exhibition of Longines Saint-Imier Collection
Oct 28	Fall-Winter launch of Qiu Hao & Masha Ma
Nov 3	Press conference of 2011 Shui On Yong Ye Cup WDSF GrandSlam Final
Nov 5	The 10th Shanghai Style Culture Symposium
Dec 2	Shanghai Xintiandi New Year Lighting Ceremony
Dec 31	New Year's Eve Countdown Party 2012

CHAPTER 9

BUSINESS OPERATION DETERMINES THE VALUE

In a fast growing but immature market, each innovation invites competitors to replicate it. A copycat strategy might work in the short term, but it will ruin any chance at long-term success.

Xintiandi has set a new benchmark for style that is fast being replicated around China, yet never been surpassed.

The problem with these copycats is that they, nothing more than architectural replicas, haven't captured the essence of the business model concept. Simply speaking, they have overlooked a critical factor in Xintiandi's success: operations. The success of Xintiandi largely depends on its operations and how they are effectively managed.

Just like mighty oaks, businesses need to be nurtured to grow. It takes many years for trees to grow, mature and bear fruit. Similarly, it may take time for businesses to become profitable.

Well-run operations are a critical, and often overlooked source of a business' success. They are often interpreted as preservation of property value or property maintenance. In fact, business operations refer to the process where greater value is obtained from the project investments and brand culture accumulates.

When analyzing development projects success factors, Shui On Managing Director Henry Cheng once said that out of the 100 points of a successful commercial property project, 20 points were for excellent planning and design, 20 points for meeting deadlines, staying on budget, and still creating high quality work, and another 20 points for successful marketing and leasing.

Business operations and management took up the remaining 40 points. Without clear, concise management of operations, a development project would struggle to remain cooperative and efficient.

A sound business plan is the road map that points you in the right direction, and well-managed operations take the goal to the finish line.

Operations management has been, together with designing and construction, incorporated in the entire business plan at the early stage of Xintiandi project planning to ensure unimpeachable quality, build a strong brand, maximize value creation and maintain design consistency. Xintiandi brilliantly differentiated itself from the competition at the beginning.

Many commercial real estate developers in Mainland China prioritize construction over operations management, steering a once promising project into a frustrating result, despite its remarkable design, that fails to deliver optimized value.

Why did some beautifully designed shopping malls stumble into a devastating cycle of dwindling traffic, lower sales and disappearing storefronts?

Successful opening of a shopping mall and a well-written marketing plan do not necessarily translate into strong retail performance. It is critical for malls to take a more active role in shaping the shopping experience to attract and retain affluent, brand-conscious customer base.

Xintiandi has tried hard to garner customers' attention and loyalty. It was in a low cultural competence stage at the startup period when this cultural attraction without walls or a ticket office were frequented by citizens pushing decrepit old bicycles along the alleys or nearby residents who used the mall's well-equipped restrooms and walked away with empty toilet paper rolls and stains all over the place. Xintiandi would have to solve these problems to attract high-end customers.

Composed of professionals that specialize in business strategies, operations management and public relations, Xintiandi

Operations Department has come up with effective solutions to these challenges through brainstorming and divergent thinking.

Habits are hard to break. It takes time and patience for new behaviors to become routine. The Operations Department was aware that proper guidance, instead of bluntly denying their entry, should be given to cultivate decent conduct and underpin a civilized community.

One to two guards were placed at each of the 15 entries of the complexes to persuade improperly dressed visitors to change their outfit before entering. Those who felt embarrassed yet refused to cooperate would be admitted though, according to Operations Department's guideline, but kindly advised that visitors be encouraged to dress appropriately. With persistent guidance and persuasion, mindset has been transformed and new habits have been fostered to envision a richer cultural experience, and the customers' impression of their experience has grown by leaps and bounds.

Xintiandi has developed a focused and competitive management plan tailored to its unique needs through continuous innovation.

Well-tailored to the taste of fashion-going young people, Xintiandi has become a popular scenic backdrop for wedding photographers and young married couples seeking a snapshot to familiar historic references. This business opportunity was quickly seized by advertising companies, design firms, wedding planners and bridal dresses shops.

Professional photographers were seen, with a whole host of gear, shooting customers seated at the outside table of a café without its permission, incurring the wrath of enraged foreign visitors.

The Operations Department, placed in a peculiar predicament, was busy handling tenant complaints while besieged by offers to rent the venue for wedding photography shots.

After careful consideration and discussion, the department turned down all the offers. Perplexed and bewildered why

With culture at the heart of governance, outdoor dining area is kept in good order and consciously separated from the pedestrian alleyway.

Xintiandi chose not to earn any profit, a Hong Kong wedding planner asked the operations manager relentlessly: "Who are you? Can you make the decision on behalf of your company?" "Although the offer is very tempting," explained the manager, "the profit is incomparable with the rental income from our 98 tenants. Taking the offer would drive our tenants away which is a 'penny wise, pound foolish' approach." Since then, it has been widely acknowledged that no wedding photography shots are

allowed at Xintiandi

How to distinguish between commercial photography and travelers taking photos just for personal use which is allowed at Xintiandi? As stipulated in the guidelines, no person shall use any public or private property at Xintiandi area for the purpose of commercial filming or still photography, including news media, without first applying for and receiving a permit from the Operations Department. Security guards patrol the area to ensure regulations are adhered to.

A Westerner was once stopped by the guards when he was shooting with a professional tripod that lasted for a long time. He then staged a protest to the Operations Department against forbidding photography at a tourist attraction. The manager explained politely, "Like a starred hotel open to the public, Xintiandi has a set of management practices to guarantee its upscale quality and prestigious reputation. We are now safeguarding our guests' privacy and portrait rights. I believe you are not allowed to take pictures of other guests dining in a five-star hotel." The foreigner nodded with an expression of dawning comprehension, "Now I get it and I like your philosophy. I finally understand why Xintiandi has been so popular. I'm actually a travel journalist and I'm going to share it with the whole world."

After Xintiandi garnered a national reputation, it has become a training venue for the provincial governors, mayors and ministers of the central government from the China Executive Leadership Academy in Pudong to study architectural heritage preservation in the process of urbanization. Xintiandi's operational excellence has caught their attention.

A mayor from China's central Hunan province spent seven consecutive evenings at Xintiandi to search for the secret recipe for its successful management. He was surprised to find that the complexes were busy, but orderly; customer flow was properly managed in a safe and secure manner to avoid congestion; passages and alleyways were spotlessly clean—free from roadside stands or stacking, no litter on the ground or mess on the walls; decorative lights came in a variety of styles and sizes that created a harmonious atmosphere; visitors were neatly dressed and behaved in a civilized and polite manner. In contrast, some of the gourmet streets and tourist attractions in Hunan province were exposed to significant environmental degradation and unauthorized food stands.

The key lies in effective operations management. China's reform and opening-up laid the foundation for a successful transition from a planned economy to a market economy oriented towards the global market. However, the administrative efforts used to manage commercial streets remained unchanged.

Rather than simply setting up a hub of restaurants and pubs, management of a gourmet street requires the capacity to honor business agreements and commitments, which refers to the "legal civilization" Mainland China has long advocated.

The establishment and improvement of market economy must be regulated and guaranteed by a complete legal regime. Nevertheless, some markets, despite introduction of competitive market economy, still follow an administrative command system, including relying solely on impromptu inspections, without establishing a self-regulatory market mechanism, which is the root cause of their failure.

Entrepreneurs always say that small businesses are often owned and managed by the same person; management of medium-sized businesses rely on company policies, while organizational culture determines how a large enterprise's employees and management interact.

An organization's culture defines the proper way to behave within the organization. This culture consists of shared beliefs and values established by leaders and then communicated and reinforced through various methods, ultimately shaping employee perceptions, behaviors and understanding. They are clear about their values and how those values define their organizations and determine how the organizations run.

Similarly, a strong culture is a common denominator in a successful neighborhood management. All have consensus at the top regarding cultural priorities, and those values focus not on individuals but on the neighborhood and its goals.

Conversely, an ineffective management by manually clearing roads and sidewalks of all impediments such as unauthorized stalls and makeshift stands can bring down the neighborhood and its leadership. The maelstrom that it has generated shakes the social order and challenged the citadels of the government. The academic term for this phenomenon is "government failure", an economic inefficiency caused by government intervention rooted in lowered cultural competence and confidence. A fundamental shift in government management can only be achieved by focusing on creating organizational culture rather than implementing lawful but harsh orders.

Culture lies at the heart of governance. This philosophy embodies the principles of wu wei, or "actingless action", one of Taoism's most important concepts. Non-action is not passivity but a way of exercising power by attuning to the rhythms of its mysterious source. It a form of natural action that reacts spontaneously to the flow of events and changing circumstances.

Culture in public spaces not only brings communities together, but also contributes towards strengthening importance of corporate reputation and personal credibility.

The key to legal civilization is that both parties demonstrate total commitment to the spirit and the words of their business agreement. Whoever breaks the rules will never again be invited. The rules safeguard the legitimate rights and interests while defining proper conduct of both parties.

Most businesses regularly comply with laws despite a variety of regulatory failures on the part of government. This level of "voluntary" compliance within society, which is ultimately based on trust in government, is a valuable asset for regulators that should not be taken for granted. Regulatory failures that undermine public trust in government are likely to have wider, longer-term implications reducing the effectiveness of government as a whole.

In fact, the vast majority of binding "laws" in those traditional commercial streets and markets were not enacted based on actual market conditions and the scope of administrative power of the government officials has been overly enlarged.

Overseas investors often complain that doing business in China can be a difficult and contentious proposition. With charges of intellectual property theft, forced partnerships, and tight restrictions, the business-unfriendly environment is hurting business confidence of the foreign investments.

On the contrary, Xintiandi's persistence in strict, fair, and civilized law enforcement has brought into play well the guaranteeing function of the rule of law that secures the foundation, stabilizes expectations, and benefits the long-term. Its practice has proven an effective management model in China's neighborhood commercial district.

Set up at the same time when Xintiandi project was launched, the Operations Department plays a distinctive role that contributes towards creating unique value and achieving core objectives of the organization.

The department has three core functions: asset management, marketing operations and property management. Therefore, the operations managers, in addition to property management, provide constant oversight on asset management, marketing promotion, and public relations.

The Operations Department makes sure that Xintiandi's ultimate priorities are being met. The objectives of the department revolve around high-quality effective operations. Its major responsibilities include:

1. Growing a luxury clientele and creating the right programs to attract the high-end clients, with as much initiative, creativity, adaptation, and resiliency as luxury hotels and airlines would appeal to their travelers. A stable high-end clientele is a key driver of Xintiandi's value.
2. Maintaining good and sustainable relationship with the tenants that boost the accomplishment of Xintiandi. Providing an excellent service to tenants and solving their issues with the highest efficiency. Running property management and equipment maintenance to ensure the cleanliness, orderliness, and safety of the environment
3. Managing public affairs in the neighborhood

commercial district, abiding by the laws of the country, building and maintaining self-discipline; fostering positive relationship with the government agencies that play a vital role in maximizing efficiency and supporting the community

Particularly worth mentioning is the management of public affairs in the neighborhood commercial district that follows the autonomous management model, while the neighborhood and community affairs of other commercial streets including Nanjing Road, Huaihai Road and Sichuan Road are handled directly by the government based on administrative management model. With government support and close cooperation, Xintiandi undertakes part of the public affairs management function.

Luwan District attempted in vain to replicate Xintiandi's management model to Huaihai Road due the conflict between the autonomous model and the national systems of governance, which is the major reason why other developers failed to replicate Xintiandi's success.

The management of the complicated public affairs which has been categorized into two major types: centralized management and autonomous control, which echo with China's notion of "harmony in diversity". Centralized management focuses on the public affairs going on in the public area of the community, including the streets, facade, etc., while autonomous control gives the tenants the authority to manage their own business operations within the rented premises.

Through centralized management, Xintiandi ensures uniformity across the neighborhood commercial district in terms of the cultural identity of the community, advertising campaigns, size of the business signs, location of outdoor seating area, planned loading and unloading times, and trash and recycling pickup schedule.

The uniform cultural identity within the commercial community is the mainstay of Xintiandi's cultural foundations.

One of the reasons why shopping centers in China are usually formulaic and lack local distinctiveness is that they have misinterpreted the "cultural identity of the neighborhood commercial district" as "cultural identity of the individual store". Each commercial street has its own distinctive characteristics representing deep historical roots and profound cultural background. However, when stores set up large outdoor signs or add huge logos to the outer walls (such as KFC and McDonald's) to captivate potential customers' attention, the streets have an uncontrolled garish look that draws nothing from their own cultures. The result is a homogeneous pastiche of commercial streets that prove to be remarkably similar.

However, McDonald's signature logo where its yellow Golden Arches rest against a bright red background has to be displayed in classy black and gold on the branch situated in the shopping arcade near the Milan Cathedral, in conformity and uniformity with surrounding signage.

The gray-brick *Shikumen* dwellings are the visual cultural characteristics of Xintiandi that must be recognized and cherished by all the tenants. To preserve the culture of the commercial community, restaurants and pubs are not allowed to attach signs to the exterior walls.

An appreciation and acceptance of the culture is an essential prerequisite for being part of the community. This is the reason why the general manager talked about history and culture of *Shikumen*, instead of rents, with the potential tenants during the interview

Xintiandi at night impresses and shows its simply more colorful side. Instead of accent lighting on the outline of the old houses, Xintiandi used dimmed lights to give off a pleasant glow and create a cozy atmosphere. Pubs also encourage you to linger with soft and romantic lighting.

Management of freight loading and unloading and the trash pickup schedule is also crucial to Xintiandi's success.

Most traditional commercial streets receive twice-daily trash collection and transportation handled by the District Landscaping and City Appearance Administrative Bureau. Collection at noon coincides with people's lunch break and the second slot from 6 pm to 8 pm happens to be the busiest time for the commercial streets. With worsening customer experience, the appeal of the streets has gradually declined.

Freight loading and trash collection, however, are only allowed after midnight at Xintiandi to avoid negative impact of noise, dirt and congestion on the pedestrian passageways.

Cooperative advertising campaigns can be difficult for traditional commercial streets as long as the key issue persists: who is going to foot the bill?

The tenants on traditional commercial streets deploy their own marketing strategies based on marketing budgets. Although most of the time, the government bears the cost of promoting the commercial community, the street tenants are

The obscuring sight of McDonald's logo conspicuously covering up the facade that undermines the cultural identity of a commercial street in Shanghai

McDonald's signature logo where its yellow Golden Arches rest against a bright red background has to be displayed in classy black and gold on the branch situated in the shopping arcade near the Milan Cathedral, in conformity and uniformity with surrounding signage.

neither appreciative nor cooperative because they believe these government-led promotional campaigns will simply fall flat.

Xintiandi, though, controls all the marketing activities and initiatives and manages a unified brand image for the entire commercial community. Expenses are included in the property management fees and shared by all the tenants.

They pool the marketing budgets aiming for a bigger bang for their promotional spending. Cooperative advertising empowers Xintiandi to utilize a more unified branding approach that creates an increased competence level of the community and gives a better leverage of best practices.

Most consumers are drawn to commercial communities that deliver quality products, seamless experience and compelling brands, which they believe are offered at Xintiandi.

This multi-faceted, imaginative approach produced by the Operations Department was a success on many levels.

The Operations Department must constantly develop and coordinate highly orchestrated touch points and micro-campaigns each week, in a way that the tenants find meaningful and trustworthy, that attract high-end customers to reach a traffic volume of at least 10,000 daily visitors.

Tenants, on the other hand, must bolster their brand awareness, attract attention and boost foot traffic, otherwise the advertising revenues being spent may have a minimal impact. The healthy competition among the tenants has pushed them to retain their competitive edge.

The benefits are a triple win: it boosts customer traffic, builds stronger owner-tenant relationship, and keeps the customers satisfied–creating goodwill and positive buzz in the community.

Endeavoring to provide a pleasant retail environment for both the tenants and customers, the whole Operations Department has a clear understanding of their responsibility to provide the tenants with meticulous support services that only a developer versed in retailing can offer.

Choosing the right tenants can be tough, yet achieving

EAST MEETS WEST

With finely wrought management practices, Xintiandi ensures uniformity of the size of business signs across the neighborhood commercial district

efficient delivery of service to the tenants is even harder. But it is those detail-oriented tenants that produce high-quality results are most welcomed by high-end customers.

Operations Department's responsibilities include:

1. Handling tenant maintenance requests as quickly as possible. The operations assistant must arrive at the site with a technician within 7 minutes—3 minutes for answering the phone call and filling in the request form, 4 minutes for the technician to make it to the scene.
2. Offering stationary patrol services to field regular inquiries of the tenants to respond to their requests promptly. Keeping detailed records of the inspections, including photographs and data entry. Operations assistants should take regular steps to monitor and improve the quality of patrol services.
3. Tracking and addressing tenant complaints in a timely manner. Creating and using an official tenant complaint form to include resolution action items, the date the issue is resolved and the tenant's feedback.
4. Maintaining a friendly relationship with the tenants. All team members of the Operations Department speak English, foster good relationship with the tenants, and make them feel "at-home" and valued.

Highly performing retail properties will typically be vibrant customer and tenant mix environments. As a retail property professional, Shui On knows how to make those things happen.

As Xintiandi exudes the typical European flair with its multitude of outdoor seating areas on the pedestrian-only streets, tenants always want to expand their outdoor dining space to attract more customers. If one places a set of tables and chairs outside the designated area, others will definitely follow suit, ultimately resulting in a narrower pavement and unwanted conflict between diners and pedestrians.

The Operations Department cleverly adopts a rent-free

strategy for the outdoor seating area so that they retain total control over the outdoor seating arrangements. Whoever breaks the rule will lose the privilege of enjoying free outdoor space. Shui On has gone to great lengths to preserve vitality of the space at the cost of a considerable amount of rental income.

There is nothing for management to gain by harping the negative. Diversified management practices give freedom in the capacity to better serve tenants and consumers, while providing space for creativity.

Taiwanese restaurant YiChaYiZuo (literally meaning "one tea, one seat") situated on the South Block has seen success through its unique management practice. The restaurant gives its customers an hourglass when they order. It should take less than 10 minutes for the first dish to arrive. If their food hasn't arrived before the time runs out then the customers get their meals for free. Consequently, diners no long complain about the slow-to-arrive food, and the pressure is naturally on the chef and the wait staff.

The well-run restaurant makes the most of every crew member's talent and takes advantage of every split-second opportunity to speed up service. The creative management approach that engenders esprit de corps is a key link in the productivity process.

Meticulously clean at all times, Xintiandi delivers an industry-defining standard of cleanliness with a long-standing commitment to rigorous cleaning protocols.

There are innumerable efforts and workforce required in order to ensure the proper cleaning of the place. In addition to cleaning frequencies, strict guidelines for cleaning have to be followed, such as keeping dust from flying in the presence of customers, using illuminating cleaning kit at night that brightens the way just enough to do the cleaning without disturbing the customers in the outdoor seating area. The operations managers often demonstrate the proper way to scrub away the bubble gum or coke stains on the ground on one knee to the new cleaning staff.

The major responsibility of the Operations Department is to

ensure that Xintiandi's operations are both efficient and effective.

Taylor Xia, who worked in the Operations Department for eight years, is well aware of their roles and responsibilities. She was transferred to the department because of her rich marketing and communications experience. She had worked in the marketing team that, through multiple marketing channels and connections, endeavored to invite celebrities and influencers to the events held at Xintiandi by sponsoring venue and funding at the beginning, in an attempt to attract and retain young shoppers. Having cultivated a high-end customer base within two years, Xintiandi is in a powerful situation with over 10,000 daily visitors and increasing venue rental income. Ferrari and BMW dealers are willing to pay 50,000 yuan a day for the event venue. The F1 organizing committee spent 700,000 yuan on a Formula One themed display for 5 days at Xintiandi to promote the inaugural Chinese Grand Prix.

Xintiandi has gradually become a hub of the city's trendiest fashion and besieged with rental requests for hosting promotional events and placing wall mounted advertising display, a lucrative new revenue stream in addition to retail rents.

Xintiandi never fails to impress the high-end customers by constantly presenting premium fashion events, which in turn magnetizes more fashion brands. Through the virtuous cycle, Xintiandi is establishing a new paradigm: one-third of the events and activities are run by Xintiandi, one-third by the tenants, and one-third by external brands.

Xintiandi's operational excellence has increased its brand value and created sustainable improvement. The 10-fold rent increase is the best testament.

One of the common misperceptions about business operations is that rent increases are expected to propel property value. However, unreasonable rent increases will only drive the quality tenants out, leading to further loss of upscale customers.

Running the day-to-day operations of a commercial property boils down to two main areas of focus: rental income and operating expenses. While having a competitive rental income is crucial, knowing how to control operating expenses is more important because it allows the business to improve its bottom line. Rent should be calculated based on the tenants' profitability to retain the good tenants and secure many years of dependable rental income and positive cash flow.

By regularly evaluating operating expenses, the business can vastly extend its cash runway. However, keeping operating costs in check by compromising its service can actually limit productivity and the potential for profit. Running a successful business is a constant battle between revenue and costs.

To thrive in the future, a smart commercial property operator is diversifying by attracting fresh, innovative stores by offering lower rents so as to adapt to an era when products and services that are cutting edge one day are outdated the next.

When it comes to operations management, market is the best teacher. Operators must relate changing market dynamics to their ability to keep exploiting existing competencies and building new capabilities.

Excellence in operations is seen as the key contributing factor in promoting value-creation and long-run competitive advantage for commercial real estate development. Does it offer valuable insight that today's urban development in China can learn from?

It is no exaggeration to say that the concept of operational excellence that allows management to plan, innovate, and focus on business growth can also be applied to China's urbanization. For a long time, we have always believed that the most significant challenge for sustainable urban development in China is the large-scale demolition and construction. A more accurate expression of this challenge is lack of solid "urban management" that led to a large number of new construction, demolition and reconstruction projects.

The traditional *Si He Yuan* courtyards in Beijing, *Shikumen* houses in Shanghai and *Arcade street* buildings in Guangzhou are rapidly disappearing and replaced by modern apartment blocks.

However, without proper urban planning, design and regulation, new buildings will also generate new hazards and extensive risks.

Without proper maintenance and care, the residential buildings built in the '80s and '90s that resemble matchboxes in Shanghai have become synonymous with dilapidated living conditions. Moreover, as the number of cars multiplies, the older, built-up residential areas often face serious parking shortages not amenable to easy solutions.

Residents also feel trapped because there is no elevator in the residential buildings built in the '90s (the number of elevators in Shanghai has reached 180,000 units). Concerned about elevator operation and safety, residents refuse to pay for elevator projects and vent frustration on government. The government, nevertheless, has neither the responsibility nor the funding to install the elevators. Residents are consequently moving to new apartment complexes just like those leaving their deteriorating *Shikumen* residences during urban regeneration, indicating a decline in the "matchbox" buildings, similar to the fate of *Shikumen* buildings.

While European buildings from the Middle Ages are still in use as they were many hundreds of years before, residential buildings only decades old in China are already in a poor

Xintiandi at night gives off a pleasant glow and creates a cozy atmosphere instead of dazzling brightness

Sunbathed Xintiandi during the daytime

condition and ready to be bulldozed.

The administrative ordinances of Prague, capital city of the Czech Republic, stipulate that the private residential buildings should be kept in a safe condition, maintenance and repair should be conducted every 5 years, and large-scale renovation should be carried out every 15 years. The public is well aware of the rules, and property maintenance companies and banks are available to provide relevant services.

Six months before the maintenance schedule, the government will send the residents a notice, reminding them to select a reputable property maintenance company and a bank if loan is needed. Residents who fail to comply with the ordinances will be prosecuted and fined.

There are no such regulations, however, in our country to avoid creating unmanageable levels of risk during urban development. There is an urgent need to promote a culture of prevention at all levels as an integral part of the urban development process.

Shikumen houses are a relic of Shanghai's fascinating history, and the overwhelming impression they give is one of charm, whimsy and poise. However, when so much of Shanghai is gleaming, shining and spit-polished, why have these delightful structures been allowed to decay into Miss Haversham-like shambles?

In a sense, the sweeping institutional changes in the country's property and housing regime sow the seeds of their demise.

During the Cultural Revolution, personal property and housing were confiscated. The resulting situation was that these unique architectural gems were slowly sinking into disrepair, and the local housing bureaus lacked the resources to adequately reverse the erosion of prior decades.

During the 1990s, the government embarked on the property and housing reforms designed to consolidate the shift to a market-based housing system in an attempt to lessen the financial burden on the authorities and improve urban living conditions of the residents. Yet no legislation on maintenance and repair of residential properties has been imposed on the property owners.

While property owners are expected to maintain their residential properties and make reasonable repairs, many residents still believe that the responsibility for maintaining and improving the common areas of the building should be passed to the government.

Some residents enjoy the service provided by property management companies but refuse to pay the management fee, let alone the share of building repair and maintenance costs. Instead, they would rather spend their life savings on a new house.

Measures should be taken to halt large-scale demolition and construction during the upgrading of the cities, along with the transformation of both civilizations and cultures.

Civilization is a series of actions taken by millions of people. Having been implemented for over twenty years, the current housing maintenance fund system which requires a one-off payment on buying the property has proven inadequate to cover the cost of major repairs including the upgrade of elevators. New regulations need to be established to define property owners' repair and maintenance responsibilities, and new rules should be set up to achieve resident autonomy, government's rulemaking authority and judicial power of law enforcement.

The culture in its simplest form refers to the ideas, customs, and social behavior of the society. The government should redefine the role it plays—from constantly protecting its people from interference to cultivating a new culture of limited responsibilities and refined management. Citizens must take responsibility for their own properties, pull their own weight and contribute to their own and the community's welfare.

The scale of urbanization in China is without precedent in human history. The country embarked on rapid urban development regardless of the shape of urbanization. The speed, scale, and quantity of urbanization are enormous. However, China's urbanization can become more efficient, inclusive, and sustainable by optimizing city operations and management.

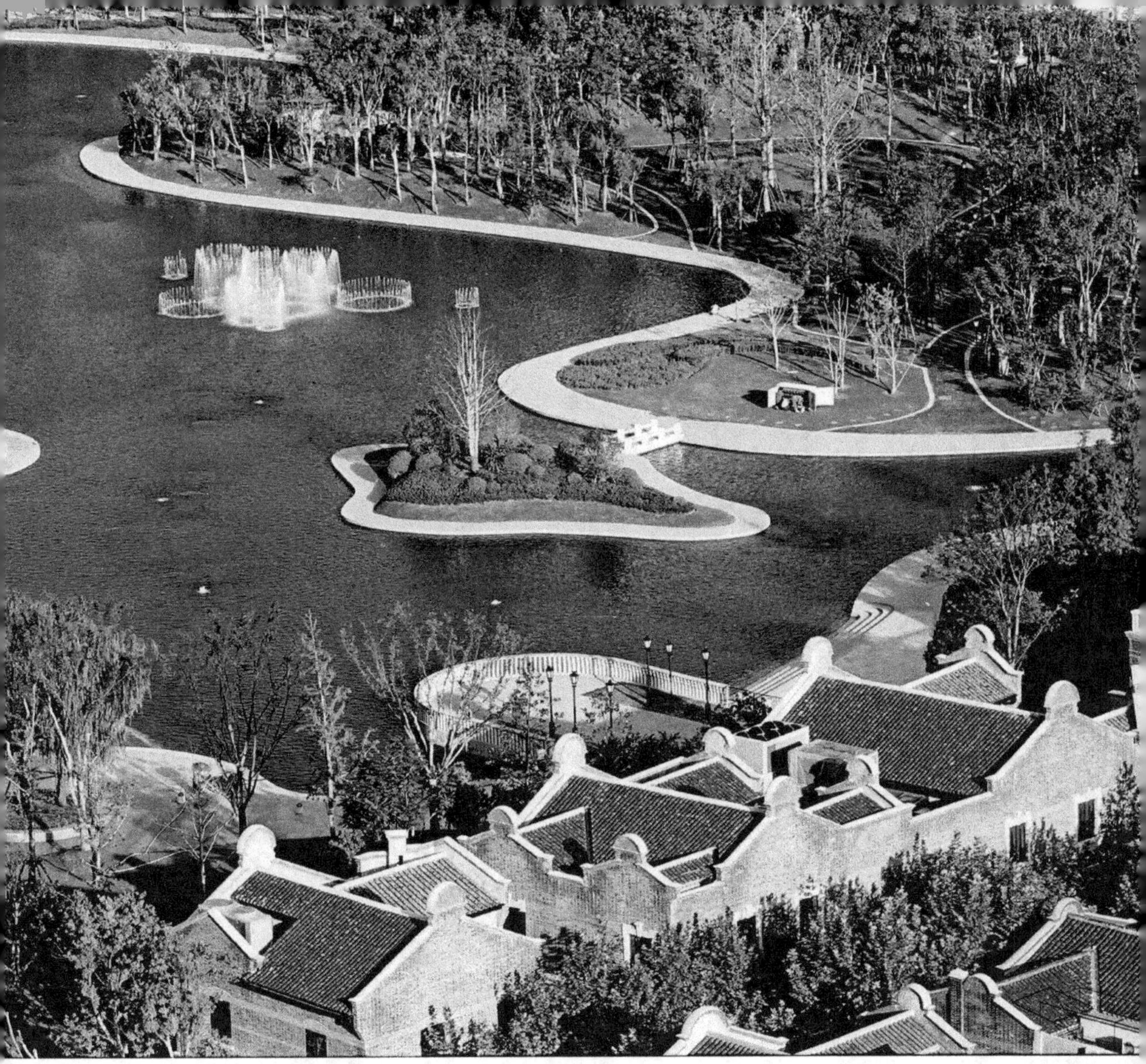

PART 3

A SERIES OF 'TIANDI' ENLIGHTMENT

While we are reshaping the urban landscapes, the city is redefining our lifestyle. Preserving the city's historic origin will bring insight into the future.

321
XINTIANDI

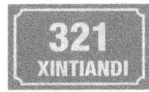

The artificial lake has restored the cultural origin of the Taipingqiao area: the water environment.

CHAPTER 1

A New Initiative

Within just a few years, Xintiandi has become a new culture and social destination as influential as the century-old Bund. What are the secrets behind the miraculous achievements?

Xintiandi project covers an area of 3 hectares and a construction area of 60,000 square meters with a total investment of 1.4 billion yuan. It will take 27 years of rent to recover the investment, which seems impossible to secure financial viability and may even result in losses. Has the chairman lost his mind, or is it actually an innovative business model?

Xintiandi turns out to be part of a larger development area called "Taipingqiao". Although Xintiandi takes up only 6% of the 52-hectare Taipingqiao Redevelopment Project with a planned total gross floor area of approximately 1.3 million sq.m., the project is commonly known by the name of its core development area, Xintiandi.

Shui On once suggested that Luwan District change the name of Taipingqiao to Xintiandi. Once a history-steeped corner of Shanghai, Taipingqiao area is believed to be permanently wiped off the map if it is renamed. To preserve the symbol of nostalgia about the local past when rivers crisscrossed Taipingqiao area, the district government decided to keep its name as well as the city's context.

Although Xintiandi alone is not profitable enough to survive in the long run, Shui On has demonstrated its determination to sustain the project as the Taipingqiao project yields a positive return on investment. What does Xintiandi contribute to the

whole project?

From an investment perspective, Shui On does not anticipate any return from Xintiandi. Instead, it is expected to improve the environmental performance and raise the value of land in the immediate area which will ultimately generate high investment returns.

According to SOM, the American firm of architects, this innovative business model has well exemplified the "smart growth" principles.

Both the authorities and the architects agree that Xintiandi has succeeded to preserve the city's historical, cultural, and geographical elements, and are in alignment with local government' urban development needs. However, critics argued at the initial phase of the project that obliterating historic structures and building new ones did not constitute preservation. Most of the old buildings of the 23 blocks in *Taipingqiao* area and half of those of the two blocks in Xintiandi area would be demolished, seemingly contradictory to the general sentiments of heritage preservation.

How come Xintiandi was conceived of as a splendid example of mixing historic preservation and commercial real estate development by the proponents and, at the same time, met fierce criticism?

Professor Sha Yongjie of the Institute of Architecture and Urban Space, Tongji University once said that unlike many other urban regeneration projects, the Taipingqiao Redevelopment Project followed a different urban planning model that featured comprehensive urban development with an agile foresight mindset.

It is necessary to review the process in the past 20 years to better understand Shui On's farsightedness.

Since 1990, Pudong New Area, where the space of cultivated land decreased as urbanization and industrialization increased, has established multiple functional zones including the financial and trade zone, export processing zone, Huamu residential and commercial area, that are well connected by highways.

This American urban development pattern has been an engine for the city's economic, cultural and social modernization. The end result is an urbanizing area with an expanding population and employment, along with the related but unavoidable impact of perennial peak-hour traffic congestion and increased contribution of vehicle exhaust to the concentration of inhalable particles represented by PM2.5. However, this rapid urbanization isn't without consequences. The expansion, together with the surging popularity of private vehicles, has led to a plague of "city diseases".

As the reurbanization of Puxi area, which faces Pudong across the river to the west, speeds up, highways increasingly take on the function of urban roads. The primary express roads form a major backbone of expressways within the city core, including several elevated highways which run directly above surface-level roadways—the Inner Ring Road which is a beltway, Yan'an Elevated Road that runs in a west-east direction straight through the center of Shanghai, and Chengdu Elevated Highway that runs north-south across the Huangpu River—that form a "申" (a Chinese abbreviation for Shanghai) shape.

The expressways encompass the downtown core of the Central Business District and cut huge swaths through our city. The sky-high cost of real estate in city center where the CBD is situated forces people to live in suburbs far from their work. China is potentially moving toward a sprawling settlement pattern in which having a long commute is unavoidable.

This urban planning idea was first proposed by a French architect who envisioned replacing crowded old cities with high-rise housing blocks and free circulation with criss-crossing highways, keeping only the major landmarks such as the Cathedrale Notre Dame de Paris and the Louvre. The design was not approved by the French government but was found favor in the United States.

The period between the 1940s and 1960s saw the heyday of this urban planning idea, called "Modern Urbanism" in the United States. Old neighborhoods tumbled, municipal zoning prevailed, and highways were running through cities. The experience of the United States demonstrates that unrestrained development can result in runaway urban sprawl, which seriously undermines the prosperity of the downtown area.

A 1961 book by writer and activist Jane Jacobs, *The Death and Life of Great American Cities* is a critique of 1950s urban planning policy, which it holds responsible for the decline of many city neighborhoods in the United States. *Silent Spring*, an environmental science book by Rachel Carson published in 1962, documents the adverse environmental effects caused by the indiscriminate use of pesticides. The 1973 Oil Embargo acutely strained the U.S. economy that had grown increasingly dependent on foreign oil. As a result, New Urbanism was developed to offer alternatives to the sprawling patterns.

Looking to traditional European towns and cities for inspiration, New Urbanism proponents are enticed by their exemplary public spaces, and walkable mixed-use neighborhoods.

Peter Calthorpe, a pioneer of the New Urbanism, points out that urbanism is the foundation for a low carbon future, and the most cost-effective solution to climate change, even more so than renewable energy — be it solar collectors or wind farms. Inappropriate urban planning will rapidly and completely destroy technological advancements.

New urbanism attempts to address the ills associated with urban sprawl and it took the American cities over twenty years to shift from car dependent, residential subdivisions toward dense, walkable, mixed-use neighborhoods.

Since its reform and opening-up in 1978, China has been learning from more advanced countries. Groups from various parts of the country conducted inspections of the monumental boulevards of Paris, the iconic skyscrapers in Manhattan, and the prime cityscape of Washington, D.C. Many of China's megacities subsequently embarked upon replication of the awe-inspiring Western architecture and city structures.

Urban regeneration in Shanghai has been generally seen as a tool to create zoning within the dwelling. In the old residences, people found themselves confined to a tight indoor existence, using the same small room of around 10 square meters for eating, sleeping, studying, cooking and even using the chamber pot. In the new apartment towers, though, spaces are divided and segregated for increased livability, such as the living room, dining room, bed rooms, study and kitchen. For local residents, a three-bedroom apartment that features a living room and a dining room creates a livable and functional modern abode.

An example of functional zoning in the city would be an area that has designated zones based on a function such as an industrial zone, a commercial zone and a residential zone, that are connected by highways.

The automobile industry and urban infrastructure investment were the two major driving forces of Shanghai's GDP growth. The automobile's mark on the land went well beyond the city core and its immediate surroundings. Roads and highways became the essential common links between people and their homes, their jobs, and their diversions.

Zoning provides the opportunity to stimulate development in specific areas. With the highest level of urbanization among all large cities in China, Shanghai set an example for other Chinese cities that wanted to follow suit.

Though, as urbanization blooms in Shanghai, many flaws follow the multiplying city since 2012. Rapid urbanization has caused large-scale proliferation in motor vehicle use, which makes the city increasingly congested and, subsequently, polluted, coupled with rising property prices, crowded concrete jungle, and exhausting fast pace of life. All these factors have increased residents' annoyance and, hence, increase complaints.

Conceived in 1996 under the influence of New Urbanism, the master plan of Taipingqiao Project was to rejuvenate the old

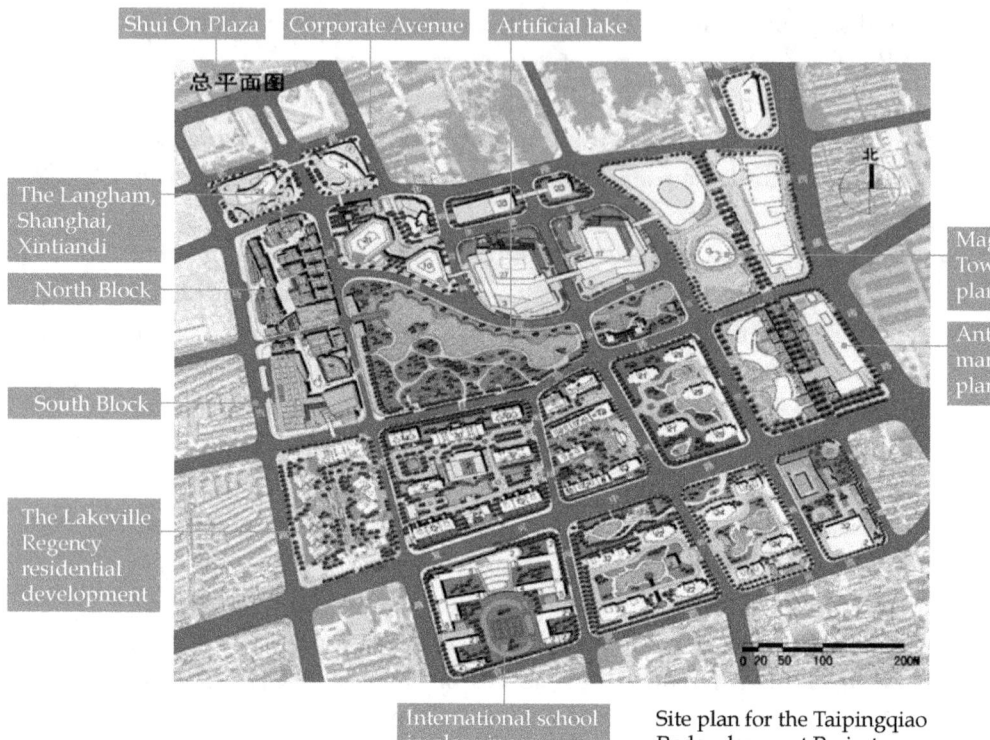

Site plan for the Taipingqiao Redevelopment Project

downtown housing quarters into a mixed-use community that encourages the development of walking networks and mass transit. Shui On was the first to introduce the concept of New Urbanism which was beginning to have widespread impact on urban development in Shanghai in 1996.

The Taipingqiao Redevelopment Project is a large-scale city-core redevelopment project with an emphasis on improving urban function level and optimizing urban spatial structure.

Smart growth serves the economy, the community, and the environment. The mixed-use community provides housing, offices, shops, and other services, easily accessible by Metro Line 1, Line 8, and Line 10. When the whole project is finished, the inner lanes in the community, which are still necessary for deliveries, will probably be reduced to snail pace with speed bumps to facilitate walkability.

A NEW INITIATIVE

The smart growth community is composed of five functional zones:

1. Public environment
In the 52-hectare project, various uses will be brought together around a central open space with a 4-hectar artificial lake to achieve a better living environment with a distinctive identity that integrates built form with landscape and enhances the central position of the Taipingqiao Lake.

2. Business
With Taipingqiao Lake sitting to their south and Huaihai Park to their north, six commercial buildings are located on the bustling Hubin Road for multinational corporations, among which is a sky-hugging ultra-tall office in the shape of white magnolia, the city flower of Shanghai.

3. Retail and culture
Xizang Road is lined with four Broadway-style theatres to provide continuity of the cultural fabric of the Taipingqiao area that featured a collection of theatres in the 1930s. The mix of retail and theatres perfectly suits the trend of both local and international elites seeking authentic, unique experiences and trendy lifestyles.

4. Historical and cultural preservation
Tucked away behind the fascinating Xintiandi area, the site of the First National Congress of the Communist Party of China and its adjacent neighborhoods have been exquisitely preserved through a holistic and integrated approach.

5. Residences
Six of the old neighborhoods were transformed into an

upscale residential development featuring a luxurious onsite clubhouse filled with premium facilities in each of its compounds. A school that offers the most modern teaching method for both local and international students completes the master plan.

On a more practical side, everything the residents might need on a day-to-day basis is nearby, including two of the most renowned hospitals in the city.

Mixing uses, however, works best when it grows out of a thoughtful plan that emphasizes the connectivity and links among the uses.

A well-planned mixed-use development is a prominent feature of urban planning, with the aim of improving urban life by keeping it on a human scale. It improves the potential for integrated neighborhoods and local social capital.

Examples of trendy lifestyles across the globe are showing that living, working, socializing and entertaining locally has multiple benefits such as shorter commutes and a more active and engaged social life. A mixed-use development can also help residents to establish frequent contact and long-term relationships with others.

The SOM architects cleverly incorporate nature into the community by inserting a relaxing, inspiring artificial lake at the center of the project that separates the different functional zones yet unites them as a whole.

The Xintiandi Project exemplifies several smart growth principles. Its car-free, individualist commercial development fosters an attractive and walkable atmosphere. Its mixed land-use pattern not only reduces transportation costs but also makes urban revitalization profitable.

The excellent ecological and desirable environment for living, working and relaxing in the community has attracted and retained top multinational corporations from around the world, such as PricewaterhouseCoopers, the largest accounting

The artificial lake links the offices and residential area in Taipingqiao community. Hubin Road, a curved sidewalk that runs along the lake bank, offers breathtaking panoramic views at every bend.

firm in the world, Walt Disney from the United States, and Sony from Japan, whose businesses radiate across the city, the Yangtze River Delta, China and Asia-Pacific region.

These multinational corporations have become an important source of tax revenue to the local government. A single Corporate Avenue building covering a gross floor area of over 70,000 sq.m. makes an annual tax contribution of 2.3 billion yuan—five or six times more than that on Huaihai Road.

Smart growth policies have been effective in improving the urban structure of the old districts. Taipingqiao area is consequently no longer a residential district attached to Huaihai Road Commercial Street, but an independent, integrated, iconic community.

In order to forge ahead with urbanization, it is useful to look at the historical record of other countries that have already gone through the urban transition and learn from their experiences—especially their mistakes.

The urbanization of Shanghai has been significantly influenced by American "Modern Urbanism". Single-use development results in the functional and spatial separation of areas in which people live and in which people work. Industrial and office parks are devoted to a single use.

Residential blocks are also largely single-use and surrounded by giant arterial roads, green median strip, and spectacular squares which detach different functions of a city and create an environment far from employment opportunities, grocery stores, schools, hospitals, theatres, restaurants and entertainment. The homes sold out to investors and buyers are not occupied by either the owners or renters. Western-themed housing developments with barely any indication of human life look like a giant museum, representing a stupendous waste of resources.

Benjamin Wood bluntly criticized this type of functional zoning. "The gardens are indeed pretty, but who wants to live in an area where there are no shops, no restaurants, no place to drink beer? All they can find are the "Keep off the grass" signs," said Wood, "people wish to get fresh bread, milk, eggs, meat and vegetables within walking distance. Why would all of it be abandoned during urban regeneration? While we enjoy a beautiful community, we want it to be more livable."

In the city of Modern Urbanism, people must deal with ever-increasing distances between work and living. Residential areas empty out during the daytime when many people are at work, and then fill up again at night when people return. The streets of Shanghai are clogged with motorized traffic with associated problems of air pollution.

The *Tiandi* model is definitely ahead of the curve, but the conventional approach of Modern Urbanism to growth remains dominant in the country where cars flood city roads and functional zoning shapes the community.

The model revolves around the core principles that aim at improving the lives of its urban residents and promoting more attractive and effective alternatives to driving—such as walking, biking, and using public transit. The *Tiandi* model preserves the environment and protects public health, but it slows the

A NEW INITIATIVE

Dinner with coworkers or friends? Work-life integration is the new norm.

development of the automotive industry and thus decreases the contribution of the automobile sector to the city's overall GDP. Moreover, there is a long delay between investment and payback that will reduce working capital turnover. As a result, the *Tiandi* model is unlikely to be popularized throughout the country.

The Xintiandi initiative sparked a series of 'Tiandi' revitalizations in places like Wuhan, Chongqing and Foshan that have all succeeded to preserve the respective city's historical, cultural, humanity and geographical elements. It takes much time and cost to maintain respect for local culture and the incorporation of local history—"Lifen" architecture in Wuhan, "Diaojiaolou" buildings in Chongqing, and "Guoerqiang" residences in Foshan, each of which contains special local cultures and is a main component exhibiting the distinct charm of the city, making the formula hard to be replicated.

Shui On has been recognized for its sustainable business model that balances financial profitability with corporate social responsibility. Its chairman Mr. Vincent Lo is known for his entrepreneurial spirit and commitment to sustainable development goals that can stand the test of time.

Albert Chan, Director of Development Planning and Design, has an article published in *Time Magazine* that poetically depicts Shui On's vision:

The *Tiandi* projects always adhere to Shui On's corporate philosophy of sustainable development. Shouldn't we enjoy a walkable, close-knit neighborhood that enables life enrichment by placing "Live-Work-Play" functions within walking distance of each other? Shouldn't we embrace the great outdoors where residents feel safe crossing the tree-lined street full of hyped-up shops and cafes? Wouldn't it be nice to bump into an old friend while we are strolling at leisure in the pedestrian friendly neighborhood? If all of the above are realized, wouldn't our reliance on cars that has led to increased air pollution decrease?

When the community is filled with lush trees, and fresh, pollution-free air, when we hear tweeting and singing from the nearby beautiful green parks, when regions of land occupied by the highways are restored for open space and community amenities, wouldn't we be living a truly sustainable lifestyle?

Prior to joining Shui On, Albert Chan worked at the New York City Department of Design and Construction where he specialized in correcting urban planning mistakes and had a more comprehensive understanding of the negative consequences of urbanization in the United States.

At an early stage in the urbanization process, urban growth was achieved by outward expansion. However, as urbanization advances, the priority has shifted to improving the quality of life for urban residents. Only until then will the *Tiandi* model become the dominant model of urban development.

CHAPTER 2

Reshaping Shanghai's social fabric

The Taipingqiao Redevelopment Project (hereinafter the Taipingqiao Project") is ahead of the curve in terms of urban development by at least 30 years. Launched in 1996, the project will probably still be at the forefront in 2026, indicating the trajectories of future urban development from at least three perspectives.

First, respect the history of the city and integrate historical and cultural resources into urban development

Second, create high-density road networks and human-scale streets that encourage walking and biking.

Third, enliven public spaces and foster community interaction and bonding through shared experiences

Achieving sustainable urban structure and growth pattern is the core of the spirit of Shanghai that echoes the leading ethical concept in Taoism.

The growth of urban development in Shanghai has been driven by the continuous increase of cars, high-rise buildings, highways and urban expansion in the first two decades. The number of skyscrapers and high-rise buildings in Shanghai reached 17,000 in 2010, 3.5 times that of Tokyo, but Tokyo still holds the position as Asia's No. 1 financial hub.

According to the analysis report presented by *Forecast Think Tank*, one of the most recognized *Think Tanks* in China, Tokyo had a population density of 14,440 inhabitants per square kilometer in 2011, similar to that of Shanghai which was 14,827 inhabitants per square kilometer. But Tokyo's per capita GDP in 2011 reached

US$72,000, 5.4 times that of Shanghai which was only US$13,000. Moreover, Tokyo's GDP per square kilometer reached US$1.04 billion, approximately 5-fold higher than that of Shanghai which was only US$188 million.

Although house prices in Shanghai have surpassed Tokyo, Shanghai lags far behind Tokyo when it comes to economic development, livability, environmental governance, traffic management and social security.

Research by the Chinese Academy of Social Sciences shows that aggressive urbanization in China has led to the decline in the marginal benefit of urban growth. Chinese cities will have to retrofit urban sprawl and implement a smart growth policy. Shanghai will take the lead in China's efforts to reshape the urban form by pursuing a "smart growth" pathway, which offers an integrated approach to development widely adopted by urban planners around the world.

The goal of sprawl retrofitting is to create a more sustainable urban environment within the context of the existing urban form. It is time for Shanghai to shift the focus from urban expansion to a more fundamental focus on improving the quality of life. Given China's limited land and natural resources, how can it enhance its citizens' quality of life smartly in a way that will ensure sustainable development?

Professor Sha Yongjie of Tongji University wrote in his book *Towards a New Chinese Urbanity* that "we should leverage the extremely rich cultural and natural heritage that cities are endowed with to make them more prosperous and sustainable".

In the first two decades of Shanghai's urbanization, developers generally placed greater value on urban land resources than on historical and cultural resources. Cultural heritage sites were damaged accidentally or deliberately as a result of development in the project area.

Taipingqiao Project has achieved a successful blend of historical, natural and cultural resources and proved that cultural heritage can make big commercial sense by finding an unconventional but reasonable way to preserve the resources and meanwhile transform them into commercial success.

Taipingqiao Project has successfully maintained a continuity of the original spatial emotion and urban fabric, while still boasting an alluring atmosphere of traditional streets that reflects the historical context and cultural climate of the city.

The urban fabric of the Taipingqiao area takes influence from the planning ideas of the French Concession in 1914. As one of the earliest European countries engaged in modern urban planning, France transported European concepts of city planning to the land which was once composed of waterways and fields by filling in the rivers to build new roads. Urban framework was consequently established, ready to accommodate houses, shops and a myriad of social and cultural amenities. The irregular flow of rivers shaped the direction of the roads—irregular but naturally beautiful. The result is a diverse, yet integrated community that retains the origin of the city's culture.

The Taipingqiao market has been demolished during the urban redevelopment. This photo shows a collection of shops and road-side stands near the market in the '80s and '90s. The streets were lined up with two-story townhouses, of which the first floor was used for shops and businesses, with living spaces above. The hustle and bustle of the busy market every morning has become part of the city's cultural memory.

Most parts of the Shanghai area are flat and belong to the alluvial plain of the Yangtze River delta. The water shaped the landscape by wearing away rock and carving out winding river courses. The network of winding rivers and waterways crisscrossing through the city prior to its first urbanization, where Xizang Road, Chengdu Road, Fuxing Road, Taicang Road, Huangpi Road and Zizhong Road now run, played an important role in the emergence of Shanghai's *Haipai* culture which is at the root of Shanghai's energy and charm.

Historically, Shanghai culture was influenced and shaped by the region of Jiangnan (areas south of the Yangtze River). After the first urbanization in the Taipingqiao area in the early 20th century, however, the natural resources and the rivers' rich history have got buried deep beneath the houses. During the redevelopment process, the architects proposed an open park, featuring a wide esplanade sweeping along the edge of an artificial lake, in an attempt to reconnect people with the lake by providing a lifestyle with water, promote quality of life, recall the city's memory, and more importantly, to perk up public spaces through good design that helps build community pride and become central to the cultural identity of the city.

Featuring 23 *Shikumen* neighborhoods and a large indoor market, the Taipingqiao area was intended to be a residential community in the French Concession in 1914. Shops were springing up around the market in the following decades. Crisscrossing streets were lined up with two-story townhouses, of which the first floor was used for shops and businesses, with living spaces above. The result was a well-known snack street with a wide range of offerings—from food commodities to household supplies, from teahouses to hotels. Not far from the street stood the theaters, schools, hospitals and department stores.

The run-down neighborhood that offered easy accessibility to daily life facilities is noteworthy for its cultural and historical variety. The redevelopment project should recognize the historic resources as valuable reminders of the city's cultural past and provide the community with a tangible connection to its history and heritage.

Taipingqiao area is repositioned to respond to evolving urban functions. The lakefront offices in Corporate Avenue and the Lakeville Regency residential buildings create a unique urban setting. The pedestrian-friendly space presents a nostalgic narrative of the once-thriving snack street. The commercial center and cluster of theaters in planning evoke a sense of history in the second half of the 20th century.

Preserving urban cultural heritage and natural resources in the process of urban regeneration not only shows respect for history, but also proves to be a smart business strategy.

Shanghai is facing a critical period of transformation of development patterns. This shift reflects policymakers' focus on attracting a skilled workforce in the post-industrial society rather than attracting business investment which was a widely adopted approach to strengthen the city's competitive position in the pre-industrial society. Nowadays, creating livable cities has become a priority for the developed Western countries to attract and retain talent.

With rapid urban sprawl, China suffers from urban decay, social dysfunction, environmental degradation, and other costly big city ills, with which attracting and retaining top talent can seem almost impossible.

Cities cannot thrive without putting people first. It's a competitive landscape that is intensifying. Success is earned by those who understand people's needs more deeply and execute to meet them better than the alternative destinations.

As the country's leading industrial city, Shanghai has taken active policies to attract, develop and retain the talent needed to drive a changing economy. Wages and benefits used to be the prime concerns for the talent to stay in Shanghai. Moving forward, the city should focus more on creating a vibrant urban community that meet reasonable and aspirational lifestyle needs of their residents.

So, what does a vibrant urban community look like?

In her book *The Death and Life of Great American Cities*, Jane Jacobs advocated "four generators of diversity" that "create effective economic pools of use":

- Mixed primary uses, activating streets at different times of the day
- Short blocks, allowing high pedestrian permeability
- Buildings of various ages and states of repair
- Density

She opposed large-scale urban renewal programs that destroyed communities and innovative economies by creating isolated, unnatural urban spaces.

The urban planners of Skidmore, Owings & Merrill (SOM), which has designed some significant architectural projects in Silicon Valley in the United States, believe that smart growth development is accompanied by walkable districts and neighborhoods with dense street network and small blocks. Innovative cities should encourage effective, efficient communication and minimize the cost of acquiring knowledge and generating new ideas. The urban planners have also discovered the similarity between the urban planning pattern of smart cities and a human brain.

Aerial photographs of London, New York, San Francisco and Shanghai have revealed a more compact urban spatial structure in the first three cities and a scattered, loose urban structure in Shanghai's Pudong and old districts. Intersections are provided every several hundred meters in urban environments in Shanghai, nearly ten times that in London.

As a World Bank study on urbanization shows, Paris has 133 intersections per square kilometer to develop better connectivity and create a more fine-grain urban fabric.

The urban design features that encouraged car dependency in

The rejuvenated Taipingqiao Park and the preserved Shikumen *buildings (at the intersection of South Huangpi Road and Xingye Road) coexist in harmony. This revitalized vernacular architecture is considered not only an integral part of the urban fabric but a vessel to carry modern lifestyle.*

EAST MEETS WEST

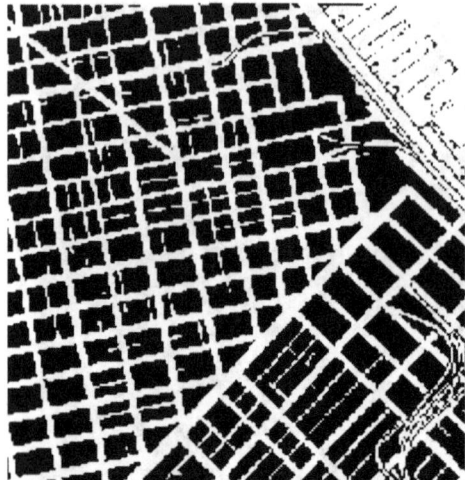
The urban spatial dimension of San Francisco

The urban spatial dimension of London

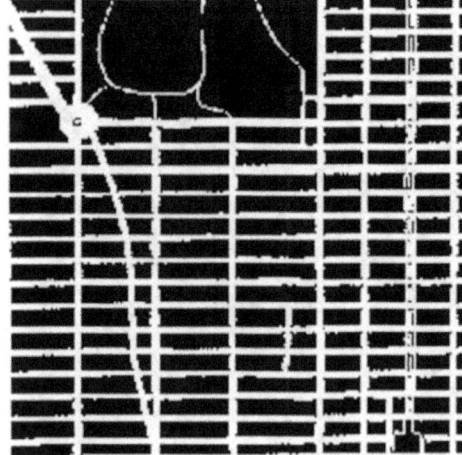
The urban spatial dimension of New York

The spatial dimension of Knowledge and Innovation Community (KIC), a large, mixed-use technology innovation community developed amid several of Shanghai's premier universities

the pre-industrial era have been shifted to a compact, walkable neighborhood that contributes to people's sense of community in the post-industrial era.

With continued urban fabric, Taipingqiao area is designed to transcend the nostalgia of historic preservation and embrace contemporary urban development. The urban landscape that features high-density road networks and human-scale streets encourages more attentive driving, reduced speed, and a better walking experience.

Another focus of Shanghai's urban transformation is on the level of citizen participation, which translates into the behavior of the citizens and their thinking habit. Much of what determines the level of citizen participation is the development of urban public culture derived from social encounters that shape the daily life.

Chinese square-dancing grannies—groups composed primarily of women in their 50s and 60s looking for ways to stay active and get out of the house—invading public spaces and rocking out to deafeningly loud music at dusk or dawn manifest a lack of appropriate urban public spaces which are the vessels to carry public culture.

During Shanghai's dramatic urban expansion since the 1990s, priority has been given to housing improvement and commercial construction. Despite their importance, public spaces have been poorly integrated or neglected in planning and urban development.

Square-dancing grannies have a strong desire for health and entertainment but lack public facilities. As a result, the dancing troupes have to take over public squares, parks, metro stations and housing estates across the city.

One of the highlights of the Taipingqiao Project that has won international praise is its well-designed public spaces that fill the urban gaps with life.

Taipingqiao Park is the largest public space and defining central feature of the Taipingqiao neighborhood, and one of the most important elements. As its core development area, Xintiandi is also a vivid example of appealing public space that empowers urban social interaction through good design. Even the Lakeville Regency residential area is where private spheres and public spaces overlap.

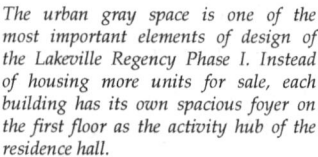

The urban gray space is one of the most important elements of design of the Lakeville Regency Phase I. Instead of housing more units for sale, each building has its own spacious foyer on the first floor as the activity hub of the residence hall.

The gray brick walls represent community interaction and bonding through shared experiences that permeate the everyday life of Shanghai locals. Through extraordinary creative pioneer cultural content, it empowers diverse social experience and builds a community with resonance and sense of belonging.

Each building features a stylistic stone arch and a well which is a symbol of Shikumen *life that provided water for the house.*

Each building of Lakeville Regency Phase I has its own spacious foyer on the first floor as the activity hub of the residence hall. The spaces are bordered by plain brick walls. Each building features a *Shikumen* style entrance and a well which is a symbol of *Shikumen* life that provided water for the house. Benches, walkways, and outdoor public balconies provide spaces for reminiscing, relaxing, and socializing.

Modern amenities such as a children's playground and an underground fitness center are also included that shows the developer's effort to give the residents a place to experience the public realm as something pleasant by blending traditional design with modern facilities.

Residents often spontaneously organize community activities to enliven public spaces by fostering community interaction and bonding through shared experiences.

Also designed by Benjamin Wood, the second phase of the Lakeville Regency residential development embodies his understanding of the *Shikumen* culture and finest contemporary architectural thought: architectural design must include all measures to respect the city's historic fabric and cultural heritage. The comfort of a city's past will anchor the excitement of its future.

New apartment blocks built during the urban regeneration provide better privacy within the dwelling which is compromised in the *Shikumen* houses. Nevertheless, the social scenarios in *Shikumen* alleys have promoted human interaction as a direct response to neighbors that is often lost in contemporary high-rise architecture. The design of modern apartment buildings often excludes publicly accessible spaces that encourage interaction between residents in the neighborhood.

Apartment life can be strangely isolating: elevators come equipped with security that only allows residents access to their specific apartments; residents don't even bother to exchange a "hello" with the neighbors who live on the other side of their walls; everyone living in the same tower retreats into their own little units.

For being so packed full of life, a modern city block can be one of the loneliest places on earth with no community identity, no shared sense of obligation and purpose.

Some of the government agencies and developers fail to notice that bulldozers have ruthlessly knocked down the decaying but close-knit neighborhoods.

Shikumen housing is a form of dwelling in an alley-structured neighborhood — to the extent that neighborhood means more than just an area, but a community where members interact with each other on a regular basis. The human scale and the arrangement of the *Shikumen* houses allow people to both physically interact with each other with their doors wide open, at the same time, provide a "neighborhood watch" sense of security that is conducive to the development of social networks. It is the urban public culture that forms the neighborhood cohesion.

EAST MEETS WEST

Large-scale urban development projects are all the rage these days in urban planning that bring positive environmental amenities to an area, but absent a thriving, urban civilization.

Without great public places, there would be no great cities. How the spaces of a city are broadly structured around a separation of public and private spaces appears to be a defining feature of these settlements: if the best architecture in a city is private homes and government buildings, and public places such as stadiums, theaters, libraries, museums and parks are walled off, then the urban spatial structure manifests the characteristics of an agrarian society that features public powers and private spaces. In a typical agricultural society, members of the community are largely self-sufficient and behave according to self-interest and personal preferences.

While we are reshaping the urban landscapes, the city is redefining our lifestyle. Urban development cannot move forward without a full understanding of the city's history and a strong belief that preserving the city's historic origin will bring insight into its future.

Shanghai has set a goal of further strengthening its role as an international financial center of global significance by 2025. In addition to economic prosperity, the city needs to attain global cultural recognition with its unique local culture rather than mimicry of Manhattan or the Champs Elysées.

Shanghai is home to commercial and residential developments inspired by western architecture in the absence of symbolic landscape of the city or the country. We must be aware that foreign cultural invasion which will create a loss of the city's identity must be avoided in the course of rejuvenating Shanghai's cultural prominence.

The residents of three decades ago, however, would not find much today that is familiar. As of 1990, the per-capita living space of urban residents in Shanghai was less than 3 square meters. Tall buildings were indeed rare, and residents were struggling to make a living and find affordable housing.

Today urban development policy no longer focuses exclusively on building more residential and commercial developments. The latest data points to a per capita living space of over 30 square meters in Shanghai. With its skyscraper boom, the city boasts more retail space per capita than European countries. What the city needs is to highlight its distinctiveness and urban differentiation with an insistence on quality and originality with deep roots in cultural heritage.

Over the last few decades, urban planning has evolved radically. Instead of a swathe of high-rise buildings, a holistic and integrated approach to urban renewal needs to take creativity, heritage, and diversity into account.

Growth is quantitative, while development is qualitative. Subtle movements of historical progress go largely unnoticed. Shanghai has reached an important turning point, a critical milestone on a hitherto unprecedented scale.

The end is where we start from.

While we are reshaping the urban landscapes, the city is redefining our lifestyle.

As the city's historic origin offers insight into what the future holds, Shanghai's uniqueness is gradually taking shape.

EAST MEETS WEST

The Taipingqiao area embodies the idea of a compact city. The city, as living organism, reflects the people who live within; tall or short, new and old, eclectic or classic, standing together to create the mosaic of our communities. Cityscape reflects life. High-rise buildings and low-rise Shikumen houses in Xintiandi stand in harmony.

References

[1] Luo Xiaowei, Sha Yongjie. (2002) *Shanghai Xintiandi: Research of the Architectural History, Cultural History and Development Model in Old District Reconstruction*, Nanjing: Southeast University Press.

[2] Sha Yongjie. (2010) *Towards A New Chinese Urbanity: Urban Design Concept of Shui On Land Developments*, Beijing: China Architecture & Building Press.

[3] Domus International Chinese Edition + Yishi Culture. (2012) *About China*, Shanghai: SDX Joint Publishing Company.

[4] Jane Jacobs. (2006) *The Death and Life of Great American Cities*, Nanjing: Yilin Press.

[5] Richard Florida, Hou Kun. (2009) *Who's Your City?*, Beijing: Peking University Press.

[6] Dai Zhikang, Chen Bochong. (2013) *High Mountains and Flowing Water: Explore the City of Tomorrow*, Shanghai: Tongji University Press.

[7] Feng Lun, Nie Jun. (2012) *Ideal Fullness*, Beijing: Culture and Art Publishing House.

[8] (Japan) Tadao Ando. (2012) *Walking While Thinking- the Life of Tadao Ando, the Architect,* Beijing: CITIC Press Corporation.

[9] Zhao Qiguang. (2009) *The Wisdom of Lao Tzu*, Shanghai: Shanghai Bookstore Publishing House.

[10] Lao Tzu, Dan Ming Zi. (2004) *Wisdom of Tao Te Ching,* Inner Mongolia: Inner Mongolia University Publishing House.

[11] Shao Longtu, Zhang Yufan. (2008) *Seeing and Discovering,* Shanghai: Shanghai Literature & Art Publishing House.

[12] Xue Liyong. (2002) *The History of the Old Shanghai Concession,* Shanghai: Shanghai Academy of Social Sciences Press.

[13] Jiang Longfei. (2008) *One Hundred years' History of Foreign Concessions in Shanghai,* Shanghai: Wenhui Press.

[14] Fu Zhiying. (2004) *Forever with You: Loretta Yang, Chang Yi and Liuli Gongfang*, Beijing: Modern Press.
[15] Xu Yibo, Weng Zuliang, Zheng Zu An. (2009) *Years - Cultural History Atlas of Luwan, Shanghai*, Shanghai: Shanghai Lexicographical Publishing House.
[16] Wang Jun. (2008) The Urban Regeneration experienced by the French, *Jiefang Daily*, 2008-11-28.
[17] Dai Yanhui. (2002) Shanghai Xintiandi, *Design Trends*, 2002 (1).

Postscript

Several years ago, when a relative of mine settling in New York told me that the original Chinese version of East Meets West was being sold on Amazon at $33, the thought of having it translated and published flashed through my mind. Globally recognized, Xintiandi has been honored with the Urban Land Institute's Award for Excellence in 2002 and elected as one of the Top 20 Cultural Landmarks All Over the World by Forbes in 2016.

I am grateful to the esteemed publishing house Earnshaw Books Limited for giving me access to a wide readership. My dream has finally come true.

Just as many people are interested in celebrities' life experience, people are fascinated by the story of Xintiandi after it has garnered much recognition for its rejuvenation of the old *Shikumen* neighborhoods. This book is the only and most comprehensive account of Xintiandi's development.

Since the birth of Xintiandi in 2001, it has received wide news media coverage both at home and abroad. Numerous writers and journalists have tried in vain to give a full account of the story behind. A professional writer from a famous Hong Kong publishing house stayed in Shanghai to interview every team member who had participated in the Xintiandi project which unfortunately led nowhere, proving the complexity and difficulty of a detailed depiction of the whole story. Books of the ins and outs of Tianzifang transformed from old-style alleyways and Sinan Mansions converted from the historical garden villa complex are already available, while the complete story of Xintiandi has never been told. I felt responsible, with the approach of my retirement in 2013, for writing down the invigorating, unforgettable experience with Shui On team by an accurate account of Xintiandi's history.

Starting from 2012, I spent half an hour each morning and the whole evening on writing. I was desperate to continue writing before inspiration slipped away from me. Sometimes I was brimming with ideas at midnight and I didn't hesitate to write them down—even on freezing winter nights.

Architecture is an art form, a material realization of artistic concepts and purposes. I strived to grasp the art of language to present the aesthetics of architecture and to provide fascinating insights into a book to sit with, ruminate over, and learn from. I spent three years devoted to writing the book which had been revised multiple times and completely rewritten twice.

Writing is like mining for treasure hidden in the hillsides of your mind. It is exhausting but rewarding when gems are discovered, strung on threads of silk, and form an elegant necklace always in style. Similarly, this book has connected various pieces of information into a cohesive written account that displays how the city's revolutionary spirit derives from its past, reverberates through its present and flourishes in its future.

The manuscript had been repeatedly reviewed and revised before both the editors of Wenhui Publishing House and I were satisfied. In 2015, the book was officially published. A professor from Tongji University said at the book launch that "this book is the most authoritative account of Xintiandi that anyone who is to write about Xintiandi again within the next 50 years has to reference".

This book has been reprinted three times, yet it is still repeatedly sold out on online bookstores. It has been collected by Shanghai Library as well as the internal library of the general office of Shanghai Municipal Committee.

This book has also become an important teaching instrument in the Class of Leadership in Urban Development, Class of Cultural Creativity, and Executive MBA program held by renowned colleges and universities such as Fudan University, Tongji University, and Jiaotong University. The case study of Xintiandi that reveals how property-led redevelopment actually works has been well received for more than a decade.

POSTSCRIPT

Through large-scale demolition and clearance, China's previous urban renewal waged a war on perceived waste—and created a new tide of it. Since the birth of Shanghai Xintiandi, the Project has started a new path of urban renewal and driven a culture shift where people realize the importance of preserving and promoting historic buildings.

The city's rapid urbanization isn't without consequences. The immense land resources devoted to housing has led to increasing housing inventory. Apartment towers built only two to three decades ago started to show signs of decay. Urban renewal is not just a trendy term, but a problem of deteriorating urban neighborhoods that the entire city is faced with. Knocking down modern apartment buildings would be much more challenging than demolishing old *Shikumen* houses two decades ago: who is going to foot the bill for the relocation?

Strategies of "urban renewal" and "urban regeneration" will inevitably stand out as key trends in China's urban development. Historic buildings have been shown to be a key ingredient in a vibrant urban community with architectural diversity and cultural identity. These are the universal issues in urban development that no country is spared from.

This book uses primary sources and crisp analysis to decode the success of Xintiandi, explore sustainable urban development patterns, and deliver insights into the city's future.

Mr. Benjamin Wood, the principal architect of Xintiandi, is very concerned with the progress of the translation work. Having already read and approved of the part about him translated by his secretary from the Chinese edition, Mr. Wood was very much looking forward to reading a complete English edition. When I invited him to write the foreword to the book, Mr. Wood said that he accepted this invitation with pleasure. I am indeed honored to have Mr. Vincent Lo, the founder of Xintiandi, and Mr. Benjamin Wood, the principal architect of Xintiandi, write the foreword for my book, and extremely grateful to Mr. Zheng Shiling, one of the leading Chinese architects and an academician of the

EAST MEETS WEST

Chinese Academy of Sciences, Mr. Albert Chan, former chairman of the ULI Mainland China Council, and Mr. Li Lunxin, former chairman of Shanghai Federation of Literary and Art Circles, for their generous recommendation of my book.

When my wife's niece Yijia Bu, married and settling down in New York, told me last year that she saw the Chinese edition was available on Amazon, I couldn't help thinking if only it had been published in English. I am greatly appreciative of the support from Mr. Zheng Naxin, Mr. Ma Xiaojun, and Ms. Jiang Yanyi to make my dream come true.

A fine translation is basically an act of recreation. One of the key challenges is the need to balance staying faithful to the original work with the need to create something unique and distinctive that will evoke the same feelings and responses as the original. The publishing house and I dedicated much time and effort to finding the competent translators.

Recommended by Mr. Yuan Jiafu, a well-known journalist, his wife, and their friend, Mr. Tao Xiangling, Ms. Xie Wen, the leading translator of the book, is well-versed in both Chinese and English and has strong linguistic background and rich international work experience. Mr. Jason Tan, the supporting translator of the book and a foreign journalist, has also made a substantial contribution to the translation work. I would like to express my sincere gratitude to all who have contributed to the translation of the book.

The scale of urbanization in China since early 21st century is without precedent in human history. Xintiandi is undoubtedly a symbolic representation of contemporary urban renewal pattern.

Being part of Xintiandi project is a true once-in-a-lifetime experience that empowered me to share this crucial piece of history with the readers and further promote it to a wider audience globally.

Zhou Yongping
July 20, 2023

www.ingramcontent.com/pod-product-compliance
Lightning Source LLC
LaVergne TN
LVHW081539070526
838199LV00057B/3720